Freedoms, Faiths and Futures

Also Available from Bloomsbury:

Religious Pluralism and the City, edited by Helmuth Berking, Silke Steets and Jochen Schwenk
Religion in the Age of Obama, edited by Juan M. Floyd-Thomas and Anthony B. Pinn
Evangelical Youth Culture, by Ibrahim Abraham

Freedoms, Faiths and Futures

Teenage Australians on Religion, Sexuality and Diversity

Andrew Singleton, Anna Halafoff,
Mary Lou Rasmussen and Gary Bouma

BLOOMSBURY ACADEMIC
LONDON • NEW YORK • OXFORD • NEW DELHI • SYDNEY

BLOOMSBURY ACADEMIC
Bloomsbury Publishing Plc
50 Bedford Square, London, WC1B 3DP, UK
1385 Broadway, New York, NY 10018, USA
29 Earlsfort Terrace, Dublin 2, Ireland

BLOOMSBURY, BLOOMSBURY ACADEMIC and the Diana logo are
trademarks of Bloomsbury Publishing Plc

First published in Great Britain 2021
Paperback edition published 2023

Copyright © Andrew Singleton, Anna Halafoff, Mary Lou Rasmussen and
Gary Bouma, 2021

Andrew Singleton, Anna Halafoff, Mary Lou Rasmussen and Gary Bouma have
asserted their right under the Copyright, Designs and Patents Act, 1988, to be
identified as Authors of this work.

For legal purposes the Acknowledgements on p. viii constitute an extension
of this copyright page.

Cover design: Ben Anslow
Cover image: Teenagers Young Team Together Cheerful Concept
(© Rawpixel.com / Shutterstock)

All rights reserved. No part of this publication may be reproduced or
transmitted in any form or by any means, electronic or mechanical, including
photocopying, recording, or any information storage or retrieval system,
without prior permission in writing from the publishers.

Bloomsbury Publishing Plc does not have any control over, or responsibility for, any
third-party websites referred to or in this book. All internet addresses given in this
book were correct at the time of going to press. The author and publisher regret any
inconvenience caused if addresses have changed or sites have ceased to exist, but can
accept no responsibility for any such changes.

A catalogue record for this book is available from the British Library.

Library of Congress Control Number: 2021932200

ISBN: HB: 978-1-3501-7956-1
PB: 978-1-3502-3754-4
ePDF: 978-1-3501-7957-8
eBook: 978-1-3501-7958-5

Typeset by Newgen KnowledgeWorks Pvt. Ltd., Chennai, India

To find out more about our authors and books visit www.bloomsbury.com
and sign up for our newsletters

Contents

List of figures	vi
List of tables	vii
Acknowledgements	viii

1	The future makers: Teens in the age of diversity	1
2	Doing away with our Sunday best: Teenagers and the remaking of religion in Australia	17
3	Mind, body and spirit: Teenagers and spirituality	37
4	A personal point of view: Discovering teenage worldviews	59
5	'A higher order out there': Seekers and the spiritual but not religious	79
6	Immanent gods: This Worldly and Indifferent teens	93
7	Awash but not adrift: Teen attitudes to religious diversity	113
8	Taking it to school: Worldviews and religious education	137
9	Harry Potter, homophobia and human rights: Teens talk about sexuality education, religious exemptions and gay rights	157
	Conclusion: The freedoms, faiths and futures of Australia's teens	179

Appendix 1: 2017 'Australia's Generation Z' national survey sample characteristics (unweighted)	189
Appendix 2: Correlates of membership in the worldview types	191
Notes	195
Bibliography	217
Index	231

Figures

1.1	Punchbowl Boys' High School students at Lakemba Mosque, March 2019	2
2.1	Religious change in Australia, 1960s–present	21
2.2	Australians aged 13–18: Current religion/denomination (% of teens)	25
2.3	Patterns of religious practice among Australian teens: 2005 and 2017 compared (% of teens in those years)	34
3.1	Australians aged 13–18: Spiritual and wellbeing practices (% of teens)	41
3.2	Australians aged 13–18: Frequency of spiritual experiences (% of teens)	52
3.3	Patterns of spirituality among Australian teens: 2005 and 2017 compared (% of teens in those years)	55
4.1	Worldview types of Australian teens (% of the population aged 13–18)	62
6.1	This Worldly teens (13–18): Identification as nonreligious (% of identity)	96
7.1	Easter picture	114
7.2	Australians aged 13–18: View of religions and Religious Nones in Australia (% of teens)	116
7.3	Australians aged 13–18: Have friends who follow a faith (% of teens)	121
7.4	Australians aged 13–18: Person lives near a place of worship (% of teens)	124
9.1	Gen Z teens' support for marriage equality versus Australian adults' support for marriage equality (% of the population)	171

Tables

1.1	Summary of birth cohorts (generations) in Australia	11
2.1	Patterns of religious identification among Australian teens: 2005 and 2017 (% of teens in those years)	27
2.2	Australians aged 13–18: Belief in higher being by religious identification (% of group)	29
2.3	Australians aged 13–18: Religious practices by religious identification (% of group)	31
3.1	Australians aged 13–18: Spiritual, paranormal and supernatural beliefs by religious identification (% of group)	47
3.2	Australians aged 13–18: Self-identification by religious identification (% of group)	57
4.1	Australians aged 13–18: Worldview type latent-class membership probabilities (% of class)	64
6.1	Australians aged 13–18: Attitudes to humanist beliefs and principles by worldview type (% of type)	99
7.1	Reported instances of religious discrimination of Buddhist, Hindu, Sikh, Muslim and Jewish teens	128
7.2	Australians aged 13–18: Attitudes to the freedom of religious expression by worldview type (% of type)	132
7.3	Australians aged 13–18: Views about religion in society (% of type)	134
8.1	Australians aged 13–18: Education and religion at secondary school (% of school type)	145
8.2	Australians aged 13–18: Sources of information about the world's religions (% of teens)	149
9.1	Australians aged 13–18: Attitudes towards education on sexuality by school type (% of school type)	162

Acknowledgements

We'd like to thank the young Australians who participated in the *Australia's Generation Z* (AGZ) study. This includes the students who took part in the school-based focus groups, the many teens across the country who kindly participated in the survey and those who agreed to follow-up personal interviews. We appreciate that you all shared something significant of your lives with us and have taught us a lot about how young people view the world today. We dedicate this book to your future.

We also thank the different secondary schools across Australia which allowed us to conduct the focus groups with their students, and our respective schools, faculties and universities: The School of Humanities and Social Sciences and the Alfred Deakin Institute at Deakin University; the Faculty of Education and School of Social Science at Monash University; and the School of Sociology at The Australian National University. A special note of thanks is due to Professor Matthew Clarke, Head of the School of Humanities and Social Sciences at Deakin University, and to the participants in the School of Humanities and Social Sciences' writing groups who read and commented on three of the chapters.

The authors gratefully acknowledge the following people for their valued contribution to the AGZ project and this book: Lisa Batten, for her first-rate and dedicated project management; Dr Ruth Fitzpatrick, for conducting the post-survey interviews with such care and skill; Dr Sulamith Graefenstein for her excellent work on project publications and assisting with this book; Olivia Kinnear, Dr Kim Lam, Dr Sophie Vasiliadis, Dr Clare Southerton and Dr Alan Nixon for their stellar research assistance at various stages and on different aspects of the project; and David Fagg for his sharp and considered editorial eye as we brought this book to completion. We wish them all the best in their academic careers and appreciate their involvement in our work. Thanks to graphic designer Lara Di Lizio for creating the infographics and figures that we have used in this book.

We are indebted to Dr Paul Myers, Dr Daniela Iarossi, and the Social Research Centre, Melbourne, for co-designing and administering the national survey, ensuring we obtained such excellent survey data.

At Bloomsbury Academic publishing, we'd like to acknowledge publisher Lalle Pursglove and editorial assistant Lily McMahon for good-naturedly shepherding this book through to publication. We are especially grateful to the two anonymous reviewers for their helpful and constructive comments about an earlier draft of this book.

Finally, we thank Professor Robert Jackson, Professor Leslie Francis and Dr Elizabeth Arweck of the University of Warwick's Religions and Education Research Unit, whose study on Young People's Attitudes to Religious Diversity in the United Kingdom greatly informed our research project.

The AGZ project on which this book is based was funded by the Australian Research Council (ARC) Discovery Grant Scheme. Project identifier: DP160102367 Young Australians' perspectives on religions and nonreligious worldviews. We thank the ARC for the generous funding on this project.

We gratefully acknowledge the copyright owners for permission to use the following material: Figure 1.1 © Lisa Maree Williams/Getty Images. Parts of Chapter 8 were published previously as Anna Halafoff, Andrew Singleton, Gary Bouma and Mary Lou Rasmussen (2020), 'Religious literacy of Australia's Gen Z teens: Diversity and social inclusion', *Journal of Beliefs and Values*, 41 (2): 195–213, DOI: 10.1080/13617672.2019.1698862. Used with permission from Taylor and Francis. The Easter picture in Chapter 7 was drawn by Mairead Spark and is used with her permission.

1

The future makers: Teens in the age of diversity

This book begins with a discussion of an intriguing photo (Figure 1.1). It shows a group of teenage boys, many of whom have Pasifika heritage, gathered outside Lakemba Mosque in Sydney's outer western suburbs. In the centre of the image are two teenagers, head bowed, foreheads almost touching. The boys are all students from the nearby Punchbowl Boys' High School, a (secular) government secondary school. They were at the mosque to honour the many Muslims killed and injured in the March 2019 terror attacks in Christchurch, New Zealand. Shortly after the embrace, the Pasifika teens sang a Fijian Christian hymn, *Noqu Masu*, and then performed the *haka*, a traditional Māori dance.

This photo, and the event it represents, is a powerful, suggestive snapshot of teenage lives in contemporary Australia – a multicultural, religiously diverse society.[1] It shows teenagers bridging religious and cultural differences in an act of unity, decrying the hatred and Islamophobia that drove the Christchurch attack. The Pasifika teens at Punchbowl Boys' High School, some of whose families are steeped in the rich Christian cultures of Oceania, have plenty of Muslim classmates.

The teens who go to Punchbowl Boys' High School encounter diversity daily. Remarkably, just about every student at the school has a language background other than English.[2] This reflects the considerable diversity of the surrounding area, the Sydney suburb of Punchbowl, where the majority of residents (54 per cent of the suburb's population) are born overseas, and Muslims represent the largest religious group (35 per cent of the population), followed by Catholics (23 per cent).[3]

Punchbowl is emblematic of recent, sweeping social and cultural change in Australia. Since the 1950s, Australia has transitioned from a mainly Anglo-European, Christian and monocultural country to a multicultural and religiously diverse nation, and one that increasingly acknowledges Indigenous peoples and

Figure 1.1 Punchbowl Boys' High School students at Lakemba Mosque, March 2019 Photo: © Lisa Maree Williams/Getty Images.

traditional ownership.[4] Now, almost a third of Australians are born overseas, and there are more Muslims, Buddhists and Hindus than Baptists or Lutherans. Compared to the late 1950s, there are more women in the paid labour market, and a greater proportion of the population live in the capital cities and have tertiary education. Social attitudes and values have also changed remarkably. For example, in 2017 – twenty years after Tasmania became the last jurisdiction to decriminalize homosexuality – the national parliament updated the 1961 Marriage Act to legislate for marriage equality for all people, including same-sex couples.

Contemporary teenagers, part of a birth cohort colloquially referred to as members of 'Generation Z' (those born between 1997 and 2016), are at the forefront of these changes. The *New York Times* recently described America's Gen Z as 'the most diverse generation in U.S. history'.[5] The same applies to Australia's Gen Zs. Statistically speaking, there is more cultural, linguistic and religious diversity among this birth cohort than the older 'Baby Boomers' or 'Silent Generation', or even 'Generation X' or the 'Millennials'. And their exposure to diversity is further amplified through their interactions on social media, at school and their local communities.

The actions at Lakemba Mosque suggest that teens are perfectly capable of building bridges across Australia's many cultural and religious traditions. Often, however, the media prefers stories that exemplify the 'risk' posed by diversity, and Punchbowl Boys' High School is a favourite target. An account of school life from a former student was published recently in the conservative, News Corp newspaper *The Australian* with the headline: 'Lebs [Lebanese students] let loose in Punchbowl "Prison"'.[6] Another strand of news reporting often raises the (unsubstantiated) spectre of Islamist radicalization among the student cohort there. A recent article in *The Australian* noted baselessly: 'And while there is no evidence it [the school] was or is, a hotbed of radicalisation, there is the potential for that to change'.[7]

Such fears about radicalization among the predominantly Muslim student cohort at Punchbowl Boys' High School reflects the fact that in recent decades there has been heightened media focus on minority religions, particularly Islam. Culturally and linguistically diverse youth are often viewed as especially *at risk* of radicalization, and therefore *as risks* to broader society.[8] The violence in Christchurch, however, suggests that Islamophobia, not radicalization, is a bigger danger in contemporary societies.

The *haka* at Lakemba Mosque contrasts sharply with the broader press coverage of teens in Western Sydney and gives rise to important questions about the teen experience of living in a multifaith society. How do Australia's teens experience and understand diversity in its many forms? How are their experiences mediated by their school, their faith *and* their geographic location? Amidst this diversity, what proportion of teens are religious, spiritual or atheist? And how different are Gen Z teens to members of older generations?

This book explores these questions. Drawing on data from a major, mixed-methods national study – the *Australia's Generation Z* (AGZ) study – it offers new ways of understanding the complexity of young people's lives and the ways they are apprehending and dealing with cultural and religious diversity. Importantly, and different from earlier studies on teen religion and diversity, one of our specific interests in this book is to learn more about how the worldviews of young people are mediated by gender and sexuality, *in addition* to their religious and nonreligious perspectives. To date, there has been no major Australian research that explores these topics together.[9] To be sure, this book spends more time exploring religion and spirituality, but discussion about gender and sexuality is certainly part of this broader conversation.[10] Religion and sexuality are often intertwined in public debates, especially when it comes to how religious schools might teach about these issues.

We must study teenagers. We know already that teen lives are shadowed by the escalating environmental crisis, the potentially deleterious effects of smartphones and social media and recovery from the Covid-19 pandemic. But religious, cultural, spiritual, gender and sexual diversity is an irreducible part of their everyday lives too. Consequently, our findings provide an empirical evidence base that can improve intercultural and LGBTQI+ understanding and social inclusion.

Moreover, if we know more about young Australians' worldviews and their attitudes to diversity, then appropriate educational programs can be developed that will equip young Australians to live more harmoniously in their diverse society. The role of education about religion in Australia has long been a controversial issue, and *young people's* voices have hardly been included in these debates. This book does not specifically analyse curriculum content or policy; rather, our interest is in *students' experiences* and subjective understanding of their education about religion, gender and sexuality. In later chapters, we argue that current school religious and sex education is founded on ways of thinking about young people that do not reflect the complexities of Gen Z's everyday experiences of diversity and their interactions with each other. We argue that certain kinds of education in schools can play a significant role in developing religious literacy, tolerance and positive attitudes to diversity.

To set the scene, in the remainder of this chapter we describe the specific catalysts for this book, with particular reference to emerging religious diversity, the recognition of LGBTQI+ rights and debates about diversity and education. We also explain what we mean by 'Generation Z' and why generational differences matter in understanding social change. We conclude by describing the AGZ project on which this book draws.

Diverse Australia

There have been some important recent research projects on contemporary Australian teens, exploring topics such as their mental and physical wellbeing, the preponderance of risk-taking behaviours, experiences of bullying (including cyberbullying on social media), labour force prospects, participatory citizenship, social inclusion and experiences of sex and sexuality.[11] Somewhat different to these studies, our interest is in how teens live with and experience religious and gender diversity.

Cultural, linguistic and spiritual diversity in Australia began at some point between 125,000 and 60,000 years ago with Indigenous peoples. Before white settlement, Indigenous people spoke over 250 languages and 800 dialects.[12]

Today, Indigenous Australians continue to have richly diverse cultures with many languages, peoples and nations.[13] Notably, before the introduction of the Immigration Restriction Act in 1901 (known colloquially as the White Australia Policy), Australia was home to sizeable communities of Buddhists, Muslims, Hindus, Sikhs and followers of Chinese religions, many of whom worked on the goldfields, in pearling industries, on sugar and cotton plantations or as camel drivers.[14] Because of this policy, some of these people were deported, and further groups of non-Europeans were largely prevented from migrating to Australia.

In recent decades, the primary driver of diversity in Australia has been large-scale international migration. While there has been human migration throughout history, its current scale and magnitude are unprecedented. Globally, the present era has been referred to as the 'Age of Migration', and an estimated 3 per cent of the world's population are migrants.[15] From the late 1940s, and following the demise of the White Australia Policy, Australia embarked on a major immigration program which extended far beyond Commonwealth and European citizens. After the UK, the major countries of origin are predominantly South Asian or Asian. Now, according to the Australian Bureau of Statistics, 'Australia has evolved into a nation of people from over 190 different countries and 300 different ancestries'.[16] Approximately half of all Australians were either born overseas or have at least one parent who was born overseas.[17]

Migrants and specific migrant communities (e.g. Sudanese-Australians) are not dispersed evenly across Australia. Rather, they are disproportionately drawn to the major capital cities, specific locales in those cities and certain rural and regional cities and towns. For example, 9 per cent of people living in the Melbourne suburb of Footscray have Vietnamese ancestry, which is nine times the national level. By contrast, in the suburb of Toorak, about a 15 km drive away, less than 1 per cent of the population has Vietnamese ancestry.

An important effect of this migration has been the emergence in Australia of genuine religious diversity. Christian hegemony was established with white settlement in the late eighteenth century, and by Federation (which included the introduction of the Immigration Restriction Act) in 1901, most people counted in the census identified as a Christian, even if they weren't going to church very often. Immigration to Australia in the post-war years has produced a flowering of religious and spiritual diversity beyond the major Christian denominations. As people migrated, they brought their religious affiliations with them. We have seen large-scale migration from majority-Muslim countries such as Lebanon and Turkey, and Asian and South Asian countries with large Hindu, Buddhist and Sikh populations.[18]

Now, census data reveal that only about half the Australian population identifies with a Christian denomination.[19] Together, followers of Buddhism, Hinduism, Judaism, Islam, Sikhism and other smaller faiths represent about 7 per cent of the population. Buried beneath these bigger 'tick-a-box' census classifications are the 'line counts' where people can write their response, and this runs to over 150 categories, from Armenian Orthodox to Theosophy and Spiritualism. There is also a staggering trend away from any religious identification: those with no religion comprise about 30 per cent of the population.

Religious communities are also characterized by considerable intra-group diversity. Australian Muslims, for example, come from over sixty-five different countries.[20] In like manner, more than a third of Pentecostals are born overseas, coming from sub-Saharan Africa, Oceania and Asia, among many places globally.[21] Today, religious diversity is Australia's 'new normal'. Importantly, the census data reveal that younger Australians are more likely than older Australians to have no religion or to be Pentecostal, Muslim, Sikh, Hindu or Buddhist. Similar patterns are found in most countries in the Global North, and particularly in the Anglosphere.[22]

Additionally, sexual and gender diversity is now an irreducible part of Australia's contemporary cultural mosaic, especially for young people. Teens are coming of age in a time when there is far greater acceptance of LGBTQI+ communities, as evidenced by the legislation of marriage equality in Australia in 2017. Benchmark Australian research finds that in the past two decades there has been an increase in young people's preparedness to be open about the diversity of their experiences of sexual attraction.[23] Fisher and Kauer, summarising data from repeated, cross-sectional national research on senior secondary students, find that the 'percentage of young people reporting some or exclusive sexual attraction to people of the same gender has grown from 6% in 1997 … to 39% in 2018'.[24] As we noted at the outset, teens are at the forefront of this experience of contemporary diversity.

Getting on well together?

To help manage emerging cultural (and religious) diversity, Australia implemented official multicultural policies under the Whitlam government in the 1970s. These policies legislated for diverse expressions of religion to be valued and tolerated. This development coincided with the cooling of sectarian antipathy between the Catholics and Protestant communities that had festered since white settlement.[25] From the 1970s to the 1990s there were significant improvements in intercultural relations in Australia. However, recent developments suggest that religious prejudice, intolerance and discrimination are rising.

Religious intolerance, comingled with racism, has been fuelled by unregulated social media, the activities of nationalistic political movements and abetted by some politicians. One Nation party leader Pauline Hanson called for a Royal Commission to determine if Islam was a 'political ideology' rather than a religion. (A recent Essential Poll found that 42 per cent of Australians surveyed agreed that 'politicians from Australia's major political parties have deliberately stirred up anti-Islamic sentiment as a way of getting votes'.)[26]

Beyond the public sphere, Australian Muslims, like others in the Global North, report that experiences of Islamophobia are not uncommon. One recent study found that Muslims experienced much higher rates of bigotry than the rest of the national population.[27] Instances of anti-Semitism are still commonly reported in the press. Given these developments, a study of how teenagers respond to diversity is timely. How responsible are they for religious discrimination, or is this largely an adult problem?

Teens, religious diversity and personal faith

To date, there have been no large-scale studies exploring how Australian teens respond to religious diversity. Two cognate studies from Great Britain that guided our research are the *Youth on Religion* and the *Young People's Attitudes to Religious Diversity* projects.[28] Both of these projects used mixed methods and included teens from many different cultural and faith backgrounds. For the most part, these projects found that British teens support the right of people of faith to practise their religions freely, and that religious diversity is viewed as a good thing for society. Of their *Youth on Religion* study, Madge and colleagues note: 'Tolerance, mutual respect and enthusiasm for integration across ethnic, cultural and religious divides contributed to the headline discourse of almost all participants.'[29] Despite being based on large surveys, neither of these important studies was based on a *national* sample, so it may be that pockets of resistance or ambivalence were missed. And as both these studies confirm, teens are certainly subject to, and sometimes perpetrators of, religious intolerance.

Further, in this book, we are particularly interested in how teens' beliefs and practices – their worldviews – are similar or different to teens of the past, and how this relates to their views of diversity. To that end, our study builds on some recent, notable social research on teen religion and spirituality. In the past three decades, there have been several major national-level or large-scale research projects on the religious and spiritual lives of teenagers throughout the Anglosphere (there are other notable studies of young adults, but these are beyond the scope of our inquiry).[30] American projects include the longitudinal *National Study of Youth and Religion*, which started its first wave in 2002.[31] British projects include the *Teenage Religion and Values*, *Teens on Religion* and the *Faith of Generation Y* studies.[32] Other large-scale research includes the Australian *Spirit of Generation Y* (SGY) project and the Canadian *Project Teen Canada*.[33] Additionally, there have been numerous high-quality, smaller qualitative projects that have explored how religious, spiritual and nonreligious youth live their everyday lives.[34]

Several of these larger studies have created typologies that codify the different approaches teens have to organized religion. This method has proved extremely helpful in identifying patterns of religious practice and belief in the population, and the sociocultural factors that condition these patterns (i.e. gender; parental religion, age). Building on this kind of approach, for this book we have created a typology of teen worldviews, using an innovative mixed-methods approach (latent class analysis *and* in-depth interviews). Our approach is novel because it gives greater credence to spiritual and nonreligious or secular points of view.

More generally, the previous research on teen religion amply illustrates how the profound cultural shifts of recent decades have resulted in a complex religious milieu, and that teens in the Anglosphere find meaning in many different places and often fragmentary ways. Importantly, an abiding theme in this research is that while teens are influenced deeply by their parents' religious and nonreligious preferences, there are also important differences between older and younger birth cohorts. The older generations, born in the decades before and after the Second World War, are more Christian and less diverse, whereas the birth cohorts who have followed them are less Christian and more diverse. As we demonstrate in later chapters, this trajectory is continuing unabated but with some surprising and unexpected turns.

And finally, our approach is informed by findings from recent research in Australia, North America, Great Britain and Europe that asserts that public and private forms of religion are in transition rather than simple decline (as per the secularization thesis), what Linda Woodhead characterizes as an 'intensified kind of pluralism'.[35] Norwegian sociologist of religion Inger Furseth describes this situation as 'religious complexity', and our mapping of worldview types seeks to explore this in the context of the lives of contemporary teens.[36] We are also proponents of the 'lived religion' approach to studying religion, as advocated by scholars like David Hall, Meredith McGuire and others.[37] According to Line

Nyhagen, a lived religion approach 'focuses on the experiences of ... individuals in everyday life ... [and] that people have an active and reflexive role in ... negotiating ... their own beliefs and practices'.[38] In this book, we are particularly interested in how teen worldviews intersect with other points of view they encounter in everyday life and what they learn and experience at school. Framing all of this are generational theories of religious change. As we describe in detail below, generational differences and dynamics are critical to understanding how teens experience religion, sexuality and diversity.

Can we do it better? Education about diversity

All of our study participants were at or had just completed school. It is an enormous part of the lives of teens, and they don't get a lot of say in the curriculum they get taught. Moreover, school is a context where religion, non-religion, spirituality, gender and sexuality are 'lived', conspicuously or not. For these reasons, we have a particular interest in education in the later chapters of this book.

Some context: Australia has three education sectors. In 2017, out of 3,849,225 students enrolled in 9,444 schools, 66 per cent of students attended government schools, 20 per cent Catholic schools and 15 per cent private independent schools (many of these have historic and/or continuing affiliations with Protestant denominations or Pentecostal churches).[39] No 'confessional' religious instruction or education (known as RI, RE or SRI, where 'S' stands for Special) in any faith tradition is allowed in Australian government secondary schools. Most Australian states, except for South Australia, allow volunteers from religious organizations to provide SRI to primary school students. Most SRI is Christian, but there are other options available in some schools, including Jewish, Buddhist, Muslim, Hindu, Baha'i and nonreligious SRI. Non-doctrinal education *about* religion is permitted at government secondary schools (we call this general religious education or GRE). By contrast, Australia's Catholic schools provide Catholic SRI and many also provide GRE at the secondary level. The third, private independent school sector, is mixed. Many of these schools are faith-based schools and provide SRI in their faith tradition and, in some cases, offer GRE at junior and/or senior levels. Most state-based curriculum bodies have GRE subjects available for Year 11 and 12 students. These subjects often include an in-depth study of nonreligious worldviews. However, very few state schools offer these subjects and they are mainly offered in Catholic or religious independent schools.

While teaching about religion in Australia's largely secular state school system has been viewed suspiciously in the past, Australian educators have begun to see the potential for educational programs that teach about diverse religions (i.e. GRE) or different worldviews (sometimes this is called worldviews education – WE). By enhancing religious literacy, and increasing knowledge about worldviews, international research suggests such programs can play a valuable role in developing intercultural understanding, social inclusion and perhaps help reduce extremism.[40]

However, the first national Australian Curriculum, which began to be developed in 2008, does not include any *dedicated* key learning areas or general capabilities focused on religious literacy. Rather, students have *ad hoc* opportunities to learn about religion and spirituality across the curriculum, confined mainly to classes in social studies, history, civics and citizenship, or health and physical education. By contrast, the Australian state of Victoria is the only state to have introduced dedicated content on *Learning about Worldviews and Religions* in the humanities. It is also part of the 'Ethical Capabilities' sections of its iteration of the national curriculum, from Kindergarten to Year 10. This education largely focuses on the main tenets of Australia's major faith traditions, as well as secular humanism and rationalism.[41]

Notwithstanding the potential of GRE and WE programs, there has been little research on its efficacy for young Australians. Consequently, in our study, we set out to ascertain existing levels of religious literacy (knowledge of religions) and attitudes towards religious diversity. We also wanted to know if teens had received SRI or GRE at school, what impact this had on their views and if they wanted more or less education about diverse worldviews.

That said, we acknowledge that issues related to religious education, freedom of religion and religious exemptions are frequently in the news, as are controversies related to gender and sexuality education. Hearing from young people about gender and sexuality should be integral to the public debate on these topics. To our knowledge, this project represents the first Australian national study which asks young people specifically about how they make sense of gender and sexual difference, as well as religious, nonreligious and spiritual difference, concerning education provision.

There is no doubt that young people in Australia are central in these debates because we compel them to attend public, private and religious schools, sometimes not of their choosing. They must find ways to navigate these spaces, encountering and negotiating religious, ethnic, sexual and gender diversity in their peer relationships, in the curriculum and through their interactions with school administrators and teachers. Too often, children and young people make the news because of adult concerns about them and their education. This book can be read as an intervention against what Barbara Baird terms 'child politics' where 'figures' of children and young people are deployed to further political and cultural agendas on the left and right.[42] In talking to young people themselves about their worldviews, they can educate us about their priorities regarding gender and sexuality, religion and belief.

Who are Generation Z and why does that matter?

In this book, we refer to the teens of this study as 'Generation Z' teens, members of a larger birth cohort that follows these cohorts: Millennials, Gen X, Baby Boomers and the Silent Generation (see Table 1.1 for details). The idea that each of these 'generations' has distinct characteristics plays well in the mass media and the market research industry.[43] For example, Sydney-based firm McCrindle Research claims that Gen Zs have a 'multi-modal' learning style, in contrast to Gen Xers, who have a 'participative' learning style.[44]

While some intergenerational comparisons don't ring true or have an uncertain evidence base, exploring birth cohort differences is nonetheless a legitimate and productive sociological enterprise. Social researcher Michael Dimock notes: 'Generations are a [helpful] lens through which to understand societal change, rather than a label with which to oversimplify differences between groups.'[45] Indeed, a common distinction sociologists make is between age, period and birth cohort.[46] Age refers to a person's stage on the life-course. (This project looks at the teenage years, a time of major developmental, cognitive

Table 1.1 Summary of birth cohorts (generations) in Australia

Generation	Birth years	Age in 2016	Size of cohort in 2016 ('000)	Proportion of popn. in 2016 (%)
Silent	1932–1945	71–84	2287.7	9.7
Boomers	1946–1964	52–70	5071.7	21.7
Generation X	1965–1980	36–51	4991.1	21.3
Millennials	1981–1996	20–35	5264.9	22.5
Generation Z	1997–2016	0–19	5786.1	24.7

Note: Percentages have been rounded.
Source: Australian Bureau of Statistics (ABS) 2016 census data.

and psychological changes.) Period refers to the time in which a person is born (e.g. a person is born in the 1940s). A birth cohort refers to the group of people who are born in the same period: this may be a one-year cohort (i.e. all people born in 1940), or a longer span, such as ten years or more (i.e. all people born in 1940–1949). A fifteen- to thirty-year span for a birth cohort is typically called a 'generation'.

As we noted above, giving different generations names is now common in both the media and among social researchers. The idea of naming specific birth cohorts, and specifically calling them 'generations', was popularized when the 'Baby Boomers' were teens. The Baby Boomer cohort was born in the twenty years following the Second World War (i.e. 1946–64). In most Western countries, there was a 'baby boom' during this period: a large increase in the fertility rate. We have followed the lead of the highly respected American research organization, the Pew Research Center, and adopted their timelines and names for the five generations shown in Table 1.1.

These generational names are widely known, save for perhaps the 'Silent Generation', which is the cohort born between the world wars, and shortly after the Great Depression. This group did not dominate the public imagination in the same way as the Baby Boomers. Table 1.1 uses data from the most recent Australian census (2016) to show how many people there are in each generation and their proportion in the population.[47] Numerically and proportionally, Gen Z is the largest generation. Our project focuses on those Gen Zs who were teens (aged 13–18) at the time of our survey (late 2017), and thus born between 1999 and 2004.

In this book, we present strong evidence for the generational distinctiveness of today's cohort of teens. We do so without glossing over or trivialising important geographic, ethnic and socio-economic differences between teens in the same birth cohort. Gen Z teens are different from teens of earlier generations when it comes to religious belief, practice and identification, attitudes towards religious diversity and attitudes towards gender and sexual diversity. They will be making a different future.

The AGZ Study: Research methods

The data in our book come from the mixed-methods, multi-stage AGZ study. Data were collected in **three stages**: (1) a series of focus groups; (2) a national survey; and (3) a tranche of follow-up, in-depth personal interviews with selected survey participants. This mixed-methods design enabled an ideal blend of research methods: the qualitative investigation in the first phase examined teens' attitudes in detail, allowing us to understand topics in greater depth. The national survey provided an accurate picture of Australian teens, which enabled generalization across the population and explored the causes and consequences of various attitudes and behaviours. The last phase, the interviews, allowed us to explore in depth some of the patterns we found in the survey, or to get some more detail about an issue. It also helped us refine our model of teen worldviews that are at the core of this book. We explain each phase in detail below.

FOCUS GROUPS: To develop a qualitatively rich understanding of everyday diversity in teen lives and guide the development of our national survey, we conducted focus groups in schools across Australia. A total of eleven focus groups were conducted in three Australian states between March and September 2017. To protect the identity of participants, and their school types and locations, we are not permitted to identify either the precise whereabouts (e.g. city/region or state) or school sector (e.g. government; Catholic; independent) of each school that took part in the focus groups.

That said, we did as much as possible to ensure we heard from a diverse range of voices in these focus groups. The schools were purposively sampled to include government and fee-paying schools, from advantaged and disadvantaged socio-economic areas, and in major cities and outer regional areas. Respondents identified variously as Christian (many different denominations, including Catholics, Anglicans and Pentecostals), Muslim, Buddhist, Hindu and Jewish, a combination of these, or nothing. Ninety-four students took part, mostly aged 15–16. We were particularly attuned to geographic location to ensure we have sufficient national coverage.

All four authors of this book conducted the focus groups (in teams of two). Each focus group proceeded along the same lines. We began with a religious literacy exercise, which involved showing the students several photos (religious, spiritual and atheist celebrities; religious and nonreligious symbols; places of worship; Indigenous heritage sites) to see if they recognized them and to find out what they thought about them. From there, we discussed aspects of diversity in their lives, at school and in their local communities, and how and what they have been taught about religion at school. Each focus group was audio-recorded, transcribed and then analysed with the assistance of the *NVivo* software program.

SURVEY: The focus groups proved enormously helpful in guiding the development of the national survey. We wrote the survey ourselves, but we also consulted cognate international projects, including two recent studies of British teens, the *Young People's Attitudes to Religious Diversity* project and the *Youth on Religion* (YOR) project.[48] We also consulted an earlier American study of teens, *National Survey of Youth and Religion* (NSYR), and Australian teens, *The Spirit of Generation Y* study, and in some instances used or adapted questions from these two surveys.[49]

The survey data were collected by the Social Research Centre (Melbourne) using CATI software, and the Centre also had input into the survey design and supplied several questions, particularly demographic ones. The survey was conducted by telephone from 23 October to 6 December 2017. Respondents from *all* Australian States and Territories were selected randomly using both mobile phone and landline numbers, and 1200 surveys were completed. The cooperation rate for the survey was 34.7 per cent. When the sample is compared with population data from the 2016 ABS Census on demographic variables such as age, gender and location, the match of sample and population is very close. To improve the representativeness of the survey, data are weighted by age, gender, location and telephone status (landline or mobile). Consequently, the sample is very representative of the population of Australian teens aged 13–18. In probabilistic terms, the maximum margin of error to apply to this survey is ±2.8 per cent.

Respondents ranged in age from 13 to 18 years old. Fifty-four per cent of survey respondents attended a government school; 24 per cent attended an independent school and 21 per cent attended a Catholic school; 5 per cent of respondents said they had an Aboriginal or Torres Strait Islander background. (Appendix 1 summarizes the sample characteristics and explains where the dataset and questionnaire can be accessed.) Data analysis and statistical modelling were done using the *SPSS* and *Latent Gold* statistical programs. For the statistically minded reader, there are endnotes in later chapters discussing technical issues and fine-grained survey details.

POST-SURVEY INTERVIEWS: Thirty in-depth interviews were conducted by phone with survey participants who indicated they would be willing to do a further, in-depth follow-up interview. These post-survey interviews allowed the research team to go behind some of the survey responses teens had given and to ask more complex questions about negotiating religious, cultural, sexual and gender diversity in their peer relationships and at school. We also used these interviews to help us refine the model of teen worldviews we derived from our survey data.

Interviewees were drawn from every state and territory apart from Tasmania and come from major cities, and inner and outer regional areas. All of these interviewees were aged 18. As legal adults, they had been able to consent to an interview without us needing to secure parental permission. These interviews were conducted by phone between April and June 2018. Each interview was audio-recorded, transcribed and analysed with the assistance of the *NVivo* software program.

Our data collection was approved by our respective university ethics committees and, where needed, by state education departments or the regional ethics committees of selected school systems. Each of the informants has been given a pseudonym and other identifying details have been changed. The data-gathering process did not give rise to any ethical issues for the participants or the team.

A final note on methods: throughout this book we've included lots of direct quotes from teens who took part in the focus groups and interviews. When talking, Australian teens tend to use lots of speech disfluencies and fillers. For example, one interview excerpt included in a later chapter was originally 670 words in length, of which the speaker said 'like' 68 times (i.e. 10 per cent). Teens also use the words 'really' and 'actually' a lot. To make the transcribed interviews easier to read we've edited them for clarity, but it should be remembered, like, really, that these excerpts differ from the spoken word, actually.

Structure of the book

In the chapters that follow, we map Australian teens' attitudes towards and experiences of cultural, spiritual and religious diversity; we identify and analyse the factors and influences shaping these attitudes; we explore the effects these attitudes and behaviours have for young people's relationships with their peers, family, schooling and wider society; and provide an evidence base that informs education about diverse religions and worldviews in Australia.

Chapter 2 focuses on how teenagers engage with organized religion, once dominant but now on the wane in Australia. We explore patterns of conventional religious belonging, belief and practice among Gen Z teens, and how this is similar or different to the teens of the past. While religion is still important to a small minority, for the most part, today's teens do not believe or belong in ways that are familiar to members of older generations. We explain why this is the case.

If most teens aren't interested in religion, what about other kinds of spirituality? Contemporary Western society is awash with alternative spiritual beliefs, practices and possibilities. In Chapter 3, we explore the extent to which teens participate in this milieu, as well as their interest in other wellbeing activities, like yoga and meditation. We find a modest-sized tranche of teens interested in or attached to different spiritual ideas and possibilities.

Teens think in many different ways about life's 'big picture'. To provide a detailed, nuanced map of this, we have deployed a new, powerful form of statistical analysis that allows us to identify six different 'types' of teen worldviews. Importantly, this approach moves beyond conventional religious/nonreligious or spiritual/non-spiritual binaries. The heart of this book, Chapters 4–6, describes these six different teen worldviews. In Chapter 4, we discuss how we arrived at our typology. We then look in detail at the two types that are connected, at least in part, to established faith traditions. Chapter 5 explores the two worldview types that are oriented towards the 'spiritual but not religious' and explores how such perspectives are related to ethics, values and outlooks. Rounding out our discussion, Chapter 6 explores the two worldview types that are 'this-worldly' in orientation and explains how such perspectives shape how teens live.

We start Chapter 7 by explaining how diversity is a fact of life for contemporary teens. What is this like for them? Do they experience racism or religious discrimination? Are teens more tolerant and open-minded than adults? This chapter explores what it is like growing up in religiously and culturally diverse contexts.

Chapter 8 takes education as its focus. What role does education play in shaping attitudes to religious diversity? And why is teaching about religion in schools such a controversial issue? Can education about diverse worldviews improve inter-religious understanding, and if so, how? And what do Australian teens think about all this? This chapter addresses these questions.

Almost 14 per cent of our survey respondents didn't identify as straight, and many more are tolerant of LGBTQI+ diversity. This is reflected in their attitudes regarding education about LGBTQI+ issues in school. As we detail in Chapter 9, on sexuality, gender and education, they told us that they wanted schools to be inclusive spaces and they sometimes felt that generational differences regarding worldviews on gender, sexuality and education were more reflective of their parents' desires than their own. The majority also strongly embraced marriage equality and this translated into opposition towards religious exemptions, regardless of religious affiliation.

The conclusion explores the implications our findings have for how education about diversity should meaningfully occur in school settings.

2

Doing away with our Sunday best: Teenagers and the remaking of religion in Australia

Whenever there is a news story about teens and religion in Australia, Hillsong Church is likely to get a mention. For example, a recent article in the *Australian Financial Review* starts with the journalist's description of a typical Hillsong Sunday night youth service, replete with a bouncing crowd, smoke machine and rock band. Another recent feature in the major dailies quotes Hillsong pastor Brian Houston: 'We've always seen young people at church because they want purpose in their lives and are looking for answers.'[1] There is a reason why Hillsong draws the media's focus – it is a rare instance of a church that attracts teenagers.

Hillsong has become a global entity, with churches in more than a dozen countries. The main campus is in Sydney's Baulkham Hills. It looks like a stadium, with seating capacity for several thousand people. Hillsong is a Pentecostal church, part of the Pentecostal-Charismatic Christian (PCC) movement in Australia. Since the 1970s, Pentecostalism has transitioned from a fringe religious curiosity to a major religious movement with many of Australia's largest congregations. Pentecostal churches like Hillsong, along with Riverview in Perth, Influencers Church in Adelaide and Planetshakers in Melbourne, draw large numbers each weekend. Previous research suggests teens and young adults are more likely to attend a PCC church than any other single Christian denomination, including the Catholic Church.[2] Australia is not unique: Pentecostalism is the ascendant Christian movement across the globe.[3]

Part of the PCC appeal lies in their non-traditional church spaces, informal service style and dynamic preaching. Most critical to their success, however, is their congregational music, which folds the Christian message into a contemporary pop sound.[4] It is played loud, and professionally. These services are more like a rock concert than a traditional church service.

Looking closely at the PCC movement, however, obscures the bigger picture. Hillsong and churches of its ilk are not attracting legions of new converts.[5] Rather, young people committed to the Christian faith are increasingly clustered in these kinds of churches.[6] In general, the Pentecostal experience, like most kinds of *organized religion*, is becoming peripheral to the lives of an ever-increasing majority of Australian teens, an argument we present in this chapter.

Here is an example of how much places like Hillsong register in the minds of Australian teenagers. As part of the data collection for this project, the research team conducted focus groups with teenagers in eleven different schools across Australia. To start the focus group discussion, we showed the students a series of photos, one of which was a picture of Hillsong. Only three students out of ninety-four, two Christians and one Muslim, correctly identified the image. A few others knew it was some kind of Christian activity, variously describing the photo as a 'church group concert', a 'conference', a 'festival', as 'Evangelical' and 'Pentecostal' worship, as 'Jesus Christian rock or something, they're like a Christian band but they're metal at the same time, pretty strange'. For the most part, however, PCC churches were not familiar to them.

One focus group at a regional high school is illustrative. The students, when asked about the photo, had the following exchange with each other:

Participant 5:	Oh, I've been to …
Participant 3:	[It's a] concert.
P1:	Yeah, kind of a concert.
P2:	Isn't it like where?
P5:	I've been to one of these in the Philippines. Yeah, because some of my family members are part of it. It's like they do the same thing as [other] Christians but they sing a lot …
P2:	So, like a youth kind of – it's like a youth group kind of thing. Yeah?
P5:	Everyone is singing and I remember because everyone was singing and all of a sudden, they started crying for some weird reason. Then afterwards we got free food. So, [laughter] that's all I remembered.
P1:	Teenage boy, free food, that's it.

Even if PCC churches remain buoyant, teens aren't signing up for this or most kinds of conventional religion.

How did contemporary Australia – once an unmistakably religious country – get to this point? And if most teens are not religious, are they atheists or humanists? Or do they follow other possibilities, like a spirituality centred around nature, or cultivate an interest in the supernatural? The next few chapters explore the religious and spiritual lives of Australia's current generation of teenagers – 'Generation Z' teens – and explains how we got here.

This chapter explores how teenagers engage with conventional religion. It begins with an overview of recent religious change in Australia. We then show how each generation has a distinct approach to religion and how important this is in making sense of what is going on. Having established this context, we use data from the AGZ study to explore patterns of conventional religious belonging, belief and practice among Gen Z teens, and how this is similar or different to the teens of the past. For the most part, they do not believe or belong in ways that are familiar to members of older generations. More teens than ever before live in a non-faith world. This chapter explains why.

Out with the old: The slow eclipse of Christian Australia

Making sense of the present involves some understanding of the past and, specifically, how the past informs the present. In the mid-twentieth century, Australia was a demonstrably Christian country, if this is measured by levels of Christian affiliation, attendance and belief, and the normality of Christianity in the public mind.[7]

Here's an excellent example: the famous American evangelist Billy Graham toured Australasia in early 1959, hosting a series of 'revival' rallies. Each rally offered the opportunity for the audience to make 'a decision for Christ'. One of the first rallies took place at the newly opened Sidney Myer Music Bowl, a large outdoor venue on the edge of the Melbourne CBD. Tens of thousands of people turned out for the Music Bowl rally. It was also televised, TV having arrived in Australia three years earlier. Graham began his rally with a prayer and then read out a letter he'd received from a self-described 'bodgie', one of Australia's notorious gangs of louts.[8] The bodgie urges Graham to hold a special rally for young people like himself, badly in need of 'saving'. Graham confirmed to his audience that he was indeed holding such an event, that coming Saturday night at the nearby Melbourne Cricket Ground (MCG), a venue that could hold a much bigger crowd. He exhorted his audience: 'Bring at least one teenager with you this coming Saturday night.' Thousands heeded his call, and that Saturday the MCG filled with the largest-ever crowd at that venue, more than 140,000 people.[9] On that tour alone, approximately 130,000 people made 'decisions for Christ', many of whom were teenagers.[10] These young people were drawn predominantly from 'mainline' Protestant traditions, including the Church of England, Methodist and Presbyterian denominations. Many Catholic teens also attended the rallies. Teens from back then are now the grandparents of today's teens and young adults.

The late 1950s was arguably the apogee of Christianity in Australia. According to historian David Hilliard: 'In the mid-1950s in every denomination, all the measurable indices of religious life – church membership, Sunday school enrolments, the number of new congregations, church income and enrolments in theological colleges and seminaries – had gone steadily upwards.'[11] The churches enjoyed strong attendances, and with their associated sporting clubs and regular dances, they played a role in the community that went beyond simply meeting people's religious needs. Almost everyone at that time had some kind of Christian knowledge and experience.

This example illustrates the importance of the era in which we grow up. The teenage years are an important time in a person's development and evolving sense of self. It is a time of important physical, social and cognitive changes.[12] Increasingly, social scientists understand that people are shaped for the rest of their lives by the social and cultural circumstances of their teen and 'emerging adult' years.[13]

The Christian mood of that time proved deeply affective for teens of the 1950s, a birth cohort often referred to as the 'Silent' generation (born 1932–45). Teenagers back then came of age when being a Christian (either Catholic or Protestant) was a normal thing for almost everyone, and a large proportion of the population was connected to a church. As we will see below, the loyalties and affiliations teenagers cultivated at this time have remained in place for the rest of their lives.

In the space of fifty years, Australia's religious mosaic has changed markedly from the Christian society that welcomed Billy Graham so enthusiastically. Figure 2.1 compares three time periods in the past fifty years: the early 1960s, the early 1990s and the present. This comparison shows the slow eclipse of Christianity, the rise of the religious 'Nones' and the emergence of genuine religious diversity.

Several important patterns are evident: the proportion of the population identifying as Christian has decreased remarkably (from 88 per cent to 52 per cent), while the proportion with no religious identification, the religious 'Nones' has reached 30 per cent. (Those who claim to have no religion are typically referred to in the scholarly literature as 'Nones'.) In the 1961 census, there was no 'No religion' option one could select. Reflecting the mood of society, this was changed in 2016 and 'No religion' was the first category in the list of

Doing Away with Our Sunday Best 21

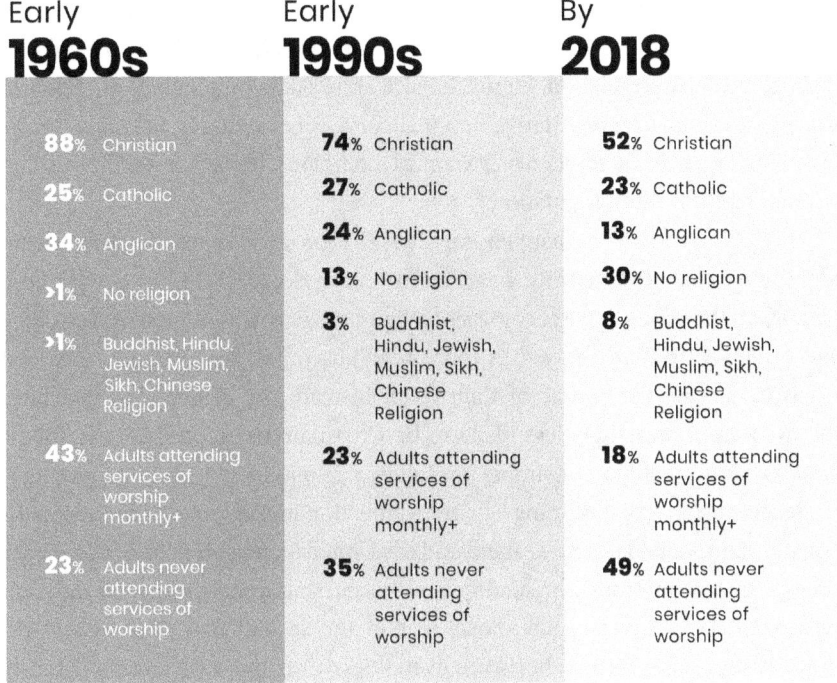

Sources: Affiliation: ABS census data for various years; Attendance: 2014 Hilda Survey; 1961 Gallup Survey. Figures have been rounded.

Figure 2.1 Religious change in Australia, 1960s–present.

religions on the census; 'Nones' are now the single largest religious grouping in Australia. Anglicans have declined precipitously and now represent 13 per cent of the population, down from 33 per cent in 1961. Other 'mainline' Protestant denominations (i.e. Uniting, Presbyterian, Methodist, Baptist, Lutheran, Churches of Christ) have also shrunk as a proportion of the population.

Among Protestants, it is only the Pentecostals who have defied this trend. Especially in the 1980s and 1990s, they benefitted greatly from religious 'switchers' (those joining from Catholic and mainline Protestant denominations) and migration.[14] The Catholic Church, buoyed by a schooling system which sustains the importance of Catholic identification, in addition to migration from Catholic countries, has not experienced a notable decline in affiliation. That said, attendance at Mass has fallen markedly, and most Catholics maintain little more than a nominal affiliation to their denomination.[15]

The other important change has been the emergence of genuine religious diversity. In the early 1960s, less than 1 per cent of the population was Jewish, Muslim, Buddhist or Hindu, among other faiths. By the 2016 census, this figure increased to 8 per cent. Australia also now boasts three substantial religious minority communities – Muslims, Buddhists and Hindus – each being at or over 2 per cent of the population. Figure 2.1 also shows data on religious attendance, drawn from three representative national surveys of adults. In the early 1960s, less than a quarter of adults never went to a religious service. By 2018, this had risen to half the adult population.

This change did not happen rapidly. The proportion of the population identifying with Christianity has shrunk every decade. This is not because people, on the whole, have become less religious, disavowing Christianity as they age. Older Australians, raised in more religious times, have largely remained Christian across the course of their lives. Instead, the generations that have followed are increasingly less likely to be Christian and more likely to follow another kind of religion or simply not follow a religion.

Recent research on declining Christian affiliation in Anglophone countries like Great Britain, Canada, New Zealand and the United States shows that the broader societal turn away from Christianity is not occurring uniformly across different birth cohorts.[16] This research shows that in the second half of the twentieth century, successive birth cohorts are overall less Christian and more religiously diverse than the preceding cohort (if measured by affiliation *and* attendance).

The same is true in Australia. In the 2016 Australian census, it was revealed that 39 per cent of Millennials are Nones; they are followed by Gen X, 30 per cent of whom are Nones, and Boomers, 23 per cent of whom are Nones. By contrast, only 14 per cent of the Silent Generation have no religion.[17] Conversely, 73 per cent of the Silent Generation identify as Christian compared to 39 per cent of Millennials. This differentiated generational profile is evident not just in the 2016 census, but in previous censuses as well. All of this indicates that **generational characteristics**, and **the time in which that generation comes of age**, are important factors in producing society-wide religious change.[18]

A case in point is the Billy Graham example from the beginning of this chapter: the Silent Generation were teens when there was broad social and peer support for their denominational affiliation and an expectation that a person attended the church at least at Christmas and Easter. Sectarian tensions between Protestants and Catholics also heightened the importance of denominational identity.[19] Even today, this generation continues to follow a model of 'old style religion' characterized by denominational fidelity and occasional attendance.[20]

Consequently, attendances at and affiliation with the Anglican, Presbyterian, Reformed, Uniting, Baptist and Lutheran Churches are disproportionately made up of members of the Silent Generation. This church-going society, defined by the hegemony of British Protestantism, loyalty to one's denomination, monocultural communities and many 'Christmas and Easter' attenders, is now long eclipsed, living only in the memories of the oldest Australians and their lifelong loyalties.

The drift in Australian society from traditional Christianity began seriously when the Boomers (the generation who followed the Silent Generation) came of age in the late 1960s and early 1970s. The Baby Boomers represented something of a population 'bulge'; there were more of them than other birth cohorts, and their youth culture developed an inexorable momentum. Theirs was a time of experimentation and questioning. Historian of religion Callum Brown notes that this was a period characterized by 'the sexual revolution; the rise of drug-taking … the loss of respect for civic institutions … the resulting challenge to authority (notably by youth in a so-called generation gap) … [and] the emergence of a new women's activism'.[21] For Australians, the Whitlam era gave full expression to this sense of social change, with reforms to the marriage act, social welfare, tertiary education and women's reproductive rights.

Emboldened, Boomers experimented with new religious movements (NRMs), the New Age and forms of spirituality characterized by fluidity, individual choice and hybridity. Boomers travelled more than their parent's generation, exposing them to different religious and spiritual options. Spiritual odysseys, to places like India, were common.[22] Less formal approaches to the Christian faith also came to the fore. The PCC churches grew markedly on the strength of Baby Boomer affiliation.

The population boom had other knock-on effects that proved deleterious to Christianity's comfortable, established place in society. Nine new universities opened in Australia between the late 1950s and the mid-1970s. In these institutions, Boomer students campaigned for a radical remaking of society. Moreover, cities expanded rapidly to accommodate the boom in families. This fractured tight-knit inner suburban Protestant and Catholic enclaves, and new parishes weren't always established in the ever-expanding commuter suburbs. Moreover, the post-war migration meant that there was greater cultural diversity than before.

By the mid-1980s, migration, mobility, consumerism and individualism further entrenched the drift from traditional forms of Christian belonging for the next generation (Gen X), and this trend continued apace for the Millennials. Shopping centres and sporting clubs replaced churches as focal points in the community. These generations also experienced a society in which cultural diversity was becoming the norm and multiculturalism, and its corollary, religious diversity, widely appreciated. And because being a None has become commonplace, we are now bearing witness to the increased intergenerational transmission of no religious identity. Gen X (mainly the parents of Gen Z) are increasingly raising Nones, something that we will demonstrate later in this chapter.[23]

This drift from traditional, institutionalized Christianity, the eclipse of Christian forms of religious belonging and participation, the rise of new spiritualities and the reality of religious diversity establishes the context for the religious and spiritual lives of Generation Z's teens. Unlike Millennials and Gen X, they are coming of age in a time of unprecedented global communication systems and live in a world defined by social media. They also live in a world in which religious institutions are to be questioned and not trusted. They are confronted regularly with grim revelations of abuses allowed by religious institutions, or the atrocities and crimes perpetrated in the name of religion. In the remainder of this chapter, we look at the distinctive ways in which contemporary teens are engaging with faith and thus how they are remaking religion in Australia.

'Old school'? Organized religion among Gen Z teens

Traditionally, social scientists have measured religiosity by looking at patterns of belonging, belief and practice. In the remainder of this chapter, we explore contemporary teens by those measures. As expected, the ongoing generational drift from Christianity is pronounced, but this does not mean that teens are wholly this-worldly. Reflecting the diverse society in which they live, many believe, and to a lesser extent, belong, in complex ways. Our data are drawn from the nationally representative 2017 AGZ survey, focus groups and interviews.

No logo? Changing patterns of religious identification among teens

The great diversity of religions in contemporary Australia is reflected in the religious identification of the AGZ survey respondents. This is shown in Figure 2.2.

Our survey respondents included Muslims (3 per cent), Buddhists (2 percent), other religions (2 per cent) and Hindus (1 per cent). Among Christians (38 per cent of the population), the single largest Christian denomination is Catholic (19 per cent of the total population; 49 per cent of Christians), followed by Anglicans

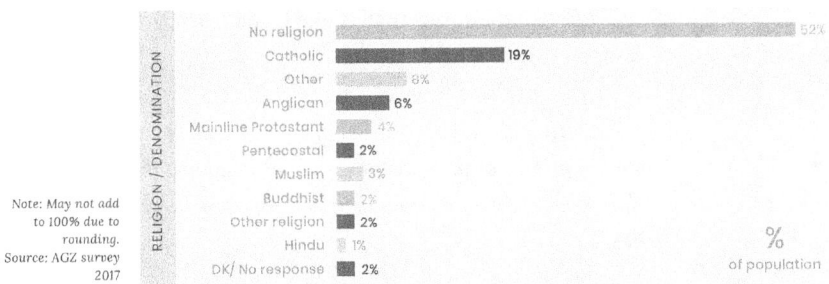

Figure 2.2 Australians aged 13–18: Current religion/denomination (% of teens).

(6 per cent of the total; 15 per cent of Christians) and other mainline Protestants (4 per cent).[24] Other Christians ('Other') counted in our survey include Mormons, the Orthodox and independents and are 8 per cent of the total.[25]

The single largest group – more than half of contemporary teens – have no religious identity (52 per cent). As we demonstrate later, being a 'None' does not mean a person has no faith or spirituality: they simply do not see themselves as belonging to a religious tradition.

Not only has the religious profile of Australia altered in recent decades, *what it means* to identify with a religion has changed remarkably in a few decades. As noted above, the Silent Generation were teens when religious identification was normative for almost everyone – a social obligation.[26] In contrast, most contemporary teens who identify with a Protestant denomination probably do so more because of a meaningful connection with that particular faith group. This was illustrated abundantly at a focus group we conducted at a Protestant denominational school on the outskirts of a major city. Although they attended a Protestant school, none of them felt obliged to identify with the school's church tradition:

Q: *But to you, the [names Protestant school name] thing doesn't matter? Doesn't mean anything?*

Participant 5: It just means the school has a chapel and we will attend services, now and then. [The school currently had no chaplain.] When we did have a reverend or a chaplain it would be like a thing where it was about, the subject would be, say respect and then he'd mention a story from the Bible or something like that which has that, the theme of respecting people. Something like that ... just using that as an example [of how] the school is [names denomination]

	or Christian … It uses that as like – you learn from this [story].
Q:	*[When I have done previous research] in … Catholic schools … the students, all there, kind of go, 'Catholic' school and we're Catholic even though they're not religious. But you don't come here and go we're at a [Protestant] school?*
P2:	No.
P3:	No.
Q:	*Doesn't mean anything to you?*
P2:	No, not really.

As we noted above, the drift from Christianity in Australia is driven by generational differences. Since the 1960s, the drift has been fairly slow: inexorable, but not rapid.

However, new evidence, drawn from our survey and comparing it to one done on Millennial teens a decade ago, suggests that the pace of change is accelerating. The first time Australian teenagers were surveyed nationally about their religious preferences was the SGY study of 2005 when a cohort of Millennial teens was surveyed. Now, the AGZ survey can be compared to that study, a reliable 'then and now' snapshot of two cohorts taken during their critical, formative teenage years. This will give an accurate picture of generational differences among the younger age cohorts in Australia and the pace of that change. The comparison is shown in Table 2.1.

This table shows that **the overall** proportion of teens who are Christian has dropped by 10 per cent in a little over a decade (48 per cent in 2005 compared to 38 per cent in 2017). Moreover, compared to teens back in 2005, a **greater proportion** of teens today identify as Buddhist, Hindu, Jewish, Muslim or Sikh (we use the shorthand BHJMS for this group) or do not identify with a religion at all.[27] The Gen Z age cohort is not only less religious as a whole but also more religiously diverse than the Millennials were at the same age.

This pattern confirms the generational account of change we posited earlier. Remarkably, big differences are emerging in the space of little more than a decade. The demise of Christian Australia is now rapid and inexorable, and teens are at the forefront of this change. For the first time since white settlement, the majority of teens don't identify with a religious group. What about other once-conventional things: belief in God and attendance at services of worship? How common are these among teens, and are they declining rapidly too, between one generation and the next?

Table 2.1 Patterns of religious identification among Australian teens: 2005 and 2017 (% of teens in those years)

Religion/denomination	Teens in 2005 (Millennials) %	Teens in 2017 (Gen Z) %
Catholic	23	19
Other Christian	25	19
BHJMS*	4	7
No Religion	45	52
Total	**100**	**100**

* BHJMS: Buddhist, Hindu, Jewish, Muslim or Sikh.
Sources: SGY Survey 2005; AGZ Survey 2017.
Note: Percentages may not add to 100 due to rounding or because small numbers of missing are excluded from the table. (Singleton, on the SGY team, thanks his colleagues on that project.)

'I guess, sometimes I believe that there is, like, a God there': Religious beliefs, practices and attitudes among Gen Z teens

The quote in the title of this section comes from one of the interviewees in this project, 18-year-old Lucinda. She talked a little about the things she believed. Like a lot of teens, she doesn't identify with a religion but maintains an openness to belief in a higher being. She said:

> I guess ... sometimes I believe that there is a God there ... I guess. I don't pray to – I don't pray to God or anything like that. I do believe [that] some things that go on ... when people are saved from things that were impossible or people come back from something ... that's a sign that there is, something out there, helping people.

Paul, 18, identifies as Catholic and believes in God – in his way. He said: 'I, sort of, believe – that there is, sort of – to label it, a higher power. Because of my upbringing, I'm happy to call it God, but I'm not – I'm certainly not a hard-line Catholic.'

We started with these quotes from Paul and Lucinda because they illustrate something of the loose, relative ways in which teens think about existential matters. While identification with a religious group is increasingly 'old-school' for most teens, belief in God – or a higher being – is accepted by a larger number. Not all of the believers in this higher being, like Lucinda, frame this within the bounds of organized religion and the practices, expectations and obligations of religious institutions. Even those who identify with a religion, like Paul, are not necessarily orthodox in their approach.

To demonstrate this, throughout this section, we explore religious practices and beliefs according to stated religious affiliation (e.g. the proportion of Catholic teens who believe in God; attend Mass). Table 2.2 shows Gen Z teens' belief in some kind of higher being, whether this is God or something else.

Looking *down* the column on the right, percentage of all teens, we present totals for each of the responses. This shows that only about a quarter of contemporary teens have no belief in God or anything else (24 per cent); slightly more than a third (37 per cent) believe in God, and just less than a third believe in a higher being or life force instead of God (30 per cent). A small proportion is not sure (9 per cent). Later, we will examine whether levels of belief in God has decreased between this generation of teens and the preceding one.

> **Digging deeper:** Thirty-seven per cent of Gen Z teens say they believe in God. **Of these believers**, about three-quarters of them think that they can have a personal relationship with God (rather than God being something like an impersonal, 'cosmic force').

Looking *down* the columns we see patterns for each group, and several things are important to note. **Catholic** teens hold a mixed bag of beliefs; about two-thirds believe in God (66 per cent), a substantial minority believe in a higher being or life force (22 per cent) and the rest are unsure or don't believe (12 per cent). Here we see the first indication that many Catholic teens have little more than a nominal affiliation with the church. Paul, whose comments were noted above, is a typical example. Teens who identify with a **mainline Protestant** denomination (i.e. the Anglican, Uniting, Lutheran, Presbyterian Churches) effectively follow the same pattern as Catholic teens.[28]

As might be expected, the **Nones** lead the way when it comes to having no belief in any kind of transcendent being or power (42 per cent), but fully more than a third (39 per cent) believe in a higher being or life force, and a small minority (13 per cent) are not sure or uncertain. This is instructive: even though these teens don't have a religious identification, a plurality believes in a higher being/God.

Table 2.2 Australians aged 13–18: Belief in higher being by religious identification (% of group)

Belief	Religious identification (%)					Total for all teens (13–18)
	Catholic	Mainline Protestant	Other Christian	BHJMS	Nones	
No belief in God/higher-being/life force	6	1	2	14	42	24
Believes in God	66	73	90	58	6	37
Belief in higher being or life force, but not God	22	21	7	25	39	30
Don't know or unsure	6	5	0	3	13	9
Total	100	100	100	100	100	100

Source: AGZ Survey 2017.

Note: Percentages in tables may not add to 100 because of rounding, or because small proportions of 'Don't know' and 'No answer' responses have been omitted to simplify the table. Unless otherwise noted, 'column percentages' are assumed – that is, in this, the number 66 in the column headed 'Catholic' means that 66 per cent of Catholic teens believed in God – not that 66 per cent of those who believed in God were Catholic. Cells with small percentages are not reliable for comparison purposes.

> **We asked the Nones in our survey:** 'Do you consider yourself to be an atheist, an agnostic, a Humanist, just not religious or something else?'. Sixty per cent said not religious, 22 per cent said atheist, 10 per cent said agnostic and 1 per cent were humanists.

Reading *across* the columns shows that the **Other Christian** category is most likely to believe in God – 90 per cent of them. This group comprises mainly Pentecostals and those who attend other independent churches. Most of these teens can be described as evangelical Christians.[29] We return to them in Chapter 4.

The Buddhist, Hindu, Jewish, Muslim or Sikh category (BHJMS) is a mixed bag. Given that not all those faiths believe in the Abrahamic God, and given the small numbers surveyed, firm conclusions should not be drawn from these data. That said, most of the Muslim teens surveyed expressed belief in Allah (this question was asked appropriately in the survey).

In sum, only about a quarter of Australia's teens have no belief at all in a transcendent being; the rest accept something, whether this is a conventional belief in God, or something more inchoate or protean – a sense that there is more to life than the material world. For the reasonable number of Nones who believe in a higher being, this belief owes little to a faith tradition. We explore the significance of this in later chapters.

Table 2.3 records attendance at services of worship and frequency of personal prayer. When it comes to orthodox religious faith, these are considered the most decisive measures of commitment, at least in the Abrahamic traditions. These data are a self-assessment rather than an outwardly objective measure (like counting actual attendance). It tells us how committed teens think they are to various traditions.

The big picture is readily apparent: almost six out of ten teens (58 per cent) *never* attend services of worship, and a further 11 per cent go once or twice a year (e.g. Christmas and Easter; maybe a special service). This means that the very large majority of teens (almost 70 per cent) hardly have anything to do with Australia's many houses of worship. By contrast, 12 per cent go weekly or more often. In terms of prayer, about 13 per cent pray often, and a further 14 per cent pray 'sometimes'.

Which teens are the ones who are most enthusiastic about these religious practices? Like belief in God, it's predominantly the evangelical and Pentecostal teens (our **Other Christian** category) who go to church and pray most

Table 2.3 Australians aged 13–18: Religious practices by religious identification (% of group)

Practice	Religious identification (%)					
Attendance at services of worship	Catholic	Mainline Protestant	Other Christian	BHJMS	Nones	Total for all teens (13–18)
Never	36	39	20	32	82	58
Once or twice a year	15	12	3	15	12	11
A few times a year	21	10	8	23	3	9
About once a month	8	5	7	8	1	4
2–3 times per month	4	8	15	9	0	4
Weekly+	16	26	47	13	1	12
Total	100	100	100	100	100	100
Frequency of prayer*						
Never / not asked	22	27	10	16 (14)	29 (54)	54
Rarely	38	19	18	21	12	19
Sometimes	24	28	31	19	4	14
Often	16	28	41	30	1	13
Total	100	100	100	100	100	100

*Only asked if respondent identified as Christian or if believed in God/higher being. Fifty-four per cent of the 'Nones' were not asked if they prayed, along with 14 per cent of the BHJMS group. Cells with small percentages are not reliable for comparison purposes.

Source: AGZ Survey 2017.

Note: Percentages in tables may not add to 100 because of rounding or because small proportions of 'Don't know' and 'No answer' responses have been omitted.

frequently. As we explained in the introduction, Australia's most religiously active (Christian) teens are clustered mainly in these traditions, even more than a decade ago. We pick up this theme in Chapter 4 when we also discuss followers of the other major faith traditions. As might be expected, most of the Nones never go to services of worship or pray.

Catholic teens are an interesting group – about a third never go to Mass (36 per cent), while another third (36 per cent) go a handful of times a year. Less than a third (28 per cent) attend with any kind of regularity – monthly or more often. This pretty much sums up contemporary Catholic teens. A substantial portion is not conventionally religious and at best are nominally Catholic or equivocal about many orthodox Catholic teachings and practices. As a cohort, they are less religious than evangelical and Pentecostal teens.

One such Catholic teen is Elizabeth, one of thirty people with whom we did a post-survey interview. She was raised Catholic and went to Catholic primary and secondary schools. She continues to identify as Catholic today. Elizabeth told us that she believes in God but doesn't attend Mass very much at all. She's curious about religion but hardly follows Catholic orthodoxy. On being Catholic she said:

> You don't have to follow the mainstream line of your actual religion, like, you don't have to go to church to speak to God like he's always there with you and everything. So, I would say that I'm a spiritual person but [not a] traditional spiritual person [such as found in the] Catholic religion … you don't need the middle man of the Church … the scriptures are there for you to take stories from it, everyone's going to take a different story from it.

Of key Catholic rituals, Elizabeth said: 'Well I've only been baptized in the Catholic faith, [but] I haven't received my other Sacrament [First Communion] by choice.' In her mind, this sets her apart from older Catholics, who she says 'wouldn't consider themselves fully spiritual unless they had received the Catholic sacraments and they go to Church regularly'.

The way a teen is raised typically conditions their religious outlook, and this is certainly the case with Elizabeth:

> So, my mother and father split and my father and his [family's] very religious and go to church … And so, on holiday day, I was forced to say grace and then we'd pray for an hour and a half and, like, I was, like, that's not cool … like, I could be playing with Barbie dolls. But then on my mother's side, it was – religion wasn't a thing … she, herself, wasn't a very religious person so our household wasn't religious but she still respected the values of the religion she is from. She

still sent all of my brothers and me to Catholic schools so we could get similar teaching.

We also asked her about her beliefs. She was interested in many spiritual ideas like karma and reincarnation and has even consulted a medium. We dug a little bit deeper on her thoughts about life after death. Again, her views don't align much with Catholic orthodoxy:

> See I struggle with that side of the religion as though. I consider myself as a very scientific person like I love science, I love biology, I love chemistry and everything like that. I don't know if I believe in a heaven and a hell and a purgatory but I believe that there should be something else because energy cannot be created nor destroyed and our body is full of energy so wherever that goes, I think, that there is something else, I don't know what ... I don't know. All I know is that dying isn't the end. Whatever comes after is fine by me ... I lie at night thinking, oh, my God what's going to happen if I die? ... But I, the whole I think, the heaven and the hell and everything like that is a way of easing the peace of mind of what's going to happen next.

While religion is still important to a significant minority, for the most part, today's teens do not believe or belong in ways that are familiar to members of older generations.

The end of faith as we know it? Millennial and Gen Z religion compared

The findings described so far need to be apprehended within the broader arc of recent religious change in Australia. The key argument in this chapter is that religious change in Australia, particularly the demise of the Christian establishment, is due to generational differences. We know that the teens of 2017 were significantly less likely than the teens of 2005 to identify as Christian and more likely to be Nones or identify with another religion. Is there a pattern of rapid change away from religious involvement also? Consider Figure 2.3.

This figure compares the teens of 2005 with the teens of 2017 on several measures: belief in God, belief in life after death, the existence of angels and attendances at services of worship. Most notable is the large decline in belief in God – 12 per cent in a little over a decade, and a drop as substantial as the fall in Christian identification. Belief in angels and life after death has also fallen, but not as decisively. It remains to be seen whether this is the nadir, or whether affiliation, belief and practice will drop even further with the next generation.

Religious beliefs
and practices

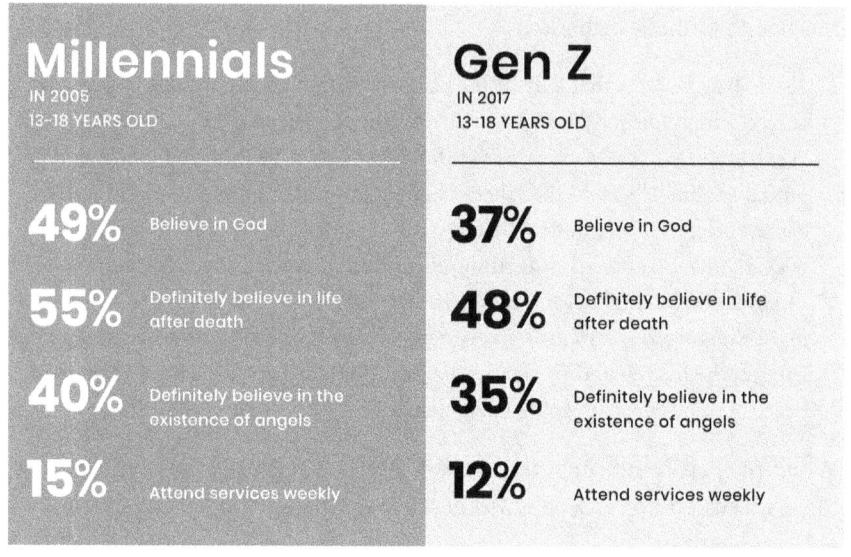

Sources: SGY Survey 2005; AGZ Survey 2017

Figure 2.3 Patterns of religious practice among Australian teens: 2005 and 2017 compared (% of teens in those years).

Each generation has its distinct profile when it comes to religious matters, which reflects the broader social context in which they come of age. We noted above that teens of the Silent Generation turned out in huge numbers for the 1959 rallies of Billy Graham, and many committed themselves to the Christian life. This event expressed the everyday realities and aspirations for a whole generation of young people. Now in their senior years, those who attended those rallies as teens still talk about that time with great affection and how it affected the rest of their lives.[30]

Recently, Billy Graham's son, Franklin, conducted an evangelical tour in Australia, celebrating sixty years since his father packed out major sporting stadiums. Mainstream press coverage of the event was negligible, limited to some op-ed pieces by Christian commentators decrying Franklin's ultraconservative, pro-Trump politics.[31] This time around, the rally in Melbourne was held at a much smaller indoor stadium across the road from the MCG. Unlike his father's rallies, Franklin drew attendees from among conservative Pentecostal congregations only. He simply couldn't get any purchase beyond this small constituency. Most teens were simply indifferent to or completely unaware of his rally.

Conclusion

Our study finds that for the most part, contemporary teens are not particularly religious in the conventional sense, if this is measured by belonging, belief and practice. A small minority run counter to this trend and are actively committed to a religious tradition: Muslim, Christian or otherwise. In Chapter 4 we look more closely at this group. But the abiding pattern is the ever-increasing drift of teens from the Christian churches, and in time, probably from all the major religious traditions.[32] Gen Z is following the patterns established by their (mainly) Gen X parents, but with even more vigour.

This does not mean, however, that teens are brokering an unequivocal secular revolution. The full-tilt 'religious package' may not have many takers, but there is still an openness to the transcendent. We've seen traces of that in this chapter, notably the proportion who believe in a higher being, even if they never go to a church, temple or mosque. After all, *only a quarter of teens have no belief in the transcendent*. Does this mean that other kinds of spiritual belief and practice have currency among contemporary teens? The next chapter explores teenagers' interest in other ways of being spiritual, particularly those which exist outside the bounds of organized religion.

3

Mind, body and spirit: Teenagers and spirituality

Health-wellbeing-metaphysical festivals are commonplace across Australia. The most successful is probably the 'MindBodySpirit Festival', held several times a year in Sydney, Melbourne and Brisbane. Staged at large convention centres, the format is the same in each location: there's the main stage, featuring lectures on metaphysical topics, mediumship demonstrations or musical performances. Dotted around the main floor, exhibitors offer an eclectic mix of things to try, see and buy, including massage therapy, Reiki healing, health foods, natural clothing, crystals, psychic services and life coaching, just to name a few.

Nestled at the back is the 'psychic reading room'. This is a partitioned area with dozens of small tables, each with two chairs. One chair is for a practitioner, the other for a sitter. Sitters pay between $50 and $100 and can choose a reading from a clairvoyant, psychic, medium or card reader (e.g. reading tarot, oracle or angel cards). Most of the readers are booked out before the event, and there are limited walk-up slots available. The stallholders and readers are addressing people's everyday concerns through spiritual, natural or holistic means. This kind of festival has been described by scholars as emblematic of the West's spiritual marketplace.[1]

One of the authors (Andrew) visited one of these major festivals recently for another research project on the religion of Spiritualism. What stood out, apart from the busy-ness of the psychic reading room, was the age range of attendees. Unlike the typical congregation at a Spiritualist church (the religion that contacts the 'dead') or the audience at a mediumship demonstration in a pub or club, there were many young people in attendance. Some were there with their parents or guardians (mostly their mum), but others were with friends. As we show in this chapter, a reasonable proportion of teens (like Millennials before them) have embraced aspects of the 'mind-body-spirit' movement.

Festivals like MindBodySpirit are the visible signs of interest in spiritual ideas, beliefs and practices that are not expressed in the *institutional* form of organised religion.² This chapter explores these forms of spirituality and the extent to which these animate the lives of Australia's teens. Traditionally, spirituality has been understood as the affective, personal dimension of religious faith.³ Increasingly, however, it refers to a very broad range of experiences.⁴ Thus, in contemporary Western usage, spirituality might be expressed through **belief** in the sacredness of the earth, a supernatural concept (e.g. reincarnation) or supernatural beings (e.g. spirits, ghosts, aliens). It might entail a **consciousness**, like a sense of 'oneness with all living things'. Spirituality is often tied to practice or **practices**, whether that be meditation, yoga or channelling. As we explain below, an increasing proportion of people believe they can be 'spiritual without being religious'.

To frame our discussion about teens and spirituality, we begin by describing briefly the emergence of the contemporary spiritual movement and the popularization of certain ideas and practices, things such as yoga, meditation, astrology, tarot, reincarnation, karma and mediumship. Turning to our data, we explore the extent to which teens take part in these beliefs and practices. We discover that Gen Z teens find a sense of purpose and meaning in all kinds of different ways, and for some, that revolves around contemporary expressions of spirituality.

The Age of Aquarius? The rise of the spiritual marketplace and the wellness movement

To set the scene for this chapter, we explain briefly the 'spiritual turn' of the past few decades. In the previous chapter, we noted the normalcy of Christianity for most teens who came of age in the 1950s. This was not to last. In the late 1960s and early 1970s, as the Boomers came of age, there was a widespread 'counter-culture' movement (e.g. the hippie and psychedelic movements) and, consequently, a kind of alternative 'spiritual awakening'.⁵ At this time, dedicated alternative spiritual communities, like the Krishna Consciousness Society (the Hare Krishnas), the Unification Church (Moonies), the Church of Scientology and the Rajneesh and the Sri Chinmoy movements all rose to prominence.⁶

Other spiritual alternatives – ones that first emerged in the late nineteenth century, like Spiritualism and Theosophy – also enjoyed a surge in interest in the late 1960s and into the 1980s. Spiritualists in Australia (i.e. those who follow the religion and philosophy of Spiritualism), for example, migrated from their inner-city churches and founded many new congregations in the outer suburbs and regional cities.

It was mainly the Baby Boomers who explored these spiritual alternatives; they were teenagers and young adults looking for new kinds of meaning outside the bounds of traditional religion.[7] Many Boomers, for example, can recall playing with the Ouija board or holding a séance when they were younger or dabbling in some way with the counterculture. Some embraced it more fully than that, founding intentional communities (e.g. Melbourne's *House of the Gentle Bunyip*), or becoming Buddhists.

In the decades after the 1960s, as the Boomers were getting older, the Human Potential, New Age and Neo-Pagan (e.g. Wicca; Druidism) movements also grew dramatically.[8] Practitioners, therapists and shops appeared, offering astrology, channelling, meditation, feminine spirituality, crystal manipulation, numerology, palmistry, Reiki, Tantra and tarot. There was also a rising interest in Indigenous spiritualities, Buddhism, Sufism, Kabbalism, the sacredness in nature, principles of interdependency and global responsibility.

This range of spiritual and metaphysical ideas, beliefs and practices is often referred to as the 'spiritual marketplace'.[9] Multiple spiritual options are now an established, normalized aspect of cultural life throughout the West.[10] People can freely cultivate a spiritual lifeworld outside the bounds of organized religion and have an ever-expanding array of resources and possibilities on which to draw. Correspondingly, research shows that many adults in the West believe in spirits, auras, energies and magic.[11]

The spiritual marketplace was largely the product of the late 1960s counterculture movement. Those in the counterculture also championed broader concerns about the wellbeing of the planet, and the impact humans have on the earth.[12] Since then, escalating concerns about the damage that Western capitalism and modernity are causing to the natural world, alongside the precarity and pressures of contemporary life, has fostered an interest in ways of living that are more harmonious with nature.[13] There are widespread, grassroots movements trying to fight global heating and cruelty to animals.[14]

Moreover, in a world that feels increasingly toxic, poisoned and stressful, there's been the proliferation of services, activities and products designed to help people 'live better'. This is the 'wellness' movement, which flourished in the 1970s, coterminous with the growth of the 'spiritual marketplace'.[15] This diffuse social movement seeks to advance mental and physical health through holistic and natural means. It spans everything from vitamin and dietary supplements, natural therapies (e.g. kinesiology, hypnotherapy, chiropractic) and adapted, ancient religious practices, like yoga and mindfulness meditation.[16] This movement can be both an adjunct to or at odds with scientific medicine. Seemingly, too, the boundaries between health, wellbeing and spirituality are sometimes blurred.

Meditation and yoga are a case in point. In Western contexts, yoga and meditation are often taught without full immersion in their foundational religious and spiritual dimensions.[17] That said, yoga and meditation do encourage inner contemplation, self-reflection, awareness and quietness. Is this consciousness 'spiritual'? If so, it is an *immanent* kind of spirituality, rather than one that requires any belief in or acceptance of transcendent and supernatural possibilities (i.e. a belief in a higher power, or supernatural entities).[18] And as we see below, practitioners and scholars are divided about whether to treat these modalities as 'spiritual' activities.[19]

The spiritual marketplace, the wellness movement and the supernatural all have a prominent place in the mass media, whether it be TV shows, films (e.g. *Ghost*), New Age books (e.g. *The Secret*) or the internet and social media (like Gwyneth Paltrow's stunningly successful wellness website, Goop). For those interested in Spirit communication, for example, there are many videos of Ouija boards, hauntings and séances on YouTube. Internationally famous mediums, like John Edward, tour and make guest appearances on mainstream FM radio and morning TV, with hosts treating such activities as completely normal. Some women's interest magazines have astrology and psychic columns. To be sure, professional mediums have been around for a long time, but arguably, these activities are subject to less opprobrium or vicious opposition than in the past.

Within the fantasy fiction genre, an alternative lifeworld is enacted through the proliferation of supernatural TV shows, novels and movies, like *Harry Potter*, *Star Wars* (think of 'The Force') and *Twilight*. The *Potter* movies, in particular, are part of an enduring genre of spirit and magic-filled media that began with the extraordinary popularity of *The Exorcist* in the early 1970s. While works of fiction, such media might sustain an interest in supernatural possibilities.[20]

In sum, contemporary Western society is awash with alternative spiritual beliefs, practices and possibilities, allied to an interest in mind-and-body wellness. How much are teens into all of this, or is it a movement mainly restricted to (now aging) Boomers and Gen Xers? We explore this question in the remainder of this chapter.

Is yoga the new black? Wellbeing and spiritual practices among teens

We begin by looking at teen interest in wellbeing and other spiritual practices, which is shown in Figure 3.1.

The first thing to note in Figure 3.1 is the proportion of teens who have practised meditation (28 per cent) or yoga (22 per cent). This figure seems high, but we were not especially surprised. During our focus groups, we showed participants a picture of someone doing yoga. There was universal recognition of the image. Like everywhere else in the West, yoga is a big deal in Australia. Interestingly, our participants told us that yoga and meditation are routinely

Source: AGZ Survey 2017

Figure 3.1 Australians aged 13–18: Spiritual and wellbeing practices (% of teens).

offered as part of health and wellbeing programs at many of the schools we visited. Here is one exchange from a focus group:

Q 1:	*Do they make you guys do yoga at school?*
Participant 1:	Yes.
P2:	Yeah, we are doing that at the moment. They are trying. Well, they try and make us do it [laughter].
Q 1:	*Do they have someone [external] like rolling in [to teach it]?*
P2:	No, they have a video ...
P5:	Yeah. You just follow it along.
P2:	Because the teachers here don't know how to do it [Laughter].
Q 2:	*So, what, you go into the classroom and they put it on there?*
P1:	We go into the lecture theatre.
P1:	And they just put it up on a big screen where 100 people across the room view it [laughter].
P2:	And we do it.

Outside school, there are many ways to practice. This includes meditation apps such as *Smiling Minds* and how-to videos on YouTube.

How 'spiritual' are these activities for teens? As we noted above, the yoga and meditation offered at school are done for health and wellbeing purposes.[21] Most of the teens we interviewed who do yoga or meditation out of school suggested it was mostly for their health and wellbeing. Previous studies show that this is how many, but not all, Western adults treat it.[22] One of our interviewees, Ferazia, an 18-year-old Muslim teen, said:

Ferazia:	I've done like yoga and meditation.
Q:	*Where did you do that?*
Ferazia:	Just in my house or at the gym.
Q:	*Where did you learn to do that ... yoga and meditation?*
Ferazia:	I have some friends who do it, so sometimes I join them or I watch YouTube.
Q:	*What drew you to that?*
Ferazia:	Just to relax me ... I did it [first] with a friend and it was nice, so whenever I feel a bit stressed, I just do that, and it just helps me to relax.

Freya is another teen who meditates and practises yoga outside of school. She told us:

Freya:	Yeah. I do both of those [yoga and meditation]. My mum was really into it all.
Q:	*Did you grow up with that around you?*
Freya:	Yeah. [When] I grew up [it] surrounded me. It's really good for the body and the blood and it feels [great].
Q:	*Do you meditate every day, every week?*
Freya:	Occasionally. I do yoga every day.
Q:	*What motivates you to do yoga every day?*
Freya:	My mum [laughs], and the feeling that I have in my body when I don't do it. You know, once you start …
Q:	*The meditation … does your mum actively encourage you or do you just see her doing it and think …*
Freya:	Oh, she usually gets me to do it with her and yes, she does encourage me … Mum's been teaching me this new one [a technique] and got me about thinking about [how] you sit with yourself. You sit with yourself for a while and then you just imagine something that you want to achieve. [Something] that you imagine yourself doing and you imagine you being there or seeing that. It's really beautiful. You've got try it a few times but it does work.

For both Freya and Ferazia, yoga helps them integrate mind and body, and they both identify health and wellbeing benefits that flow from it. We recognize too that for some practitioners it can be interpreted or experienced as a deeply spiritual accomplishment, or helps individuals attain a state of mind they think of as spiritual.

Some teens come to meditation because of an interest in Buddhism. Andrzej's mother was a Buddhist for a time and that served as his introduction to meditation:

Andrzej:	My mother had a look into Buddhism for a while and I was involved in a community. Every year we'd go off to a retreat for a week, and the kids would go do their own kid [meditation] thing.
Q:	*Did you like that?*
Andrzej:	Yeah, it was good fun and I made friends through it and it was good fun, we were camping.
Q:	*And have you kept up that meditation at all?*
Andrzej:	I don't consciously practise it but I would say it's influenced the way I deal with things and stress. Because I've had that experience I know it's influenced how I calm down or how I manage things a little bit.

That said, the majority have come to meditation because it is an allied health practice and do not engage with its religious roots (it is a part of many religious traditions) or its spiritual possibilities. This is the case for Jack:

Jack: As a kid, I was picked on because I suffer from a learning disability. So, growing up I wasn't the most popular kid in class. I was picked on for what I said, what I did, how I did in a test. How I did sport. As I grew older I attempted meditation, when I was 15. I attempted meditation and that's when I spiritually found peace within myself and those around me. So that I can just move on from what has happened in the past, look more to the future as a person making better life decisions, making better choices as a person and as a man.

Q: *Wow, that's great. How were you introduced to this meditation?*

Jack: Ah, through doctors. I do a lot of sport and I did a lot of acupuncture – the ancient Chinese acupuncture – and she [the therapist] recommended meditation. When I was 15, so I tried it and I enjoyed it.

Q: *What sort of meditation did you do?*

Jack: Just basic meditation, I just sit in a room quietly for half an hour and just …

Q: *Like mindfulness of your breathing?*

Jack: Yes.

Q: *And you've found that to be quite transformative?*

Jack: Pretty much.

Of the teens we interviewed who are practising either yoga and meditation seriously, all agreed it had led to some personal transformation, which in some cases is deeply consequential.

Looking at Figure 3.1, we see that teens are less interested in the alternative spiritual practices of horoscopes, séances and tarot cards. Unlike yoga and meditation, which are immanent activities, a deep commitment to these other practices presupposes the acceptance of unseen forces that can affect us – like the cosmos, fate or the spirit world. While horoscopes are ubiquitous – a staple of magazines and newspapers, or via phone apps – we found that these are not especially popular: 18 per cent of teens have seriously consulted their horoscope for guidance.

Even less common among teens are tarot or angel cards (6 per cent). A couple of our interviewees use these cards. Freya, who is generally attuned to all things spiritual (her mum runs tantric workshops) said:

Freya:	Tarot cards I've got. I mean, I've got about four different decks. I do them properly, but [also] they're always interesting to play around with.
Q:	*Are your friends into that too?*
Freya:	Yeah. A lot of the times when we hang out, we'll just have, you know, a glass of wine [she was 18 when she did the survey and interview] have the crystals around us [and do] tarot card readings.

The use of these cards is not a frivolous activity. Take Jana for example. She described herself as spiritual, which led to further conversation about tarot cards:

Jana:	I'm kind of spiritual, I guess.
Q:	*How do you find expression for that … exactly what do you do?*
Jana:	Well [I am] new age kind of religious. I use tarot cards and things like that.
Q:	*How do things like tarot cards, or the other practices you have mentioned, how do those activities make a difference in your life?*
Jana:	I think that most people turn to religion because it's like if you're stuck and you don't know what to do you kind of look for answers in something. So, the tarot cards are something [I use] if I don't know what to do in a certain situation. I would use them like get some clarity and that stuff … Usually, I write most of it down in a book as well. And I like going back and looking at it and it's 'Oh.' So, it's pretty good.
Q:	*It gives you confidence?*
Jana:	It does.
Q:	*With this stuff, has there ever been any life-changing experiences?*
Jana:	Everything that I think I've done has changed the way that I live my life. [Once I got a] new set of cards and then the first a reading I did it was really like – do you know, it made me cry actually. I don't know why, I can't even remember but, I guess, it was emotional or something like that.

Q:	*Yeah. It was significant for you?*
Jana:	Yeah. Sometimes it's just like, maybe the energy that I can feel when I do things like that.

Lucinda found both horoscopes and tarot cards helpful but maintained a somewhat critical stance towards both:

Lucinda:	I like horoscopes and stuff like that, they're not always, like, correct but I like looking at them [and] being like, 'Maybe that'll happen'. Or, I've had the tarot cards [read] or however you say it. It's nice to have an opinion on what might happen in the future … [that's] cool.
Q:	*Do you think you can tell the future?*
Lucinda:	I think you can tell a version of the future. When they read your cards they're just reading, like, your future based on what you're doing at that moment, so there's no accurate representation of what's going to happen because it might change every single day with the choices that you make. Yeah, it might be along those lines – it won't be exact.

Almost absent among contemporary teens are activities that involve communicating with the dead (4 per cent had consulted a medium or psychic; 3 per cent had been part of a séance). While séances may have once been a popular pastime for teens and young adults (in 1967, after the patent had been acquired by Parker Brothers, Ouija boards outsold the Monopoly board game), this is not the case now. One of the authors (Andrew) recently sat in on a darkened séance on the far outskirts of town for another project he is doing.[23] Twenty people had paid $120 to be there. And despite the promise of apports and ectoplasm, no one there was under the age of 40, and most of them were over 50. It seems there are more popular ways to spend a Saturday evening than testing the Ouija board or the powers of the spirit world.

Ghosts, aliens, angels: Teen belief in the spiritual, paranormal and supernatural

A modest-sized proportion of teens have an interest in the spiritual and the supernatural, and beliefs derived from Asian religious traditions. Interest in karma, reincarnation and other spiritual ideas are shown in Table 3.1. As in the previous chapter, we will explore belief according to stated religious affiliation. In the previous chapter, we saw that Nones (those with no religion) are not

Table 3.1 Australians aged 13–18: Spiritual, paranormal and supernatural beliefs by religious identification (% of group)

Teen believes in	Religious identification (%)					Total for all teens (13–18)
	Catholic	Mainline Protestant	Other Christian	BHJMS	Nones	
Karma (our actions come back to us in another life)	61	44	31	63	49	50
Ghosts	35	21	31	35	31	31
Reincarnation (people have lived previous lives)	34	28	15	29	31	29
The possibility of communicating with the dead	31	17	24	23	25	25
Astrology (that stars and planets affect people's fates)	21	20	15	28	18	20
UFOs	18	10	13	20	25	20

Source: AGZ Survey 2017.
Note: Percentages shown are *only* those who expressed belief.

completely irreligious. Interesting patterns also emerge when it comes to various spiritual beliefs, particularly among Nones and Catholic teens. The importance of this is discussed in the next chapter.

Looking down the last column to the right, we see some interesting patterns. The most popular belief, by far, is karma (50 per cent of all teens believe in it). Reincarnation is also widely accepted (29 per cent of teens in Australia). While Australia's geographical proximity to, and long history of migration from, Asia may have helped popularize these concepts, previous research shows that most teens who believe in karma and reincarnation do not follow, or even know about, Buddhist and Hindu teaching on these doctrines.[24] This table shows that among those who identify with a religion, Catholic teens are those most likely to believe in metaphysical possibilities, while a solid subset of Nones also believes in these things.

Like yoga and meditation, belief in 'karma' can't be treated as solely 'spiritual'. In the public mind, karma seems to have become a shorthand way of taking personal responsibility and accepting that there are consequences for one's actions, an idea also expressed in the popular phrase 'What goes around comes around'. Here is an instructive exchange with an interviewee, 18-year-old Brandon:

> Brandon: I believe in karma, that's something I believe in.
>
> Q: *You do, right.*
>
> Brandon: I believe in karma, in [that] things happen for a reason. I always try to keep my karma good if that makes sense. I always try and do a good deed for anyone.
>
> Q: *That's good. How did you get influenced by that notion? Karma is really in the popular culture now, but it's not like you're Buddhist?*
>
> Brandon: Yeah, no, I'm not Buddhist or anything like that. I first heard of it on a show and I watched it, and it was on karma, bad karma, good karma. I wondered what that is, so did a bit of a Google and looked it up. This is when I was very young. … Basically, you do good things, you have good karma, things should happen nicely. You do a good deed, something might happen nice to you. Same thing with the bad as well. When I've done something bad … I'd say there's always a bad consequence. If I do something good, I'm always complimented with a smile or something, something good, that's all karma.
>
> Q: *That is something that you can have faith in because you've experienced it?*

| Brandon: | Yeah, yeah, I'm not heavy on it, I'm definitely not heavy on it, you know. I keep my karma good, that's pretty much it. |

There may be some metaphysical underpinning to this sense of karma, as if the universe, God or some higher power ensures we are responsible for our actions. But it is hardly about setting up irrevocable consequences for the next life. That said, it provides someone like Brandon with a framework for living, conditioning his actions and choices to be more ethical and considered.

> **Spiritual eclecticism:** Many teens hold various supernatural/spiritual beliefs. Many also practice *spiritual eclecticism* – mixing-and-matching beliefs and ideas that come from disparate sources.[25] In summary, 31 per cent of teens don't believe in any of astrology, karma, contact with the dead, reincarnation, ghosts and UFOs; 23 per cent believe in one and **47 per cent believe in two or more**.

In our interviews with teens we got the sense that for the most part, these beliefs (karma excluded) don't make much difference to how they live their everyday lives, something explored in previous Australian research.[26] Rather, they reflect a latent openness to spiritual possibilities. This seems particularly true of Catholic teens, who lead the way when it comes to belief in karma, ghosts, reincarnation and contact with the dead (see Table 3.1).

But this does not mean that these beliefs are necessarily trivial or insincere. Vivien is a Buddhist who believes in reincarnation. (We hear more from her in Chapter 5.) She told us about the death of someone very close to her:

Vivien:	I think that it was 100 per cent a life-changing moment and that was where the Buddhism side came in because that also helped me. Because when you are talking about reincarnation … because when [the death] happened I was 14 and I was just so like lost … In the family, I was the one that was closest to him. I found that whenever any sort of significant event was happening a butterfly would always appear. One hundred per cent I think he came back as a butterfly. Whenever I do anything important or significant a butterfly always appears.
Q:	*Yeah.*
Vivien:	And I think you know that this sounds so ridiculous.

Q:	*No.*
Vivien:	*Like 100 per cent …*
Q:	*Not at all.*
Vivien:	*Fully if he came back he would [be a butterfly].*

Lucinda told a ghost story, but more profoundly, her experience consolidated her belief in transcendent possibilities:

Lucinda:	I had a school excursion to the [names place] up at [names place] and, it's supposedly haunted, it's where [early settler migrant] boats came in. That's where [the authorities] would take them when they were so sick they had to be quarantined and a lot of people died there because they'd have showers in acid [carbolic acid showers] to try and get the sickness off them and stuff like that. We went during the day and they have ghost tours at night so, and we went into a shower area where they had the acid showers and, we were just in there. A few of the girls started coughing and sneezing and they all had asthma and they started having real asthma attacks. People that had hay fever were sneezing and everything and then their eyes were watering. Then there was banging going on so we all ran out! I was fine, I was personally fine because I don't have asthma or hay fever or anything like that but it was really weird. I believe in ghosts [and thought that was the cause].
Q:	*So, you read that as being, well, is this place is haunted?*
Lucinda:	Yeah. When we went in there on the tour – the tour guide did say that this is one of the spots during the ghost tour where they get the most activity and then he started talking about history and stuff. That is when things started happening so … there could be something there, otherwise, it is a [very] strange coincidence.
Q:	*And did that impact you?*
Lucinda:	Well I believed in ghosts … [they are] something like a spirit or something like that [but] they're not trying to hurt us, they're just letting us know that they were there so, yeah, there was something there.
Q:	*And did others share your … interpretation of it?*
Lucinda:	Yeah, everyone was, like 'Whoa that's so weird.' 'I can't believe that happened.' 'I didn't believe in ghosts before but

	I do now.' And then the people that were affected by it were really, really affected. My friend, she had asthma and hay fever so she was having an asthma attack and sneezing and everything [and] she was traumatized by that experience and she said, 'I couldn't control it. I felt something on me.' She's a part of the ghost club now, I guess.
Q:	She's part of a ghost club?
Lucinda:	Well, not *a* ghost club ... she knows she believes in them. Like fully believes in them now.

These kinds of stories suggest that belief in ghosts, UFOs or reincarnation shouldn't necessarily be dismissed or trivialized. Rather, it is evident that a subset of teens, in everyday, private and non-institutionalized ways, believe that there is more to life than meets the eye.

Sensing the invisible: Spiritual experiences

Thus far, we have explored 'spirituality' as it might be expressed in beliefs and practices, or ideas about the self. People also commonly report having *experiences* of the spiritual or the sacred. These are sometimes called transcendent experiences. Examples might include seeing a ghost, an ineffable sense of awe and wonder in nature, sensing the presence of a loved one who has died or having an out-of-body experience. In our survey of Australian teens, we asked about the prevalence and frequency of three experiences of this ilk. We asked teens how often, if ever, they have: experienced a connection with nature; felt a connection with the universe; or been aware of a presence or power (whether they called this the presence God or not) that was different from the everyday self.

The first two items are self-explanatory. The last item has been asked for decades by social researchers in Australia, Great Britain and America.[27] It has no set meaning: a religious person might think this involves an answer to prayer; others might think it includes the experience of seeing a ghost (remember that 31 per cent of Australian teens believe in ghosts) or something else again. Irrespective of how it is understood, it points to experiences of the 'numinous', 'mystical' or 'otherworldly': something beyond the material.[28] The proportions having these experiences are noted in Figure 3.2.

Figure 3.2 shows that the most common experience teenagers have is feeling close to nature, something that three-quarters of all teens have experienced at least once (18 per cent said they have this experience often; 58 per cent said once

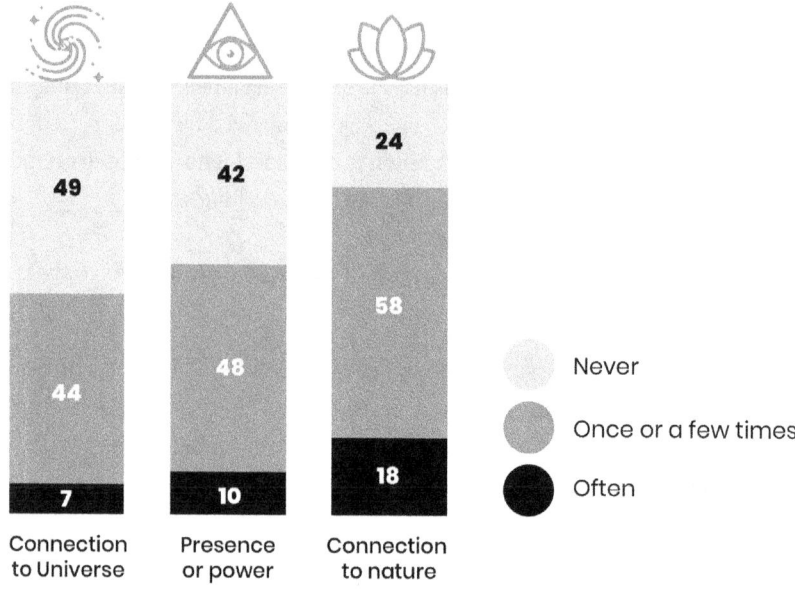

Source: AGZ Survey 2017

Figure 3.2 Australians aged 13–18: Frequency of spiritual experiences (% of teens).

or a few times). Of the other experiences, a majority of teens have experienced a presence or power at least once (58 per cent) or felt a connection to the universe (51 per cent) at least once.

But clearly, feeling connected to nature is the most important of these experiences for teens. One of our interviewees, Noah, said: 'I do very, very much like the river. So, I've been on [names the river] before and I just felt, on the river, on a really warm day … I just felt this is where I belong, I like this. [I felt it] strongly'. Lucinda described the effect that certain places have on her:

> I like going to the beach because it's calming. So if I've had a crazy day or something like that I'll go to the beach or I'll go sit on the beach in the afternoon or go swimming. It's a calming place it's not really [but] I wouldn't [use the word] sacred [to describe it].

Elizabeth also discussed nature as her 'favourite' place for thinking and reflection:

> Elizabeth: I have places that are my favourite place. I think there are places I can relax and reflect on things but none of them is religious or anything. I have a fascination with heights where I like being up high as well. I think that's a way of

	being able to be free and think whatever I want without anyone being around.
Q:	*Yeah. So how do you get up high?*
Elizabeth:	Well we have a massive hill right in the middle of my town and I just climb it.
Q:	*Yeah. Right. And you do that to get a sense of reflection there and solitude?*
Elizabeth:	Exactly.

Freya's most sacred place is sitting high up in a tree:

Q:	*[Are] there any places or kind of things that are particularly sacred to you?*
Freya:	I've got a few. Yes. One is the at the very top of – you know the giant pine trees? I live on the coast and there's just one … [it] looks like this giant bird's nest at the top. I'll just sit in that and look over the ocean and it's just pristine. I'm really about getting out into nature and nurturing myself in the sun.

For some of these young people, their connection with nature has had other consequences for their lives.[29] Jana is a vegetarian, concerned about the 'bad conditions' experienced by animals in the 'mass production of meat'. Freya also explained how environmental issues were a significant concern for her and that she had 'been to a few protests … mainly logging ones'. She also added that 'I definitely, I agree with protesting and, you know, making your actions towards saving these things'.[30]

There is no relationship between religious identity and whether or not a person is more or less likely to report experiencing a connection to nature or a connection to the universe. But it does make a difference when it comes to experiencing a 'presence or power'. Teens who identify with a religion are much more likely than Nones to report having had this kind of experience.

Are spiritual practices and beliefs on the rise? Millennial and Gen Z spirituality compared

In the previous chapter, we discussed the eclipse of Christianity. Does that mean that spiritual beliefs and practices are increasing? Is spirituality replacing religion?

This idea plays well in the popular press. Stories are frequently written about the rising interest in astrology or psychics.[31] One journalist wrote recently: 'It's part of a broader shift, one that finds magic and mysticism referenced regularly in popular culture.' This kind of argument forgets history, ignoring the wild popularity of Spiritualism in the late nineteenth century, the spike in astrology belief during the 1940s or the vibrancy of the 1960s spiritual awakening.

One way we can get a sense of change is by comparing birth cohorts. Figure 3.3 compares the teens of 2005 (Millennials) with the teens of 2017 (Gen Z). Are alternative spiritual ideas and practices more popular among Gen Z teens than they were for the Millennials when they were teens?

Although there are slight differences in the proportion of Millennial and Gen Z teens who believe in reincarnation, astrology and spirit communication, these are not statistically significant (i.e. the margin of error between the figures overlaps). In effect, **nothing much has changed** between these two birth cohorts. Acceptance of these beliefs and practices is holding firm among teens, rather than increasing or decreasing. (Karma is missing from this comparison because it was not asked of 2005's teenage cohort.)

By contrast, yoga and meditation practice has risen dramatically. This may be due in part to their incorporation into school life – something not happening in 2005 – and because these activities are genuinely becoming more popular.

The emergence of the 'spiritual but not religious' identity

Thus far, we have explored the 'spiritual' through reference to discrete beliefs and practices, most of which are about connecting to something 'greater than the self', or 'the transcendent', no matter how that is personally construed. Additionally, many people in contemporary society also see themselves as 'spiritual' people, a way of being in the world that denotes an openness to larger connections.[32] Here is an exchange about the meaning of spirituality from one of the focus groups:

P1: Spirituality is just finding a connection …
P6: Well that's what religion is for a lot of people. I think it [spirituality] is answering questions you can't answer and being part of something bigger, like, everyone wants to be a part of something bigger than themselves.

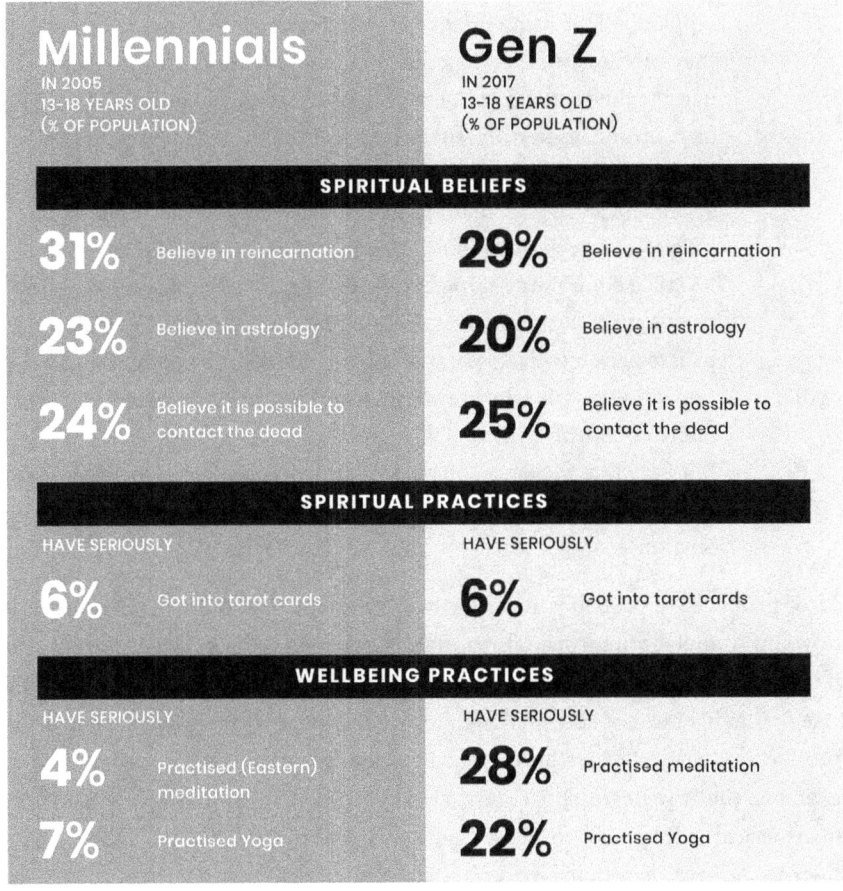

Figure 3.3 Patterns of spirituality among Australian teens: 2005 and 2017 compared (% of teens in those years).

Historically, and when higher proportions of the population actively participated in Christian institutions, spirituality was *implicitly* understood in theological and public parlance to be the personal, interior and affective dimensions of religious faith.[33] This is no longer the case. Now, it is widely agreed that people can happily conceive of a spiritual lifeworld outside the bounds of organized religion and are finding new ways to be spiritual, whether that via the New Age, through Buddhism or something else. We suggest that understanding of spirituality – something distinct from religion – is the view of most Australian teens. Here's an instructive exchange that took place among a group of mostly Jewish teens:

> P6: I think we have a – a bit of a misconception that spirituality and religion are the same things, they're not the same thing … I mean, they can be associated together and religion often goes hand-in-hand with spirituality but it's not a two-way street. Spirituality has nothing to do with religion most of the time. There's a new kind of millennial craze. I guess you could classify it as self-awareness and self-actualization and that strays from the whole religious and religion mould. It's a lot more personal. I mean, it's still a community thing but it's about personal reflection and personal connections to nature and literature. And it's not really in association with a creator or a God or Gods, it's very internal …
>
> P7: I do know people who are spiritual and it connects – like, intertwines with their religion.
>
> P1: But I say that they're associated, but religion is often associated with spirituality but spirituality doesn't have to be associated with religion.

Most people have probably heard of the phrase 'spiritual but not religious'. It is now commonplace in most contemporary surveys on religion to ask participants if they think of themselves this way, or if they see themselves as being something else ('religious but not spiritual', 'neither'). This research suggests an increasing proportion of Westerners agree that they are 'spiritual but not religious'. For example, the Pew Research Center found recently that approximately a quarter of American adults now think of themselves as 'spiritual but not religious', an increase of 8 per cent in five years.[34]

There are two ways to understand the popularity of this phrase. There may be an actual increase in the proportion of the population who believe they are 'spiritual but not religious'. These might be people disaffected with or alienated from organized religion but still open to transcendent or non-material possibilities. It is possible too that as social scientists and journalists have studied this concept, a previously unrecognized or misunderstood group sees it as applicable to them. A recent book by sociologist Robert Wuthnow demonstrates amply how social scientific categories, especially on religion, have shaped public opinion.[35] Either way, it is now a concept that has cachet throughout the West. For the first time in Australia, it is possible to declare how teens relate to these labels (see Table 3.2).

Table 3.2 Australians aged 13–18: Self-identification by religious identification (% of group)

Belief	Religious identification (%)					Total for all teens (13–18)
	Catholic	Mainline Protestant	Other Christian	BHJMS	Nones	
I am a religious and spiritual person	27	31	50	32	0	16
I am religious but not spiritual	28	33	18	17	0	12
I am spiritual but not religious	13	15	6	25	29	22
I am none of these things	10	6	10	12	60	35
Can't choose	22	14	15	11	11	14
Total	**100**	**100**	**100**	**100**	**100**	**100**

Source: AGZ Survey 2017.

Note: Percentages in tables may not add to 100 because of rounding, or because small proportions of 'Don't know' and 'No answer' responses have been omitted to simplify the table.

Looking down the column on the right, we see that about a quarter of teens say they are religious in some way: either just religious (12 per cent) or spiritual *and* religious (16 per cent). Slightly less than a quarter (22 per cent) say they are 'spiritual but not religious' and about a third say they are none of these things (35 per cent). Fourteen per cent can't choose. (Thus, about half of teens are indifferent to, uncommitted or not interested in 'spirituality' in any form.) In Chapter 5 we explore this category of 'spiritual but not religious' in much greater depth, but for now, we see that it is an important self-descriptor for a reasonable proportion of teens. Instructively too, almost a third of the Nones see themselves as 'spiritual but not religious'. As we noted above, many Nones also believe in reincarnation, ghosts and UFOs. There is more than meets the eye with this subset of 'nonreligious' teens.

Conclusion

The overview of the religious and spiritual lifeworlds of contemporary teens presented in the two previous chapters shows several distinct patterns. As expected, contemporary teens are less conventionally religious than the teens of previous generations. The long, slow eclipse of Christian Australia is continuing, one generation following another. For the first time, the majority of teens do not identify with a religion. Only a small proportion of teens are deeply committed to conventional religions. Interest in the metaphysical and the spiritual is holding firm, neither rising nor sinking.

However, they are not a generation of atheists or humanists. We've shown in this chapter that many of the Nones believe in something – it's just not conventional. In the next two chapters, we fill out this picture, explaining some deeper patterns we have discerned in our data. We do so using an exciting new methodological approach that stitches together many of the themes we have explored in the previous two chapters, revealing the existence of six distinct types of teen worldviews.

4

A personal point of view: Discovering teenage worldviews

In the course of researching this book, we had the opportunity to go to different schools and talk to teens about their experiences of religious and cultural diversity, among other topics. During these focus group conversations, they told us a little about the shades and complexities of their own lives when it comes to religious and spiritual matters. For example, this exchange took place among a group of 15- and 16-year-olds who mostly identified as Jewish:

Q:	*Can you begin by telling us a little bit about your school in terms of how diverse it is both, culturally and religiously?*
Participant 1:	Not very.
Q:	*Not very?*
P1:	I think most people at [NAMES SCHOOL] are progressive and Jewish and Caucasian, well Jewish-Caucasian.
P2:	It's Jewish-Australian, yeah – Jewish-Australian.
P1:	But not everyone's Jewish at the school.
Q:	*Not everyone is Jewish?*
P2:	No there is …
P1:	But the majority – like the largest [group] …
P3:	There are a few people in every level that aren't Jewish.
P1:	Or don't associate with any religion.
P3:	Yeah.
P1:	Yep. And even though we're all Jewish we all celebrate our Judaism very differently.
Q:	*Yeah? Can you say a little bit more about that?*
P1:	Well, some people have more a spiritual connection [with the faith], some people have more of a … I'm personally very aware of my cultural connection to Judaism rather than [religious connections]. A lot of us are atheist.

There's a lot of going on here, and indeed, being Jewish has many layers for them. One teen said:

> I don't consider myself being religious except for, I do keep Shabbat [the Sabbath]. I think a big thing [for Jewish people] besides [the] spiritual and religious [things] is the cultural stuff … like, every Friday night, even if I could choose the way I want it, I'd still have a Shabbat dinner.

Most of the teens in that focus group agreed that while they followed a religion, and often partook in religious practices, they weren't spiritual. By contrast, in most of the government schools we visited, it was abundantly clear that the large majority in the room had no personal religious convictions. At one government school, a teen said:

> I feel like a lot of people I know [at this school] aren't religious at all. And they don't come from religious families so I don't actually know many people who are Christian or any form of religion at all. Most people I know don't follow a religion.

And yet, four of the seven students in that room agreed that they were 'spiritual but not religious'.

To provide a detailed and nuanced map of the ways teens think about and experience religion, spirituality and nonreligious matters, we have deployed an emerging, powerful form of statistical analysis that allows us to identify different 'types' of teen worldviews. This approach considers beliefs, practices and life outlooks, and, most importantly, moves beyond thinking of a person as being either 'religious' or 'nonreligious'. To ensure the types were more than computer-generated assumptions, we interviewed in depth at least five teens from each group, checking that our types made sense (thirty interviews in total). You will hear their voices in the next three chapters.

This chapter introduces the different types of worldviews we have detected. We begin with a summary of these and explain how we came up with our formulation. From there, we explore in detail two types that are indebted, at least in part, to established faith traditions. We also explain why teens grow up to have one orientation and not another. The next two chapters explore the other types.

The big six: The worldview types of Australian teens

We should begin by stating what we mean by 'worldview'. A 'worldview' is how a person understands the world and their place in it. It's a personal 'frame of reference'—a latent orientation that helps give meaning to life experiences.[1] Shaped by culture, lived experience and individual psychology, our worldviews orient us to think in particular ways about politics, social issues and our lived, everyday experiences. We draw on our worldviews all the time to provide a frame of reference for whatever is going on around us. For example, a ghost sighting for one person is explained rationally by another; a coal-powered future is thought of as inestimably bad by many teens and yet is seen as viable by a smaller group of right-leaning, politically (and financially) motivated adults.

Figure 4.1 maps the different worldview types of Australian teens and the proportion who fit into each type. The different types are conceptually related to one another, and the distinctions between them are not necessarily hard and fast – there is some fuzziness around the edges, hence the small overlap shown in the diagram.

Briefly, the types are as follows:

Religiously Committed. Making up 17 per cent of Australian teens, the Religiously Committed stand in stark contrast to the rest. Religious faith, whether that is Christian (mainly Pentecostal and evangelical), Islam or something else, is a big part of their lives.

The very large majority of this group attend services of worship regularly and believe there is life after death.

Nominally Religious. Twenty per cent of teens. This group is largely culturally religious, following the religious identity of their parents, guardians or community. Certainly, they identify with a religion and believe in God, but faith is not very important in their daily lives and they don't often go to a temple, church or mosque.

Seekers. An intriguing group are the exploratory Seekers, making up 8 per cent of teens. They almost all describe themselves as 'spiritual'. Seekers have an eclectic worldview, seeking out their spiritual truth. They might consult their horoscopes, believe in reincarnation, or both. At the same time, they identify with a religion.

Spiritual but not religious (SBNR). Next is a group we call Spiritual but Not Religious (SBNR), representing 18 per cent of teens in Australia. God, faith and religion are not important to them, but the door is open to other spiritual possibilities.

Indifferent. As might be expected, one group is largely indifferent or undecided about all of it: religion, spirituality and atheism. We call this group Indifferent. They comprise about 15 per cent of Australian teens.

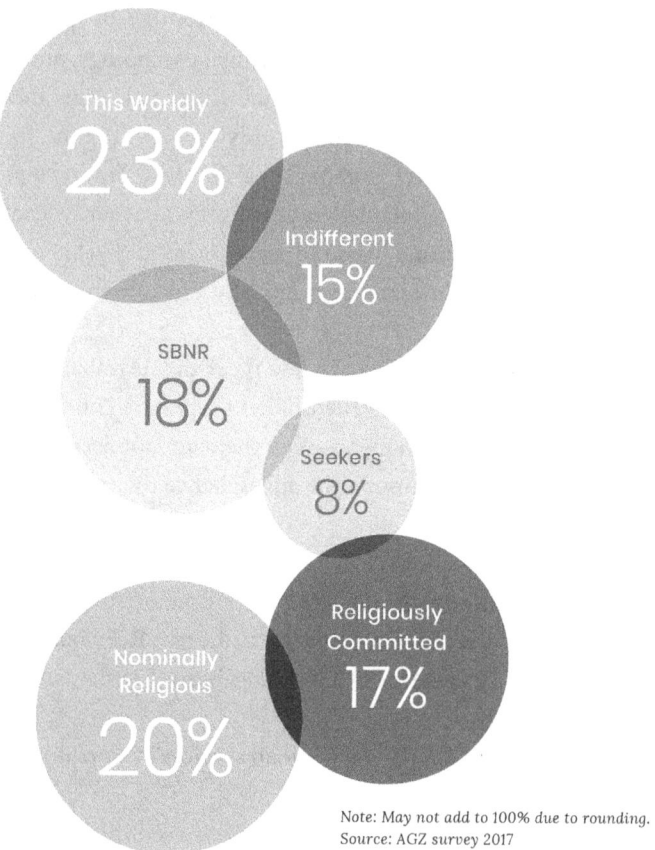

Figure 4.1 Worldview types of Australian teens (% of the population aged 13–18).

This Worldly. This largest group accounts for 23 per cent of Australian teens. This Worldly teens have no space in their worldview for religious, spiritual or non-material possibilities. They never go to services of worship and don't identify with a religion. None of them believes in God. They have no truck with other spiritual possibilities, whether that is the belief in reincarnation or horoscopes. Their thinking is entirely 'this-worldly'.

Our worldview types are *implicit orientations* that teens have towards religious, spiritual and humanist beliefs, practices and ideas. Why did we choose this approach? Most typologies in our field are created by American scholars and concentrate solely on religion, focusing on how religious (or not) their teens are.[2] But this doesn't make sense in a place like Australia, where teens are much less religious and more spiritual and nonreligious than their American counterparts.[3] Thus, we sought to build a model that could distil types that were variously 'this-worldly', religious, spiritual or a combination of these. There is also complexity, uncertainty and equivocation in regards to these kinds of matters. The statistical approach we employed readily accommodates this.

Individuals within each type may not accept or agree with the labels we gave them, or even think it applies to them. Our process simply gives the best indication – at this moment in time – of how they approach broader existential matters. Next, we describe how this model was built.

Devil's in the detail: Uncovering the types

Why bother with types? It is the best way of finding out how *groups of people* in the population are similar or different from each other when it comes to any broad area of interest. This can be reading practices, politics, learning styles or even adolescent development. Once we know this, we can work out why people fall into one group and not another.[4]

Our set of types was developed using the innovative method of 'latent-class statistical analysis' (LCA), which is often described as a 'person-centred' approach.[5] This means we discover a person's profile (how they answered a set of survey questions) and then identify how similar or different they are to other people in the population. The analysis produces a map of distinct groups in the population.

In our model, people are assigned to one group and not another based on their answers to a range of different questions. To improve the reliability of our model, we cross-referenced the types through in-depth interviews with teens who had done the survey. Indeed, after conducting the first batch of interviews, we increased the number of types from five to six, disentangling the SBNRs from the Indifferent. The full analysis, including all the survey questions we asked of all the groups, appears in Table 4.1.

How to read this chart: the top row of the chart shows the proportion of teens in each type (e.g. 23 per cent of teens are classified as This Worldly, 15 per cent are Indifferent, etc.). The column on the left-hand side has all of the items (i.e. survey questions) included in the model. Looking down the column on the right, we include *totals* (i.e. the percentage of all teens aged 13–18) for each of the ten items. For example, the item 'belief in life after death'. This shows that about half of all teens believe in life after death (48 per cent), 30 per cent do not believe and 22 per cent think 'maybe'.

The other columns show how each type answered the question or questions. For example, 76 per cent of This Worldly teens have no belief in God or a higher

Table 4.1 Australians aged 13–18: Worldview type latent-class membership probabilities (% of class)

LATENT-CLASS PREVALENCES (%)		This Worldly	Indifferent	SBNR	Seekers	Nominally Religious	Religiously Committed	Total for all teens (13–18)
		23	15	18	8	20	17	100
ITEM-RESPONSE PROBABILITIES (%)		This Worldly	Indifferent	SBNR	Seekers	Nominally Religious	Religiously Committed	Total for all teens (13–18)
Belief in a higher being	No belief in God or higher being	76	18	13	2	5	0	24
	Believes in God	0	1	13	65	66	99	37
	Belief in higher being but not God	15	44	71	30	23	2	30
	Don't know or unsure	8	37	3	3	5	0	9
How important is religious faith in shaping how you live your daily life?	Extremely	1	2	0	8	0	52	10
	Very	4	2	6	14	14	37	12
	Somewhat	18	52	42	70	77	11	42
	Not at all	77	44	51	9	10	0	36
Which of the following statement best describes you?	I am a religious and spiritual person	0	0	0	42	5	71	16
	I am religious but not spiritual	0	2	0	10	41	16	12
	I am spiritual but not religious	12	26	54	31	10	5	22
	I am none of these things	85	43	36	4	13	0	35
	Can't choose	3	28	9	13	30	6	14
Attendance at services of worship	Never	86	81	84	36	42	2	58
	Rarely	13	15	15	48	38	10	21
	Monthly	0	3	0	13	14	26	9
	Weekly	0	1	1	4	5	62	12

		This Worldly	Indifferent	SBNR	Seekers	Nominally Religious	Religiously Committed	Total for all teens (13–18)
Identifies with a religion?	None	97	84	91	7	2	--	52
	Religious ID	3	13	6	92	95	97	46
Been aware of a presence or power, whether you call it God or not, that was different from your everyday self	Often	0	1	13	31	4	25	10
	Once or a few times	12	65	58	60	52	60	48
	Never	87	33	29	8	42	12	41
Do you believe in life after death?	Yes	6	13	75	87	48	88	48
	No	86	15	9	4	23	8	30
	Maybe	8	73	15	10	29	4	22
Number of alternative practices (horoscope; séance; mediums; tarot)	None	86	76	60	23	94	87	77
	One	11	22	26	45	6	10	17
	Two+	3	2	14	32	1	3	7
Number of alternative beliefs (astrology; reincarnation; contact with dead)	None	87	69	4	0	61	62	53
	One	13	31	31	35	29	27	26
	Two+	0	0	65	65	10	11	21
Agreement with the statement: The physical universe is the only thing that exists	Disagreement	32	53	84	89	65	87	65
	Neither	3	11	0	3	6	1	4
	Agreement	60	23	13	4	21	11	26

Source: AGZ Survey 2017.

Note: Percentages may not add to 100 per cent due to rounding or because small numbers of 'don't know'/missing have been omitted from the table.

being; 77 per cent of them declare that religion has no importance in shaping how they live their daily life. Reading across the row indicates how one type compares with the others in response to any given item. Unlike 'This Worldly' teens, 99 per cent of the Religiously Committed believe in God and not a single one thinks that religion is unimportant in shaping daily life.[6]

Ten items are included in the model. The chart starts with religion. We were interested in how much religion plays a part in teens' outlooks. Looking at Table 4.1, it is evident that the model features well-recognized measures of conventional religiosity: belief in a higher being; the importance of faith in daily life; attendances at religious services; and identification with a religion. (We have data on other religious practices, like prayer, meditation and fasting, but these were only asked of those who followed a faith tradition.) We've also included a general item about whether a person sees themselves as 'spiritual but not religious', 'religious or not spiritual' or none of those things.

We haven't referenced any particular religion in these items. We thought long and hard about how to treat those who identify with the many different religious traditions in Australia. Keep Muslim, Hindu, Christians, Buddhist and Jewish teens separate from each other in the analysis, or look for common ground? In the end, we decided on the latter approach. After a careful review of the survey and interview data, we felt that the Australian teens who follow a faith tradition in a dedicated way have much in common (see below).

Reading on down the left-hand column reveals other things in our model: we've included a few items that explore different aspects of spirituality. We asked participants how often they have 'been aware of a presence or power, whether [they] call it God or not, that was different from [the] everyday self'.[7] It can be interpreted differently: a religious person might think this involves an answer to prayer; others might think it includes the experience of seeing a ghost (remember that 31 per cent of Australian teens believe in ghosts). Irrespective of how it is understood, it points to experiences of the 'numinous', 'mystical' or 'otherworldly': something beyond the material.[8]

The next question, belief in life after death, is also open to individual interpretation. A committed Muslim or evangelical Christian teen will probably believe in life after death and imagine this as continued existence in Paradise or heaven.[9] Others, particularly those who are less inclined to follow a religion, might imagine life after death as involving reincarnation or the continued existence of spirit in another plane. Either way, belief in life after death indicates an openness to transcendent or non-material possibilities.

Two items are designed to explore engagement with the contemporary spiritual marketplace. We count the number of spiritual practices a person has ever done seriously (read their horoscopes; participated in séances; consulted a medium) and the number of spiritual beliefs a person holds (astrology; reincarnation; contact with the dead). In effect, these are measures of spiritual eclecticism, mixing-and-matching beliefs and ideas that often come from disparate sources. The earlier SGY study found that the most 'spiritual' teens were the ones who were the most eclectic or experimental in their approach to spiritual matters.[10] This fits with the logic of the contemporary spiritual marketplace we described in the previous chapter.

The last question indicates agreement with the statement 'the physical world is the only thing that exists'. In our survey, we included five questions that were designed to explore how humanistic teens were in their everyday thinking (these are discussed in greater detail in Chapter 6). One of the objectives of LCA is to find a model that best achieves class separation. Of the five 'humanist orientation' questions, this particular one seems to be the most decisive measure of a materialist worldview.

This six-type model best encapsulates how teens think about a range of existential matters. It allows for some fuzziness around the edges, and a teen is assigned to their type based on the *totality* of their answers across all of the items. Thus, a teen can be 'This Worldly' and still claim to believe in life after death (which is the case for 6 per cent of This Worldly teens) because their answers to the other questions place them with generally like-minded people. The model is also very accurate – various statistical tests we applied show that there is a very high chance that teens are classified correctly, and a very high probability that this model is true of the teen population of Australia.[11]

Having introduced broadly our types, in the remainder of this chapter we explore two in greater detail: Religiously Committed and Nominally Religious teens. To a greater or lesser extent, traditional religion is part of their worldview.

'If you're religious you're already pigeonholed': The Religiously Committed

Australian teens' everyday lives centre around school, sport, friends and social media. Religion and spirituality often aren't a high priority; remember that only 12 per cent attend services weekly. It takes time to go to the temple or church, to pray or fast. One informant put it this way: 'No one cares that much in our age group about [it]. They mainly want technology and their connections on Facebook and other social media.'

This is the prevailing standpoint. Nonetheless, a reasonable minority (17 per cent) of teens in our study defy this trend. We call this group Religiously Committed. Religion is a central part of their everyday lives, suffusing their home life, friendships and schooling. And as we will see in later chapters, this orientation makes a big difference in their attitudes and values.

Following a faith tradition with conviction, this group are often seen as outliers among teens in Australia. These teens understood themselves to be in the minority, commenting on how being religious made you 'automatically different', or 'stick out', and was something that 'takes some guts'. They also explained how 'declaring yourself [as religious] is always going to be difficult', 'because … God is like a foreign concept' to so many of their peers. For all of that, however, they all belong to communities and often attend schools that sustain their worldview.

Looking down their column in Table 4.1, it can be seen that almost nine out of ten attend services of worship monthly or more often and rate religion as being extremely or very important in shaping their daily life. All of them believe in a higher being (which is God, Allah, etc.). They also resist the spiritual eclecticism favoured by the Seekers and SBNR teens: they have very little belief in or involvement with alternative spiritualities.

Not shown in Table 4.1 is the frequency of prayer, but this is something we asked about in the survey: almost 60 per cent of the Religiously Committed pray often, and a further 30 per cent pray sometimes. No other type comes anywhere near this frequency of religious practice.

Religiously Committed teens typically cluster in some religious traditions and not others. The majority are not members of the traditional, mainline Christian denominations, like the Catholic, Anglican, Uniting or Lutheran Churches. (Catholic and Anglican teens are twice as likely to be Nominally Religious than to be Religiously Committed.) Instead, most of the Religiously Committed teens attend mosques (more on this below), Pentecostal, Mormon and independent churches (which are often evangelical), a smattering of evangelical Anglican and Baptist congregations, and some conservative Catholic churches. None of this is surprising, particularly concerning Christian teens. The mainline denominations have struggled for several decades to retain young people. Newer kinds of churches, with their ambitious outreach, contemporary congregational songs and less formal style, are more appealing to teens.

In the main, Religiously Committed teens belong to religious traditions that are 'high demand'. Participants are encouraged to take an active part in a range of religious and social activities (e.g. youth/outreach groups), and at the same time, a strong commitment is also expected of them. Madelyn's story is one such example. She's a member of the Church of Jesus Christ of Latter-day Saints (LDS Church), known colloquially as the Mormons. Raised a Mormon, Madelyn goes to services every week and prays often. She talked a little about the importance of the Mormon missionary experience as a marker of that expected commitment:

> In my particular religion, boys and girls at the age of 18 or 19 can go on a church mission. So, the church mission is that you get to serve in a particular place, or country, and you serve for two years for boys and a year and a half for girls. You have a random person as your companion who you work with and you preach about the gospel. My cousin [also a Mormon] left to go to Argentina and [was] learning a whole ... different language. That was insane for me. I was thinking, wow, how brave, how amazing is that to just leave your whole family for two years and to ... just live with God. So that was inspiring to me.

Typically, too, Religiously Committed teens count like-minded teens among their friends. Madelyn, for example, said:

> My two best friends that I have, they are part of my church. They weren't always my best friends when I was younger. You go through life and ... a lot of your school friends slip away and for some reason, they've come more closely into my life, which I'm very grateful for ... It's really good to talk to them because they ... both see what's going on in my life. They're like, OK, so you're doing this [outside of church] but here's a point of view from the church.

Looking again at Table 4.1, we can see that more than any other group, Religiously Committed teens report regular religious experiences. In response to the question about being aware of 'a presence or power different from the everyday self', 25 per cent claim to have this kind of experience often, and a further 60 per cent once or a few times. By contrast, only 12 per cent couldn't remember such an experience.

Here is an example of that kind of religious experience, told to us by one of our interviewees. Ashleigh is a committed Catholic teen and told us about two of these kinds of religious experiences, both from her childhood. She was raised in a Catholic family and attended Catholic primary and secondary schools. Now at university, she still lives at home with her parents, both of whom are also

Catholic. At the time of the survey, she attended Mass every week. Here is one of her stories:

> I don't remember … my age, but … my siblings and I were going for a walk with the dog, and it was school holidays. We had some money that Mum had given us. It was $50 … it was quite a lot for young people to have. I think we were walking up to the shops or something to get some DVDs and some lollies. So, we were told [by her mum] not to bring the dogs, because they are large dogs, and our parents didn't think we could control them by ourselves. My brother and sister went running with the dogs, and my sister had the money in her pocket, and when we stopped running, we decided to walk to the shops, she went to check her pocket and the $50 had disappeared. It had fallen out of her pocket while she was running. And my dad always said to me [that] when I lost things to pray to St Paul [most Catholics are taught to pray to St Anthony when things are lost]. And so – we looked everywhere, we re-traced our steps and we were nervous now that we hadn't found this money. We decided to take the dogs back to the house, put them back and then look again. And we still we could not find it. This was at a park, a humongous park that's right next door to my house. And my sister said, 'I'm freaking out now' because we would have been in a lot of trouble. So, we all sat down and we held hands and we prayed to St Paul, and, on the way back, we found the $50. And that – that to me was like it might have been a coincidence, but a young age it like – it's something that I remember a lot.

These kinds of experiences, which both confirm and scaffold faith, are an integral part of the ordinary lives of the Religiously Committed teens.

Most of the thirty-five Muslims teens in our survey were classified as belonging to the Religiously Committed type. (Not so for the small number of Buddhist, Hindu and Jewish teens in our survey, who were mainly classified as Nominally Religious or Seekers.)[12] Deniz is one of the Muslim teens who did our survey and was happy to do a follow-up interview. He was born in Turkey, arriving in Australia less than a decade ago. Deniz lives in the outer suburbs of a major capital city, in an area where a lot of other Muslims live. There's a mosque nearby. His home is also in one of the most socially disadvantaged postcodes in the city. Both his parents are Turkish: his mum is 'highly religious', but 'not my father, no'. Spending his younger years in Turkey, Deniz recalled the following about religion and everyday life:

> I was born overseas. So most of the stuff [on religion] was based on … the community's [religion]. So, there wasn't much freedom [for] what everyone

wanted. But I do have the sensation, where, there was freedom where you can believe what's to be believed but there was that sense yet again you were to be judged. You weren't fully free.

Since moving to Australia as a 10-year-old, he thinks his faith hasn't wavered, but it's not completely the same either, mostly because of living in a diverse, multifaith society:

I've always been a person who believed ... the [holy] books and what I've always been taught. [But] when I came to Australia my thoughts were not changed. But I would say they were reconsidered, because of what other people's religions were.

Living in religiously diverse communities is a theme we explore a little more in later chapters. These days, Deniz maintains an active commitment to his faith. On getting to the mosque he said:

I'm a full-time uni student [we surveyed him when he was in high school and then did the interview a few months later] and I do have a casual job so it's kind of a bit hard for me to go, but when I do have the time and the option to go I do go. I also follow the practices at home. *[Q: Yeah, right. You do those daily?]* Correct.

On doubt, and his enduring commitment to Islam, Deniz said this:

There were times when I had doubt. But, I do believe there is something [there] and [that is responsible for] how everything is created. But, there are times that I would be growing and thinking, I would think about it [whether God is real]. But I wouldn't fully think of it [the doubts] or think about it all the time as it could change my beliefs and I don't want to go through that experience.

As the stories of Deniz, Madelyn and Ashleigh illustrate, family, culture and religious experiences play an important part in the faith of these teens. And while Deniz's experience as a Muslim in Australia has its unique contours, the background factors that are important to his story are common among many of the Religiously Committed. We follow this thread in the next section.

Finding and keeping the faith: Explaining religious commitment

In previous chapters, we traced the arc of recent religious and social change in Australia and how this has created possibilities for the six different worldview types we have outlined. How is it that a teen comes to follow one path and not another? Why is Ashleigh still a committed Catholic when so many others in that tradition only have a nominal affiliation? What makes a person a Seeker? Beyond cognitive, psychological and developmental factors, survey research can instructively provide important clues about those sociocultural factors (like gender, age, place of residence, parental place of birth) associated with being a member of one type or another.

Not all of these sociocultural markers are equally important, and some are not as significant once other factors are considered.[13] For example, it might be that where a person lives has more influence on worldview type than their parents' religiosity. We have used statistical techniques that take into consideration a whole range of factors to find out which are strongly associated with any given type and which are not.[14] In this and the next two chapters, we will comment on the important sociocultural factors that are 'associated' with the different types.[15]

Below, we describe the factors strongly associated with being Religiously Committed:

Parental religion. Teens with religious parents are much more likely to be Religiously Committed than teens with nonreligious parents. Most studies show that parents are the single biggest influence on the religious outlook of an adolescent.[16] All of the teens featured in this section have one or both parents who are committed to religion and have grown up in households where religious activity is normal and expected. This generally, but not always, develops into adolescent religious faith.

Notably, the Religiously Committed teens we interviewed emphasized that their faith was their own, something that had deepened and matured during adolescence. Madelyn, for example, like Deniz and Ashleigh, was 'raised religious' but also felt that her faith was something that she had come to own herself:

> [Since] I was young ... from a baby on I've been part of that religion [LDS] and then there was a point in time where I was like, you know when you're a teenager and you're thinking, there are so many options for me, what's going on, is this real, is this right, is this true? It did hit me [at one point] and I was like, what am I doing? But I had a hard think ... I didn't want to just go into life and be like yeah, this is the religion that I'm in and just be like a follower. It was more like I wanted to make my choice and to see for myself if it was making me happy and myself me.

It is a familiar story with Vincent. Both his parents were born overseas, and both are committed and practising Catholics. He said:

I think I was 12 or 13 when I went to this summer camp. It was called Jesus camp or something. And, that's when, I sat down and had a conversation with God and – it's – because I've always believed in God, going to church was a bit [laughs] ... I didn't see the point and like all the priests were old and I didn't understand what they were talking about. Anyway, and when I was told about this camp, I sat down and thought about it. And [on camp, he saw] the power of Christ and [had the chance to talk to] people about God. And that started my journey my two – oh, just two-year journey on becoming what I call, like a conscious Catholic. I wanted to do this ... it was sort of the beginning of the journey ... my journey of choosing to believe in God, choosing to go to church. Then we got a new priest and his homilies were good and they explored themes of identity and growing inwardly and having an affinity with God, and why that is important, and having a dialogue.

Each of the Religiously Committed teens we interviewed insisted on their agency when it came to their outlook. For them, it was a faith of their own.[17]

Age. Younger teens are about twice as likely as older teens to be Religiously Committed. Thanks to some excellent recent American studies, we know that as they transition through adolescence, most teens don't lurch suddenly from being strongly religious to atheist, or vice-versa. However, among the most devoted there is some cooling evident in the transition through adolescence: teens often establish some independence from their parents as they grow older.[18] That helps explain our finding about a person's age. (We will discuss more on this in the next section.)

But we should note that our Religiously Committed interviewees, including Vincent, Ashleigh, Deniz and Madelyn, are all older. That makes them a little different. Among those *maintaining* high levels of religious commitment through the teen and young adult years, research suggests several factors are important: having religious parents; having regular religious experiences; and partaking in regular religious practices, such as attendance at services of worship, and prayer.[19] Looking at the profile of the Religiously Committed, it is clear that a lot of this is already in place.

School type. Teens who attend independent private schools are twice as likely than teens who attend government schools to be Religiously Committed. We have to be careful with attributing cause and effect here. We are not saying that going to such a school necessarily has an influence – simply that Religiously Committed teens are more likely to be found at independent private schools. Interestingly, there is no defined statistical effect for Catholic schools – as we explain below, Catholic teens are more likely to be other types, like Seekers and Nominally Religious.

Independent schools have far greater latitude than state schools when it comes to making religion part of the school experience, but how much religion plays a part in school life varies (see Chapter 8). Moreover, it is unclear the extent to which religious activities in school (e.g. religious instruction, chaplains) help or hinder faith development.[20] But being in a context where *being religious* is OK, or even expected, may have some overall positive impact. A handful of schools in Australia are like this. These are known as Christian or religious schools (e.g. Islamic colleges) and are different from 'Church' schools (denominational schools that have a Christian ethos).

Two of the authors conducted a focus group at an independent Christian school. The team had already been to nine other schools before visiting this one. These teens were in many ways no different to teens we encountered elsewhere: similar life aspirations, open, engaging, happy to be part of our research. But religious activity permeated school life in ways that could never occur in a government school.

Where most schools in Australia host a 'formal' dance or a debutante ball, students here did a 'blessing', which one student described as: 'It's … like [a ceremony] for us going from being a girl to women or boy to a man.' Others described it this way: 'It's like a deb [debutant ball] but at a deb, you have to dance and stuff, there's no dancing. You sit down, you eat, you get blessed and you leave.' And: 'There are people performing stuff, so there's the worship performer and we have to [sing congregational songs].' The students were entirely comfortable with this, and with the weekly school worship service (featuring a band and Pentecostal congregational songs) held in a church adjacent to the school.

Later, we did a focus group at an Islamic college. Here too, religion framed the everyday experiences of the students and afforded them a place where it was acceptable to be a Muslim. As one participant commented: 'Like when you celebrate Eid and Ramadan, we know you can talk about the food that we eat in Ramadan and the traditions we have in Eid, it's the families and that's what we discuss usually in class or something.' We should also note that sending a child to a dedicated religious school is often a reflection of how seriously parents take their religion – they are willing to sacrifice financially to provide a religiously supportive environment for children.

Parental place of birth. Teens whose parents are both born overseas are about twice as likely as those whose parents are born in Australia to be Religiously Committed. Many of the Religiously Committed teens come from religious traditions that have prospered, in large part, because of migration. The recent growth of Australia's Muslim community is largely the result of migration from Muslim-majority countries. Similarly, a growing proportion of Australian Pentecostals are migrants, and many of the newer independent churches are founded by migrants.[21]

In sum, religious parents, age, school type and country of birth (or parental place of birth) all seemingly inform the orientation of Religiously Committed teens. These are not necessarily in play for the next type we examine, the Nominally Religious.

Following in the family's footsteps: The Nominally Religious

In the Australian census, a large proportion of people – more than half of the adult population – select a religion when offered the choice and yet rarely go to a church, temple or mosque. They are prepared to nominate a religion when asked but do not follow that faith tradition with much vigour. This is particularly true of those who follow the mainline denominations, particularly the Anglican and Catholic churches.

About 20 per cent of Australia's teens fit the same mould: they have a broadly religious orientation, but for the most part, they don't take religion too seriously. This is evident when reading down their column in Table 4.1 and comparing them to the Religiously Committed. For the Nominally Religious, faith is a flicker rather than a flame. But their worldview is still primarily indebted to religious influences: more than three-quarters of them (77 per cent) think that religious faith is 'somewhat' important in shaping daily life. Significantly, they are not interested in other ways of being spiritual and otherwise reject a secular path.

Almost *half* the Catholic and mainline Protestant teens in our survey (Anglican, Lutheran, Presbyterian and Uniting Church) are Nominally Religious. (The other half fall into different types: Seekers, Indifferent and Religiously Committed.) Tom, by way of illustration, identified as Catholic, telling us he 'went to a Catholic school so I kind of ... fall under that [being Catholic]'. These days he never attends Mass and prays only rarely. For him, being Catholic is a legacy of his extended Catholic family. Unlike Religiously Committed teens, religious practices are a thing of his past. It was mainly via his primary school that he ever went to church, telling us: '[My primary] school had a church on site as well, so I think we went every two weeks to that.' He only ever went to his local parish 'for ... the special religious events like confirmation, communion.

If my friends were getting their [first] communion, that's the only time we'd go.'
And as for prayer:

> Tom: When I was at primary school, we would ... [pray] at school and then because it was kind of a recurring thing, every day at school. Sometimes at home as well ... But not very often.
> Q: Yeah. And what about as you've gotten older?
> Tom: Ah, got less and less so yeah, not any more.

Even growing up, Tom's parents had little enthusiasm for regular Mass either, noting: 'My parents are ... more like me.' His grandparents are more devoted but keep their opinions private: 'You don't hear them say anything but I think they'd like us to go more and stuff like that but we don't hear about it.'

Religious faith is not important in his everyday life. It is there, in the background, exerting some influence on his values. For the most part, however, Tom sees himself as having a mathematical and scientific orientation, saying: 'I am more of a science person.' As a result of his Catholic heritage, however, he still believes in God and thinks that God relates to humans in a personal way. He can reconcile this with his scientific orientation, saying: 'Having studied all of that it's kind of hard to not think that there's a higher power making all that happen ... with a lot of things there's too much of a coincidence.'

Why lukewarm for religion? Explaining nominal religiosity

In the previous section, we examined a range of factors that are associated with being Religiously Committed, such as age, school type and parental place of birth. For Nominally Religious teens, age, gender and the kind of school they attend are not huge influences on their religious development. Rather, their worldview is shaped by the religious tradition they follow (e.g. Catholic and mainline Protestant affiliation rather than Pentecostal) and by whether their parents are religious. Our statistical analysis shows that if only *one* parent follows a faith tradition (rather than both), then that greatly increases the likelihood that teen will end up Nominally Religious rather than Religiously Committed. And as Tom's case shows, if the parents are lukewarm for faith, then chances are that the teen will turn out the same way too. (His grandparents are more religious, though, showing the generational drop-off we discussed in Chapter 2.)

Importantly, adolescence is a time of profound cognitive, emotional and physical development. This can affect how a teen thinks about and relates to their religious enculturation. Research shows that as young people pass from older childhood into adolescence, traditional worldviews and values, inherited from family sources, are not only questioned but also frequently suspended.[22] Annie, for example, was raised in a mainline Protestant denomination and went to Catholic schools. She grew up in a very religious household, and while she still identifies with that religion, now in her later teens, she is leaving that commitment behind.

Q:	*[As a child] Would [you] go to church regularly?*
Annie:	Yeah.
Q:	*And still to this day?*
Annie:	Oh, well, yeah, providing I'm not busy.
Q:	*What other elements would you see as quite central to your practice of being Christian?*
Annie:	Nothing… I'm not an extreme … I just do what my parents want me to do.
Q:	*Do you think you would, even as you get a bit older, continue going to church, do you think?*
Annie:	Probably not, no.
Q:	*Do you pray?*
Annie:	No.
Q:	*No?*
Annie:	No, oh God … I said, 'Oh God'. My parents would like me to [pray], but no.

And of her peers at school, Annie said: 'I think they were just the same as me, like their parents, forced them [to attend church] mostly.' For now, she fits the profile of the Nominally Religious. Neither a secular or spiritual outlook beckons her. This places her in stark contrast with another group whose religious enculturation catalyses seeking spiritual inspiration outside the bounds of the religious tradition in which they were raised – the Seekers. This group, alongside the Spiritual but Not Religious (SBNR) group, are the subject of the next chapter.

Conclusion

This chapter has presented an entirely new way of thinking about teen worldviews, using a cutting-edge statistical approach and underpinned by in-depth interviews. Our final model settled on six distinct types, one that reflects the different, but sometimes related, ways Australia's teens think about the world. We then discussed the two major types whose worldview is indebted to conventional religion. It was clear from this discussion and analysis that family and family tradition are key factors in shaping how teens think about the world. This thread remains consistent in the next two chapters when we explore the four remaining worldview types.

5

'A higher order out there': Seekers and the spiritual but not religious

Vivien is an 18-year-old university student who lives with her parents in the inner suburbs of one of Australia's capital cities. Both her parents are from South East Asia. Vivien was a participant in our national survey and is one of thirty teens we phoned a few months later for an in-depth interview. She had indicated in her survey responses that she identified as a Buddhist, but her religious and spiritual worldview was much more complex than that. She's what we describe in this chapter as a 'Seeker' – someone interested in a spiritually eclectic and exploratory way of being. Among other topics, we called her to find out more about her outlook on life.

Vivien identifies as a Buddhist because that's the religious tradition of her extended family and part of her cultural background. She told us:

> My dad, actually I think – I only saw this a bit later on in my life, maybe early high school – I think he's [got] atheist views but he will do the [Buddhist] ceremonies and traditional stuff, just for the family's sake. But my mum is slightly more active in the community [but] I think she's pretty chill and lenient on it. I think it's because her oldest sister, my aunty, is super into it, the Buddhist traditions, and I think we kind of do it for the family's sake.

Vivien goes with her family to the Buddhist temple once or twice a year but doesn't immerse herself too much in the rituals, saying: '[I will] sit on the floor and do the chanting [but] I won't know the words or anything. I will just stay silent and just bow whenever everyone else bows.' When we asked how Buddhism influences her outlook she began by talking about karma:

> I am a firm believer in karma and if you do good things in the world you will receive good things. So, I think that's definitely from the Buddhist side … everyone wishes for good health and good prosperity and whatnot. And I think

that's something that I do actually, might, believe, occurs from doing the prayers and stuff. Yeah, I don't know … When I have incense in my hand and I'm asking for good luck and everything … I really do believe that it occurs from doing that. And doing other sorts of good things in the world.

Notwithstanding her Buddhist heritage and the fact she identifies as Buddhist, Vivien doesn't see herself as religious. She said: '[While] my parents are Buddhist [and] I've been raised sort of Buddhist, we went to temples and we did the … incense at home. But I wouldn't say I am religious. But I would say I am spiritual.' As we noted in Chapter 3, the idea that one can be 'spiritual but not religious' is an increasingly popular way of identifying in the West. So how does this find expression for an Australian teen, loosely raised as a Buddhist? Vivien shared these thoughts:

> I guess for me if someone says they are religious, it means they actively practise their religion. They actually, make an active involvement to attend … if you were Catholic, a Sunday service. Or going to the temple. I would say spiritual is more [if] you believe there is a higher order out there somewhere … I do believe that there is something out there. But, I wouldn't say that's – a Buddhist thing … I think it's more just a general broad spiritual [orientation]. Sounds so airy-fairy – I don't know how to word it [laughter].

Beyond this understanding of the transcendent, Vivien has done yoga, tried meditation, believes in reincarnation and has had other spiritual experiences. Part of this mix includes her education in the Catholic school system, at both primary and secondary levels. Of this, Vivien says: 'My values are based on Catholic values … treating others as you would [want] to be treated. That kind of basic, parable type thing.' Vivien feels no obligation to follow any religious or spiritual tradition in an orthodox way. She picks and chooses what feels right to her, with a nod to her cultural and religious background.

According to the matrix of types we presented in the previous chapter, Vivien is a Seeker, a worldview type that comprises about 8 per cent of Australian teens. This group, alongside the 18 per cent we call 'Spiritual but Not Religious' (SBNR), represent the teens who are most oriented towards spiritual, metaphysical, transcendent or holistic ways of being in the world. **The main difference between these two types is that Seekers have a 'home' of sorts in a religious tradition, and SBNR teens do not.** This chapter explores why these teens, and not others, are interested in 'spirituality', and how much their worldview informs their everyday lives.

'I am spiritual ... I believe in the things out there': On being a Seeker

We began this chapter with Vivien's story: born into a Buddhist family, schooled in the Catholic education system and now interested in wellbeing practices and other spiritual ideas. She represents a type we call 'Seekers'. These teens are largely raised in or with inherited religious traditions but they search more widely for existential meaning and are open to many different beliefs. They almost all identify with a religious group *and* most also describe themselves as spiritual.

Table 4.1, which was in the previous chapter, presents their profile in detail, but we reprise it here briefly. Almost all Seekers identify with a religion and claim that religion is in some measure important in shaping their daily lives (22 per cent said it was 'extremely/very important'; 70 per cent said it was 'somewhat important'; only 9 per cent said it was not at all important). Like the Nominally Religious type, they do not attend services with any regularity. Unlike the former group, however, they have an openness to spiritual possibilities. The overwhelming majority responded affirmatively to the question asking them if they have ever 'experienced a presence or power', and **more than any another type**, they are spiritually eclectic, blending beliefs into a self-styled worldview.

We have chosen to label this group 'Seekers'. They have a 'home' in religious traditions but are not bound in any way by that tradition. Instead, that seems to give them an openness towards the transcendent, spiritual or holistic. Seekers are the type most likely to engage in spiritual or holistic practices and beliefs. Not shown in Table 4.1, but important nonetheless:

- Seventy-four per cent of Seekers believe in reincarnation;
- Eighty-eight per cent of Seekers believe in karma; 65 per cent believe in angels; 58 per cent believe it is possible to contact the dead; and
- Two-thirds (65 per cent) have consulted their horoscope for guidance.

We interviewed several teenagers who fit the Seeker profile, and it was quickly evident that organized religion has played a formative role in their upbringing. Like Vivien, 18-year-old Ferazia is classed as a Seeker, born in Australia to migrant parents. She's raised in the Islamic tradition and identifies as Muslim. As a child, she would attend her mosque infrequently ('We'd go every now and then'), and of her parents, she says: 'They're ... more religious than I am.' These days she will fast during Ramadan. But that's about it. She never goes to the Mosque, and said: 'I don't pray five times a day ... I don't ... wear a headscarf (i.e.

hijab).' For these reasons, Ferazia told us 'that's why I wouldn't say I'm religious'. Her parents are OK with this.

But this enculturation has resulted in a legacy of openness to the spiritual. Ferazia said: 'I am spiritual in terms of like, I believe in the things out there, so like God and ... all that kind of stuff.' For her, that 'kind of stuff' includes belief in astrology, ghosts, angels and contact with the dead. When asked if she believed in reincarnation, she equivocated for a while before saying: 'I'd like to say yes, but no.' She's also tried yoga and meditation.

Mariella is similar. One of her parents was born in South Asia (to preserve confidentiality we won't identify which country) and she was one of the fifteen self-identified Hindus who participated in our survey. In many ways, she embodies the new possibilities of a religiously diverse Australia. Mariella said: 'I am Hindu, but it's kind of difficult because I'm – I'm from two different cultures' with a 'Western mum' (who was raised in a Christian country) and 'my dad is South Asian'. As a child, she remembers 'going to ceremonies and, things like that, just the little rituals, going to temples and stuff'.

She doesn't follow the Hindu tradition when she is in Australia, but when she goes to her father's country of origin she says: 'It's nice to have that kind of ritual.' Mariella explains this further:

> I think it's nice to just kind of have [my background] – because the belief and story of that religion, are really interesting to me. Or just anyone's religion in general, just because religion is so old and they have different stories. I find it interesting, just – I wouldn't say I am religious, but I do really enjoy learning about other religions and kind of going into that.

She is adamant, however, that 'I'm just not really religious'. Of her heritage and experiences, Mariella observes: 'I did really enjoy and I still do, just because it is a very community atmosphere there [father's country of origin]. It is really nice and I think it's nice to be a part of something like that. As with any religion.' Mariella doesn't believe in God, 'maybe' believes in karma and angels, but believes in a higher being, reincarnation and astrology, evidence of a curious, eclectic approach to existential matters. Above all, she thinks she is 'spiritual but not religious'.

To be a Seeker is to have religion as just one point on the compass. Ferazia, Mariella and Vivien all felt comfortable self-identifying as 'spiritual' and see this being about *more than* just religion (although for them it was also *inclusive* of religion, which is not the case for the SBNR teens, see below).[1] At least for the Seekers above, their openness to many beliefs seems to be mediated by their experiences as the children of migrants. They are impacted by the religious traditions their parents or grandparents brought with them to Australia, but not sufficiently to adopt this for themselves. They are also situated in families that are adjusting to new ways of seeing; these young people are open to new experiences, but at the same time they are not wedded to anything specific in the old or the new. Thus, their overall worldview is syncretistic.

In Chapter 3, we described the emergence of the spiritual marketplace and the myriad ways in which Westerners can enact a 'spiritual but not religious' ethos if they choose. None of the three we've talked about so far can reasonably be described as wholly embracing the 'New Age'. They do not practice another holistic or spiritual modality, like Reiki or channelling. For the most part, that is a path trodden more by members of the two preceding generations, Baby Boomers and Gen Xers.[2] However, some Australian teens do lean quite seriously into this milieu.

We briefly encountered Jana in Chapter 3 in the discussion of tarot cards. Like her peers above, Jana also has migrant parents. Because she still identifies with a religious tradition (Orthodox Christian), she was classified as a Seeker. When asked if she was 'spiritual or religious', she responded: 'Maybe not religious exactly. I don't really have my own religion. Maybe I'm kind of spiritual, I guess.' When asked how that found expression for her, she replied that she was: 'Yeah, maybe, well, like New Age kind of religious. Yeah.' This led to the extended discussion of tarot cards, which is something she takes extremely seriously, noting: '[Once I got a] new set of cards and then the first reading I did it was really like – do you know, it made me cry actually.' Jana is vegetarian, motivated to do so because of a concern for animal rights. Above all, however, it is her card-reading practice that is central to her spiritual outlook. Jana said:

> I think [why] most people would turn to religion ... [is] because if you're stuck and you don't really know what to do you kind of look for answers in something. Or you try to get help with [it], so the tarot cards are something. If I don't know what to do in a certain situation, I would use them and then try and like get some clarity. And I think that's probably what people do with religion too.

Tarot becomes a type of religion for Jana – searching for clarity through this medium.

Why a Seeker? Explaining why some choose a seeking path

In the previous chapter, we explored the relationship between membership in the Nominally Religious and Religiously Committed types and factors such as age, gender, migrant status and the type of school a teen attends. Some similar themes emerge with teens who end up on a path of 'seeking' rather than 'dwelling'.[3] This is what we know about Seekers:

Parental influence. Teens with parents who identify with a religion (one or both parents) are about three times more likely than teens with nonreligious parents to be Seekers. The Seekers we have met in this chapter have experienced religion as part of their family story, but it was never especially important to the parent or parents. This has attuned them to spiritual possibilities but hasn't left a legacy of strong commitment. This subtlety is captured is this exchange with Jana, when we asked her about first getting interested in tarot cards:

> Jana: I think it was my sister, again mostly. And my dad as well is into that sort of stuff.
>
> Q: *How did he get involved in those different practices and ideas?*
>
> Jana: Yeah. Actually, I'm not sure. But I know that he used to, well Mum told me before [he had children] he went through a few different religions. He was like, I think he was really into Christianity at one point and then he was really into Buddhism and stuff like that. And then, I guess, he kind of stumbles upon these kinds of things and that's what was the best for him.
>
> Q: *And what about your mum then?*
>
> Jana: She's not really interested at all, I don't think.
>
> Q: *And did you ever go to church or were you ever involved in any religion formally?*
>
> Jana: Because my dad's Greek, so my brother and dad are pretty Orthodox Christian. So, we – I've been to the Greek church a few times, but just on like Christmas and, well funeral-kind of events.
>
> Q: *Just quite occasional things?*
>
> Jana: Yeah.

She also describes her response to learning about religion as being like that of her father, saying: 'I feel like my dad a little bit. Whenever we would learn about different religions [when Jana was younger] I was like, oh, I want to be that now.'

Age. Older teens are about twice as likely as younger teens to be Seekers. Older teens seemingly display a greater openness to a 'spiritual+religious' eclecticism than younger teens. Older teens are at a developmental stage that sees them becoming increasingly independent, exploratory and curious. This might dispose them to a more eclectic outlook on life and to move beyond the family's orientation.

Gender. Females are twice as likely as males to be Seekers. As sociologists, we argue that there's no inherent reason for this gender bias. It is instead a reflection of larger societal norms and expectations. Lots of contemporary spiritual activities are about self-care, introspection and emotional awareness, and in Western culture, these traits are more strongly associated with the 'feminine' rather than the 'masculine'.[4]

School type. Teens who attend Catholic schools are about twice as likely as teens who attend independent schools to be Seekers. Also, among those who identified as Christians, it is Catholic teens who are more likely than any other denomination to also be Seekers. Why is this? There are a couple of possible explanations. Perhaps a Catholic upbringing 'attunes' a teen into spiritual possibilities – it's they just don't want to accept the whole Catholic package. Or it might be that Catholic teens – more than any other Christian tradition – will hold onto that identification even if they don't believe or belong in other conventional ways.[5] That fits with our profile of Catholic teens we presented in Chapter 2.

For example, Elizabeth is a Seeker (she says she is 'spiritual and religious') who was raised Catholic (her mother is Catholic, father a 'None') and attended Catholic schools. She believes in God and enjoyed RE at school, but she also believes in reincarnation, astrology and karma. At some point, she realized, however, that she didn't need 'a middle man of the Church'. Elizabeth also considers herself to be a 'very scientific person' and this has led her to question some of the traditional Catholic beliefs in things like 'hell and purgatory'.

Parental place of birth. Teens whose parents are both born overseas are almost twice as likely as those whose parents are born in Australia to be Seekers. Being a Seeker is intertwined with having a religious background (some of the Hindu, Muslim, Christian and Jewish teens are Seekers), which in turn is related to their cultural background. But Seeker teens are moving beyond their parent's religion. Could mobility and diversity be another factor in what drives people to become Seekers? Negotiating new cultures as part of the transition to Australia may encourage the development of a Seeker religious profile.

'I believe we [humans] are a spirit': On being SBNR

In Chapter 3, we discussed the emerging popularity of the phrase 'spiritual but not religious' and how this references 'a way of being' in the world that denotes an openness to transcendent possibilities beyond religious belief and practice. We felt the phrase helpfully described one of our six worldview types. Like

Seeker teens, SBNR teens (who comprise 18 per cent of Australian teens) are oriented towards the non-material and do so in eclectic ways.

Table 4.1 presents their profile in full, but here we summarize some notable points. While almost all SBNR teens believe in a higher being, only a few call this 'God'. They don't attend services of worship, nor do they identify with a religion or think that faith is important in shaping how they live their lives. The overall orientation of their worldview is towards a range of supernatural and spiritual beliefs. For example:

- Seventy-five per cent of SBNR teens believe in life after death, and a further 15 per cent 'maybe' believe;
- Seventy-six per cent of SBNR teens believe in reincarnation;
- Sixty-six per cent believe in ghosts; and
- Sixty-two per cent believe it is possible to contact the dead.

For most SBNR teens, like the Seekers, these beliefs are not held exclusively – 65 per cent believe in some combination of astrology, reincarnation and contact with the dead. (Remember from the previous chapter that a person is assigned to their type based on the *totality* of their answers *across all of the items*, which is why, for example, not a 100 per cent of them believe in reincarnation.)

We've called this group SBNR because of their *latent* interest in various spiritual beliefs and practices, or because this is how they identified in response to that survey question. But how committed is this group to 'being spiritual', and how vital is this commitment in their everyday lives?

When researching 'spirituality' or a 'spiritual orientation', it is often difficult to gauge exactly how coherent or meaningful it is for someone, and how often it is enacted in their daily decision making. There is little collective agreement in the public mind about what it is for a Westerner to be consciously 'spiritual' – it is simply too personal and self-authenticating to be 'nailed down'.[6] For example, if we asked all the practitioners at a yoga class if they are spiritual, or even engaged in a spiritual activity, we would receive highly varied responses.[7]

We have seen from the interviews that some teens can give voice to *why* they said in the survey that they are 'spiritual' and how, if at all, this is enacted in their daily life. Others might be surprised to see themselves classified this way – they simply said 'yes' in a survey to holding some disparate beliefs and may have never contemplated that it might add up to something. So, we are not claiming to be measuring teens' *commitment* to a spiritual pathway – we've simply discovered that a group of teens are oriented towards certain 'spiritual' ways of being. That said, *under the broader SBNR umbrella*, there appear to be two kinds of teens – **spiritually oriented believers** and **spiritual marketplace participants**.

First are the **spiritually oriented believers**, which comprise about two-thirds of the SBNR group (and thus 12 per cent of all Australian teens overall, given the SBNR group is 18 per cent of all teens). They are open to spiritual, paranormal or supernatural beliefs but *not* the common or familiar 'alternative spiritual' practices. For example, none of them had participated in any of the following: a séance; seeing a psychic; reading their horoscopes; using tarot cards; practising either yoga or meditation. We are not sure how consequential their latent belief in ghosts, reincarnation or astrology is in their everyday lives, but it probably varies from a lot to a little for this subgroup of SBNR teens.[8]

The other main cluster of SBNR teens is **spiritual marketplace participants**. This group represents about a third of SBNR teens (and thus about 6 per cent of all teens overall). While the term 'spiritual marketplace' might be construed as somehow dismissive of or negative about young people's spiritual commitments, we deploy this metaphor to signal how central the idea of consumer-oriented choice is to how young people explore their interests, construct identities and share culture.[9] These teens aren't just predisposed to participate in the spiritual marketplace; they are also likely embedded in this market through their use of various forms of social media. It's a key thread in the fabric of their lives. Teens with a marketplace approach not only hold an eclectic mix of spiritual, paranormal or supernatural beliefs but also have engaged in some kind of practice too, with varying levels of commitment and seriousness. The most favoured activity, by far, is consulting a horoscope for guidance. Less common, but still somewhat prevalent among this group, is tarot card reading.[10] The tiny handful of Australian teens seeing psychics, mediums or doing séances are either in this **subgroup of SBNR teens** or are some of the **Seekers**.[11]

Freya is one of these kinds of teens – a sometime participant in spiritual marketplace activities. We introduced her briefly in Chapter 3 as an enthusiastic meditator and reader of tarot cards. Freya is also among the 14 per cent of Australian teens who identify as LGBTQI+. She was raised spiritual, as her 'mum was really into it [yoga and meditation] all'. She explained how her mum rebelled against her own 'totally Christian' family by first becoming a 'party animal' and then getting into spiritual things. Freya further recounted how she regularly attended an ashram with her mum and that this gave her a sense of community that she really appreciated:

> Freya: I was surrounded by her spirituality. Like, I've been to an ashram many times [in Australia] and … those kinds of things … we went up to the ashram twice a year … When I was about, ah, nine to 14 … I really loved it … It was really nice to be part of something.
>
> Q: *Yeah, right. It's a sense of community and belonging?*
>
> Freya: Yeah.
>
> Q: *Yeah, right.*
>
> Freya: And great food… Well, it's something, like, they don't force you to join in… it was just… very beautiful.

Both Freya and her mother had friends at the ashram, who looked out for them. They openly spoke about spirituality together, and even now among her peer group, she says that discussing spirituality is 'pretty comfortable terrain. It's nothing, like, huge. Like, it doesn't feel like anything big to talk about.' She also added that growing up 'it didn't really matter [about anyone's point of view] because we just hung out … regardless'. When asked whether she identifies as spiritual or religious or neither, Freya replied:

> Oh, more so on the spiritual side, but I don't really identify as anything. I believe we are a spirit and, you know [we] go on to another life … but I haven't, you know, given my entire life over to trusting in that.

Lucinda, like Freya, is another SBNR teen who has mixed some practices with belief in spiritual and supernatural things. We introduced also her briefly in Chapter 3 as someone who talked about liking to read her horoscope and was curious about what this might say about the future: 'I like horoscopes and stuff like that, they're not always, like, correct but I like looking at them being like maybe that'll happen.' She's also responsible for the ghost story we featured in Chapter 3, and she believes in ghosts. Lucinda grew up in a nominally Christian family who weren't particularly religious, although she and her brother were baptized. Like other SBNR teens, she had her own, self-authenticated ideas about existential matters:

> Lucinda: I don't agree with how Christians believe they can do something and God will forgive them … I don't believe in that sort of God but I believe there's someone up there, and, he or she is, kind of, taking – not taking care of us but … there's something there, it doesn't just finish here, there's something up there but not as, as a God as the Christians put it, he is our

> Saviour and all that stuff ... because if he was, he wouldn't let all the terrible things that happen, happen...

Lucinda also believes in reincarnation, albeit in a particular way:

Lucinda: Yeah, I guess ... I feel like depending on the person, it depends on, like, what happens to you after you die ... some people may go to heaven or some people may be reincarnated into other people. I believe, our spirits might go to heaven but then, like, half of us might stay here ... and get reincarnated into someone else, it's really, up to each person [to decide].

In terms of activities, Lucinda reads her horoscope and has done yoga. Sometimes she's had her tarot read for her by a friend. She's also done some mindfulness meditation, which began at school:

Lucinda: At school as well we got taught about how sometimes you need to take a break and just relax [for] 10 minutes. Headspace [a mindfulness app] is really good. So it's more like, just that stuff, breathe, just taking a break, letting your mind rest, like, that was really good during [her final year of school] and just taking 10 minutes out of your day to think about nothing and, yeah, stuff like that, not really, religious [or] religion-related.

Q: *Would you think of it as spirituality?*

Lucinda: Yeah.

Q: *Do you meditate with your – your group of friends did you say? ... Or just a couple of you?*

Lucinda: Well, at school ... once a month we had meditation in the hall. My whole year group [was there] where we just laid there and it was, like, they just talked to you about breathing and stuff like that. And my friend from our school she does it, every Sunday morning or something, just, 10 minutes and [she] listens to a video about breathing and stuff like that. So if I have a sleepover at her house and we do it on Sunday morning.

While she is not a consistent practitioner of any spiritual modality, she is 'OK' with these activities because they fit with her self-view:

Lucinda: My friend that does the meditation she's also into the tarot cards and her family as well, they're all into crystals and stuff

> like that. [It] opened me [to it] as well. So it's really like, I'm not really into one thing, I kind of just experience it when people are talking about it. Like I won't be, like, oh, no, I don't want to do that and walk away, I just like, [to] be a part of it but won't invest in it.

Among the teens with whom we talked, these activities were not necessarily done in private or kept especially secret, at least not from friends. Indeed, Lucinda views spiritual marketplace practices as common, mainstream and acceptable:

> Lucinda: When I first saw that [my friend] had, the crystals and stuff I was, oh, that's a bit weird … when I was growing up I just thought … [it's] weird people that believed in, crystals and all this, strange stuff but then, it's pretty normal … it's more a well-known thing that people are into that kind of stuff now … astrology and, crystals and stuff like that … so it's not that weird anymore … but I wouldn't do it, I wouldn't do it every single day or anything like that.

Both Freya and Lucinda have dipped into the possibilities of the spiritual marketplace and done so with openness and curiosity, willing to learn about themselves and others. They do not subscribe to any one convention or absolute rule, which is probably one of the main reasons the phrase 'spiritual but not religious' sat comfortably with them.

In Chapter 3, we described the burgeoning spiritual marketplace that has flourished in contemporary Western society in recent decades. Considering the evidence we have presented, it is likely that less than *one in ten* Australian teenagers are passionate, serious and committed to a 'New Age' lifestyle familiar to many Baby Boomers and Gen Xers (i.e. as dedicated, regular practitioners of palmistry, Reiki, Tantra, channelling, astrology, mediumship and tarot, or as regular consumers of these modalities). Most of these activities are client-based, expensive and are not pitched at teenagers.

However, SBNR and Seeker teens embrace the logic and approach of the spiritual marketplace more than any other worldview type. Their worldview is characterized by an openness to spiritual possibilities beyond mainstream religions and a willing eclecticism to this openness (which can include wellness activities). Judging from the interview data, this has a low-key and sometimes ephemeral quality. Perhaps in time, with increased age and income, more of them will embrace specific spiritual practices or holistic lifestyles. Though we don't see this as the next step in terms of spiritual maturity but rather another possibility afforded to people who are interacting with the spiritual, cultural and financial economies often associated with the 'spiritual marketplace'.

It is also helpful to think more expansively about 'spirituality'. It can also refer to the 'higher' values and principles that animate a person, and which leads people to care about certain issues or take particular actions. In the in-depth interviews, we asked teenagers about their social concerns. The issues most commonly nominated were: gender and sexual equality; mental health (including bullying); environmental issues and global conflict. SBNR teen, Freya, said this about the 'anxiety epidemic':

> Some of [my] worries are just, society, you know, how society isn't really a society anymore, because society needs a group of people and we're all quite separate these days ... Also the rape culture. That is a huge impact on so many people, and it's just so normal ... It's just, the amount of unhappiness that is happening at this current point in time, it's out of this world really.

Freya also described to us her commitment to environmental issues, particularly stopping deforestation. However, the survey took place before 'the Greta effect' unfolding internationally. Greta Thunberg's school strike for climate and the catastrophic 2019–20 Australian bushfire season will no doubt have influenced teen responses on such issues but unfortunately, we can only speculate about the significance of these events in shaping teen worldviews. That said, caring about society or the environment wasn't the preserve of any one worldview type, and teens are motivated to care and act for many different reasons. The research wasn't designed to establish causality regarding these issues, though in later chapters we do explore the relationship between worldviews and attitudes to religious and sexual diversity.

Why SBNR? Explaining why some teens have an SBNR outlook

Seekers and SBNR teens, while equally spirituality eclectic in outlook, come at religion differently. This difference is reflected in those sociocultural factors that are most strongly associated with the SBNR type:

Parental influence. Teens whose parents don't identify with a religion are about five times more likely than teens with religious parents to be classified as SBNR. SBNR teens have no place for religion in their worldview, mainly because they have minimal religious influence in their extended family lives.

Although we don't know precisely how much their parents influence their eclectic outlook, we can infer from this study, alongside earlier studies, that SBNR teens would likely have a worldview that mirrors that of their parents' fairly closely.[12]

School type. Teens who attend government schools are about twice as likely as teens who attend Catholic school to be SBNR teens. SBNR teens have no foundation in religious traditions. Teens with religious roots are more likely to be found clustered in the independent and Catholic school systems, and nonreligious teens (SBNR, Indifferent and This Worldly) are more likely to cluster in the government school system.

Gender. Females are twice as likely as males to be classified as SBNRs. For the reasons we noted above in the section on Seekers, young women are more open than young men to most alternative spiritual beliefs and activities about which we inquired—except belief in UFOs (which is not part of our worldview types model).[13]

Conclusion

This chapter has explored the lives of Seekers and SBNR teenagers. Above all, we found that SBNR and Seeker teens have a spiritually open and eclectic worldview. Among them are the Australian teens who engage, sometimes deeply, in a range of spiritual, wellbeing and holistic practices, such as horoscopes, meditation and tarot cards. They undertake these spiritual practices to calm their minds, and also for fun. They practice on their own or with their parents or friends, sometimes at school and occasionally in spiritual communities. In this way, their spirituality often has a social dimension. Importantly, it is their own decision making – not just the spiritual economies in which they are circulating – which regularly prompt them to enter into the marketplace to see what's on offer.

So far, our exploration of worldview types has covered a substantial proportion of the teen population. Importantly, however, a plurality of Australian teens cares very little for religion, or spirituality, and makes sense of the world in other ways. This Worldly and Indifferent teens are the focus of the next chapter.

6

Immanent gods: This Worldly and Indifferent teens

British philosopher Alain de Botton's bestselling book is called *Religion for Atheists: A Non-believer's Guide to the Uses of Religion*.[1] It explores ways that nonreligious people can 'promote morality, engender a spirit of community ... train minds and encourage gratitude' without religious belief and religious communities.[2] Perhaps inspired by this nonreligious mission statement, in 2013 a group of London atheists inaugurated the Sunday Assembly, intended to be a network of 'godless congregations' and 'a global secular (nonreligious) movement for wonder and good ... We meet to celebrate life together in secular congregations around the world'.[3] Their motto is 'Live better, help often and wonder more'. They aim to foster communities that engender these aims, while consciously rejecting religious belief.

Congregations were established in cities throughout Western Europe and America, along with four in Australia. Each month, attenders come together and sing secular congregational songs (i.e. pop songs), listen to speakers and affirm nonreligious creeds. After, they are welcome to stay for refreshments. It is, in effect, a 'secular church'. Unsurprisingly, the Sunday Assembly was the subject of extensive press coverage in the first few years of its existence.

Like many Christian denominations in the West, however, the Sunday Assembly is faltering. Numbers are dwindling and some congregations are closing. Three of the Australian chapters are dormant or finished. An article in *The Atlantic* highlights some of the reasons for these difficulties.[4] This includes a lack of volunteers to organize the services, the cost of staging services, even monthly ones, and leaders without church-growing skills. There is no professional clergy class either, able to knit the community together in the days between each service, through pastoral visits and small-group and social activities.

Another stated cause is something deeply familiar to Christian churches – the preponderance of other interesting things to do at the same time the service is on. *The Atlantic* piece notes: 'people have plenty of other options on a Sunday morning. Boot camps. SoulCycle. Brunch.' Something else seems to be missing too. A careful look at photos of congregants on social media and in the press reveals few young faces. It is not surprising that the Sunday Assembly has a muted appeal to young people. If it looks like a congregation and sounds like a congregation, then it probably is a congregation, God or not. We have already seen in this book how hard it is for religious communities to connect with young people. Moreover, without young people, religious (and nonreligious) communities are fated to falter and fade away.

Seemingly, following a church model couldn't inspire a large-scale, nonreligious movement dedicated to altruism and community beyond anything that exists already (recognizing the long history of humanist, atheist, secular, free-thinking and philanthropic organizations). However, the existence of the Sunday Assembly in different places, even if only briefly, does illustrate a deeper truth. Religious Nones do have 'nonreligious belief systems',[5] or 'worldviews' (our preferred term). These kinds of worldviews might involve an individual's latent orientation (like a commitment to caring for the environment), or it might involve fidelity to a secular creed, ideal or philosophy (e.g. humanism; Marxism). Sometimes this orientation is expressed with others in a dedicated community.

To that end, this chapter explores the values and outlooks of teens we call 'This Worldly' and 'Indifferent', people who have 'embraced religion's other' and live nonreligious lives.[6] Our objective is to be 'positive' when describing the lives of nonreligious teens. Previous survey studies that identify clusters of nonreligious teens have done so using a 'deficit model'.[7] That is, teens are grouped in typologies solely because they reject religious and spiritual beliefs and practices (i.e. no belief in God, no attendance at services of worship) rather than their commitment to a nonreligious ideal, or some other positive assessment of how they see the world. While our model does acknowledge that, say, not believing in God, is an important part of many teens' worldviews, we also identify the types of thinking these teens *affirm* and teased this out in our in-depth interviews.

Consequently, this chapter explores the things that animate the lives of Indifferent and This Worldly teens. What are the sources of meaning for them, and what difference does it make to their life decisions and attitudes to others? Thus far, this book has focused on religion and spirituality, but now we move in a different direction.

'Very science-y and not very religious': On being This Worldly

During the interview we did with 18-year-old Noah, he was asked to describe his peer group at school and noted they were 'very science-y and not very religious'. To Noah, these two things are related. His outlook on life, which he said was grounded in scientific thinking, precluded transcendent or metaphysical possibilities. This is why we gave the name 'This Worldly' to teens who have strictly nonreligious or non-spiritual lives. This Worldly teens are the single largest group in our model, comprising 23 per cent of Australian teens. Their full profile is revealed in Table 4.1 (Chapter 4), but notable points include:

- This Worldly teens don't believe in God. The large majority also don't believe in a higher power (76 per cent); some believe in a higher power (15 per cent), and a further 8 per cent are unsure;
- Eighty-six per cent of This Worldly teens never attend services of worship, and the rest go only 'rarely', mostly because they are obliged to go;
- Most This Worldly teens (nine out of ten) have *never* been aware of a presence or power different from their everyday self. The same proportion don't believe in life after death, reincarnation, astrology or contact with the dead; and
- Sixty per cent of This Worldly teens agree that 'the physical universe is the only thing that exists'. They are somewhere between three to fifteen times more likely than any other type to express this point of view.

These data suggest that religion or spirituality plays little part in their daily lives, whether that is rituals, practices or beliefs.

As a team we spent a good deal of time trying to settle on an appropriate name for this group, with rejected suggestions including: 'Here-and-now(s)', 'Seculars', 'Materialists' or 'Humanists', among others. We felt that 'This Worldly' positively described the key characteristic of their worldview. These teens are growing up without metaphysical beliefs or attendant practices of any kind, or as scholars Jesse Smith and Ryan Cragun put it, they have 'an understanding of reality that simply does not require or imply theistic ... beliefs'.[8]

While they are technically atheists (i.e. lacking a belief in the gods or a God), we didn't want to call this group 'atheists' for two main reasons. First, atheism is not a system of belief, and our aim in this book is to shine a light on the things different groups of teens believe.[9] Second, and perhaps surprisingly, most This

Worldly teens don't identify or see themselves as atheists. When our Gen Z teen cohort were children, the 'New Atheist' movement was flourishing. Bestselling books were published by high-profile atheists such as Richard Dawkins, Christopher Hitchens and Sam Harris. In 2006–7 their books sold more than a million copies combined in the United States alone.[10] Around the same time, Pastafarianism, a spoof religion whose followers worship the Flying Spaghetti Monster, became a popular internet meme. Atheists organized 'Global Atheist Conventions', placed advertisements on buses to promote non-belief and staged campaigns in the UK and Australia to encourage people to select the 'no religion' option in the census.[11] Between 2006 and 2011, there was a rise in the number (and proportion) of Australians who identified in the census as 'atheists' (which is done by writing in the space provided), although this dropped between 2011 and 2016.[12]

Notwithstanding the growth of New Atheism and of Nones, 'atheist' is simply an unpopular identifier among teens. In our survey, we asked all those who didn't identify with a religion if they otherwise describe themselves as an atheist, agnostic, humanist, something else or simply 'not religious'. Figure 6.1 shows how This Worldly teens responded (it is only showing teens in this type, not all the Nones in the sample. That data are reported in Chapter 2).

This figure shows that half of This Worldly teens see themselves as not religious; 33 per cent consider themselves atheists and 8 per cent are agnostics. Only three people in the entire survey described themselves as humanists.

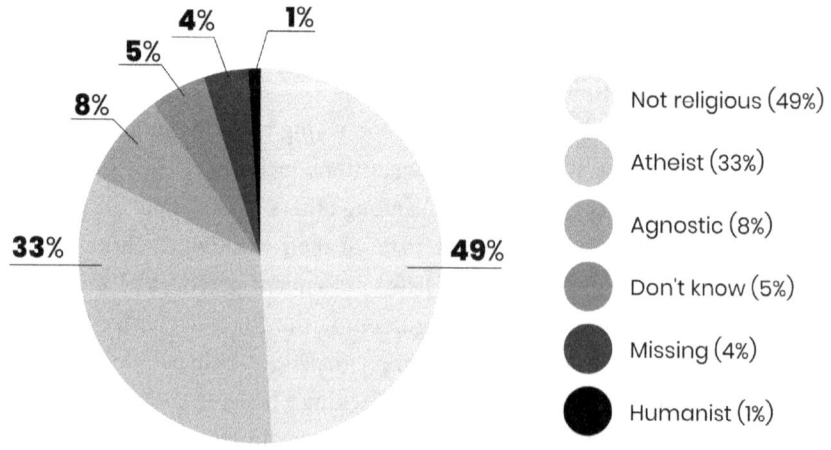

Source: AGZ Survey 2017

Figure 6.1 This Worldly teens (13–18): Identification as nonreligious (% of identity).

To be sure, some This Worldly teens are 'out and proud' atheists. The following exchange took place at one of our focus groups, in response to a question about religious diversity at school. One of the respondents, a 15-year-old boy, is a proud Pastafarian. He adopted this spoof religion because it is emblematic of his feelings about faith:

Participant 1:	Well, to an extent in school there's a really open idea about religion like religion has become a very loose term. Like there's a religion about a giant spaghetti monster in the sky, and it's classified as an actual religion.
Participant 2:	Weren't you part of that religion?
P1:	I still am.
P2:	Oh, nice.
Q:	*You indicated you're a Pastafarian, is that right? How did you convert to Pastafarianism?*
P3:	What is that?
P1:	Oh, the god is the Flying Spaghetti Monster.
Q:	*It's the religion that follows the Flying Spaghetti Monster.*
P2:	Not familiar with this monster.
P1:	It's a big monster that's made out of spaghetti and meatballs.
P3:	And what are your values and beliefs?
P1:	Ah, there's actually a list. I can't remember them.
P3:	Isn't there a bible?
P1:	Yeah, there is, the Loose Canon. It was made in 2011 I believe. I think somewhere in the United States, after …
P2:	Is this real?
P1:	This is real, yeah. It's classified as a religion. It started in the United States after someone, protested that their son had to go to, I think it was some religious thing. I think it was a Christian youth group I believe somewhere in the United States and so he wrote this letter to the school saying, 'Why can't my kid follow the Church of the Flying Spaghetti Monster?' as a joke and now it's become a real religion.
Q:	*It was a movement where they wanted to stop the teaching of Intelligent Design in high schools in the United States. They wanted to teach this [Pastafarianism]. How did you come across it?*
P3:	Internet?

P1: It was. I came across it on the internet. I heard about it on a radio program I listen to and it sounded interesting to me, so I followed it up. I found … an internet meme which had [a picture of] the human nervous system and nothing else but the brain, the eyes and the human nervous system and it looked like a giant flying spaghetti monster. It said if you look at the [human] body without everything then we are basically flying spaghetti monsters, [so] go follow Pastafarianism. That's how I looked into it.

This exchange took place in a friendly, humorous way. We didn't encounter bitter anti-religious sentiment in the interviews or focus groups. As we explain in Chapter 7, Australian teens are just not like that when it comes to religion or non-religion.

In contrast to most of the previous quantitative research on nonreligious teens, we were committed to discovering more about how trust in science, humanism and reason figured in teen worldviews.[13] Accordingly, we asked our survey participants a few questions designed to tap into this kind of mindset. Responses are shown in Table 6.1. We designed some of these statements ourselves; others are principles propagated by various rationalist and humanist societies.

A majority of all teens agree with the first two items, 'Human beings can live ethical and fulfilling lives without religious beliefs' (83 per cent agree), and 'When something strange or unusual happens, I always think there must be a rational explanation for it' (77 per cent), but This Worldly teens are somewhat more likely than any other group to agree with these propositions.

The sharp point of difference lies in the two items: 'Science provides the only reliable source of knowledge about this universe' and 'The physical universe is the only thing that exists'. This Worldly teens are the *only type* where the majority agree with these statements (not shown in this table, but only 5 per cent of This Worldly teens 'strongly disagree' with the latter statement). The differences between This Worldly teens and the Seeker/Religiously Committed teens are particularly pronounced. In short, This Worldly teens possess a worldview that affirms the primacy of science as *the* reliable source of knowledge and meaning. This was a repeated theme in interviews we did with This Worldly teens. The following exchange took place with Jade:

Q: *Do you feel like dreams might have the capacity to tell you things or other things beyond just the empirical, tangible world?*

Table 6.1 Australians aged 13–18: Attitudes to humanist beliefs and principles by worldview type (% of type)

Item	Response	Worldview types (%)						Total for all teens (13-18)
		This Worldly	Indifferent	SBNR	Seekers	Nominally Religious	Religiously Committed	
Human beings can live ethical and fulfilling lives without religious beliefs	Disagree/strongly disagree	4	5	5	18	13	33	12
	Neither	1	7	1	5	3	7	4
	Agree/strongly agree	94	87	94	76	80	57	83
When something strange or unusual happens, I always think there must be a rational explanation for it	Disagree/strongly disagree	14	17	25	19	20	20	19
	Neither	1	4	3	5	3	6	3
	Agree/strongly agree	84	79	71	75	76	72	77
Science provides the only reliable source of knowledge about this universe	Disagree/strongly disagree	22	42	57	68	52	81	51
	Neither	2	7	2	2	6	4	4
	Agree/strongly agree	76	46	40	29	39	14	44
The physical universe is the only thing that exists	Disagree/strongly disagree	32	53	84	89	65	87	65
	Neither	3	11	0	3	6	1	4
	Agree/strongly agree	60	23	13	4	20	11	26

Source: AGZ Survey 2017.
Note: May not add up to 100 per cent due to rounding or because small numbers of 'don't know' responses have been omitted.

Jade: I'm very much ... I believe in science.
Q: *Science?*
Jade: Yeah, I don't necessarily believe in souls or [that] dreams having meaning. I just feel like sometimes, I feel humans kind of want that kind of concept, you know, 'Your dead relative is still here' like they're not just completely dead. I feel like sometimes there's that feeling inside me that I want them [too], I want to have a heaven or something like that. [But] my belief is more scientifically [oriented] there's no evidence for it [an afterlife] yet.

This Worldly teens do not embrace religious and spiritual ways of thinking. Meaning is made in other ways. This is not an affirmation of the doctrine of scientism (a perspective that dismisses other philosophical approaches). Rather, it's just how they feel the universe should be explained.

Some This Worldly teens, like Jade and Noah, have a reflexive and well-articulated worldview, grounded in humanist philosophies, though this is not true of all. They have ethics or values, but these are not consciously related to any particular philosophy. For example, David is an 18-year-old who lives in a regional town. A substantial proportion of the town's population works in a primary industry, and the place is neither particularly socially advantaged nor disadvantaged. His parents own a medium-sized retail business. This Worldly teens are found all across Australia: in remote locations, regional towns and the inner suburbs of the biggest cosmopolitan cities, in all school systems and across all socio-economic classes. David attended the government high school in his town. He told us that his favourite ways to relax and unwind are watching 'a movie or something, just a TV show, I like watching TV shows ... just sitting back'. His main source of news was the TV, followed by social media.

To get a broader sense of our interviewees' values and attitudes, we asked them to discuss the social issues that are important to them, including how they felt about inequality between very wealthy people and those struggling financially. David was a little hesitant at first, but then warmed to the question after a while, saying:

David: I don't really know much about it, can't really comment on it but I – I feel like there – there should be measures in place – well, there are, like welfare and stuff like that, to help out people who are struggling. As I said, I don't really know the statistics of what is happening at the moment ... There should be, maybe medical services that should be sent to remote rural

	areas that have high levels of poverty and stuff like that. So essential services.
Q:	*Do you think that particularly wealthy people have any obligation to help less fortunate people?*
David:	Ah, no. It's their money. Like, they don't have an obligation. It's nice if they do but it's really their lives and they can really do whatever they want with it.

We discuss other attitudes to social issues later in this book, but it is worth noting that David supports marriage equality and LGBTQI+ rights, and affirms that students are entitled to learn about LGBTQI+ issues at school. He is like most This Worldly teens in this regard. David said: 'Everyone should be free to express how they want to live their lives … it's their lives,' and of same-sex partnerships: 'People [who might be critics] [should] just deal with it, it's their [LGBTQI+ people's] decision.' And on the idea that a teacher could be sacked because of their sexual or gender orientation, he was unequivocal: 'I don't agree with that.'

In talking to David about existential questions, it was clear that he just didn't think in ways that might be characterized as 'religious' or 'spiritual'. He was sure he was neither of these things and certainly didn't believe God, or life after death, reincarnation or astrology. He'd had some religious education at primary school, 'but that was ages ago and I can't really remember anything from it anyway'. David never goes to church and is uninterested in yoga, meditation or astrology. Unsurprisingly, neither of David's parents are religious.

We were curious about teens' relationship to places—whether there are places that are especially important to them, or even 'sacred'. David demurred when asked to name places that are sacred to him, and instead described the Egyptian pyramids, stating:

> They've been around for a long time, the pyramids and stuff, you know. You can't knock them down. They're pretty sacred … just things that have a great history around them. I think they're pretty sacred … You can't do anything to them.

It was clear that thinking of things as sacralized or sacred wasn't in his frame of reference. He was adamant he had no places in his own life that were sacred to him: 'No. Not really. No. I don't really feel that fondly about places. I think they're just, you know, I don't have any, really, attachments to any places or anything like that [i.e. sacred] or [any] items.'

All the This Worldly teens we interviewed were hardly Richard Dawkins facsimiles when it came to talking about religion and its place in society. Being stridently anti-religious is simply not their thing, and it is fine for people to be religious if they want. On this, David said: 'You know, it's their right to follow whatever they want to feel. As long as they don't impose it on others that are against it, it's fine.' This attitude is typical of most teens in Australia, something we explore further in Chapter 7.

Unlike David, who lives in a large country town, Alice lives in the inner suburbs of a capital city. She went to a Catholic school and lives in a socially advantaged area. Alice's interview was full and frank, and she spoke articulately about a range of social issues and concerns. She was particularly interested in addressing social inequality:

Alice:	I do think we could do a lot more, as a society, to help people who aren't making as much money to be able to live comfortably. I … do believe that the super-rich don't always contribute in the most satisfactory way they could. And I think it would be nice if they did do a lot more to help society. Because, I mean, I think it's one thing to just live richly, but I think, also, to help others is a good thing. And people should do more.
Q:	*How you think that could be best achieved, like higher taxes or …?*
Alice:	I think making sure that people who have enough money, do pay their taxes and don't skip it. Like, I know there have been reports of a few people doing that [not paying taxes]. And I think if you have the money, you might as well pay your taxes and it's not going to harm you at all, is it, honestly?

Alice went to a Catholic school, and she talked about how this gave her an appreciation of religion and some of the values it promulgates:

> I do know they teach a lot about, you know, the Christian religion or the Catholic tradition, about Jesus and what-not, or Moses and at my school it was that. And I mean, they do have good values like treat others how you want to be treated. I do believe that my school was good at that.

Nonetheless, the religious elements of her schooling (e.g. Mass, religious education) didn't 'move the needle' for her. Because she was raised in a nonreligious home, the chances are that she would also follow this path (see below). Where David's parents were largely quiet about religion, Alice's are more forthright. Her dad is a self-identified atheist, and:

Alice:	He's quite open about that, which sometimes drives some people mad but, I think, generally, overall, we follow – I mean, we don't follow – we share the same views on religion.
Q:	*In holding an atheist view he's as tolerant as you are to religions generally?*
Alice:	I think I'm more tolerant than him, to be honest.

Tolerance of religion is widespread among This Worldly teens. We've already seen that David expressed this attitude, and Alice was similar:

> Yeah, I think it's fine to practise your religion as long as you're not harming others, but usually, you're not. So, it's fine I think or whatever. If you want to follow a religion, if you don't want to follow a religion it's OK … I think it's OK as long as you're not, going out and hurting anyone else or forcing people to follow that same religion.

Interestingly, she raised the spectre of religiously motivated terror in her answer. In Chapter 7, we see that any attempt by a religious person to impinge on the liberty and rights of others is viewed dimly by many Australian teens, none more so the This Worldly group.

Strictly no gods or ghosts: Being and becoming This Worldly

In the two previous chapters, we have looked at those sociocultural and demographic factors that are demonstrably associated with the different worldview types.[14] Our statistical analysis reveals that the following are significantly associated with the This Worldly type, accounting for the effect of factors like gender, age, school, place of birth and parental religious identification:

Nonreligious parents. Teens whose parents are Religious Nones are six times more likely than teens with religious parents to be This Worldly. The majority of This Worldly teens have not left a religious tradition behind or even know that much about religion at all (something we explore more in Chapter 8). We saw in Chapter 4 that there is a very strong association between parental attitudes and those of their children, and this is true of This Worldly teens as much as any other group. Chances are, if the parents or guardian have a This Worldly orientation, the child will follow the same path. Christel Manning, who researches how nonreligious parents raise their children, observed: 'The families I studied … were not lacking in values. Many could articulate systems of belief or practice that, even if not religious, are just as effective in offering them meaning and ethical guidelines for how to live their lives.'[15] Children come to learn these values in myriad ways, both explicitly (asking existential questions of the caregiver) or implicitly (following examples, mimicking statements).

Occasionally, a child will take a different path to their parents and guardians, particularly when it comes to *not* professing the religious identity of their parents. Most This Worldly teens have been raised nonreligious their whole lives, though some, like Noah, have parents who have some religious history. Noah is a self-described atheist, and he has completely disavowed his parents' religious perspective: 'It [religion] was kind of taught to me,' he notes, 'and I just kind of went, that doesn't really make sense.' For various social, cultural, developmental and psychological reasons, some teens don't follow their parents' convictions.[16] Sometimes the parents are not very committed to their putative religious worldview, or they are not effective at transmitting this to their children.[17] This is Noah's experience:

> Noah: Yeah, pretty much, like they're [his parents] religious, but they don't go to church all the time.
> Q: *Sure, so when you kind of say, religious, do you mind me asking like, what does that mean, like how do you see them as being religious, through what they believe in?*
> Noah: What do you mean?
> Q: *What makes you say, 'Oh yeah, they're religious'?*
> Noah: I don't really know how you say it, I just know that they are [religious] because they've said that they are and show it every now and again.
> Q: *Sure.*
> Noah: They say grace before meals, or before dinner, don't do it before every meal, but just before dinner.
> Q: *Yep and is the fact that you have different views to them, is that any issue at all with them?*
> Noah: Not with Mum, I'm not sure about Dad actually. I don't think I've ever pointed out to him that, 'Yeah, I'm not really religious at all'.

Age. Older teens are about twice as likely as younger teens to be This Worldly. This is in contrast to the pattern among Religiously Committed teens we identified in Chapter 4. It relates somewhat to the finding about parental influence noted above. A small cluster of This Worldly teens once believed in God. Previous research shows that this distancing is more likely to occur in the later teenage years when parents' influence on their children decreases and other influences (especially peers) come to more into play.[18]

Gender. Males are twice as likely as females to be This Worldly. Why are males disproportionally drawn to a nonreligious outlook? One intriguing theory proposed by Penny Edgell and colleagues in their study of American non-believers is that it is 'socially risky' to be a non-believer and that men are more prepared than women to accept that risk.[19] Such an explanation hardly makes sense in Australia, where Nones are now the single largest group of any affiliation. Normative gendered expectations are the more likely reason for these observed gender differences. The secular worldview has long been associated with traditional 'masculine' values and norms, such as 'reason' and 'rationality'. At one point in his interview, Noah talked approvingly about tech entrepreneur Elon Musk and his 'Big Fucking Rocket' project, which aims to colonize Mars.[20]

School type. Teens who attend government schools are somewhat more likely than teens who attend Catholic schools to be This Worldly. In previous chapters, we haven't attributed too much cause and effect when it comes to school and how this influences a teen's worldview. Simply, This Worldly teens are clustered more in government schools than Catholic schools (who prioritize enrolling Catholic students, many of whom fitted into the Nominally Religious type). That said, peers and friends are an important part of school life and do play a role in consolidating how teens think and react.[21] As Noah, who went to a government school, puts it: 'I don't think there was any particularly religious people in that [his school friend] group.' Moreover, in our study, we asked participants how many friends of faith they had (that is, someone who identifies with a religion), and This Worldly teens are far less likely than Religiously Committed teens to have two or more friends who identify with a religion.

'I'm just somewhere in-between': Indifferent teens

Whether it was during the phone survey, in-depth interviews or focus groups, it was clear that some teens just didn't have that much to say about religion, or spirituality, or even what it meant to them to be nonreligious. For example, one survey interview went like this:

Q:	*Do you believe in God, or not, or are you unsure?*
Respondent:	Unsure.
Q:	*Do you believe in reincarnation?*
R:	Maybe.
Q:	*Do you believe in life after death?*
R:	Maybe.

Q: *Do you believe in ghosts?*
R: Maybe.
Q: *Do you consider yourself to be an atheist, an agnostic, a Humanist, just not religious, or something else?*
R: Not religious.
Q: *To what extent do you agree or disagree [that] science provides the only reliable source of knowledge about this universe?*
R: Neither.

Some teens didn't have a decisive answer to these kinds of existential and philosophical questions or were simply undecided. In her study of nonreligious American adults, Manning found a tranche of people who are 'just plain indifferent to the kinds of questions we usually ask about religion'.[22] This is a group of Nones who are:

> Not atheists but are indifferent to the very question of religion, spirituality, or secularism. They often cannot tell you whether they believe in God because they have not given it any thought ... unlike atheists and humanists, they do not reject religion; they ignore it.[23]

We found a group of teens who are like this, and following Manning, we called them 'Indifferent'.

In our *initial* latent class model, we identified five categories of teens (This Worldly, SBNR, Seekers, Nominally Religious and Religiously Committed) in our survey data. The Indifferent type was not there. Next, we tasked one of our research assistants, Ruth Fitzpatrick, to do extended, follow-up interviews with a selection of teens who fit into each of the five types. (About 130 of the 1,200 teens who participated in our phone survey had agreed to be contacted again in case we wanted to do an in-depth interview with them.) In that first model, the SBNR and This Worldly groups were larger (29 per cent each, respectively) and assembled using a slightly different set of variables to the ones that comprise the final model.

In speaking more expansively to some of these teens, we saw shades and qualifications that the statistical analysis was missing – a cohort uninterested in anything 'spiritual' but not strongly committed to a nonreligious point of view either. The exchange below took place with Mitch, a teen who lives in the hinterland around one of the state capital cities. It began when he talked about meditation:

> I tend to follow the sciences, and, yeah, they say that meditation does – it does do things, whether it's for the reasons [spiritual] people that meditate say or not but it does seem to do stuff, so I'm not against it.

Then he discussed belief in God:

> Mitch: Well, as a kid it's not that I – I believed but, I don't deny the existence of a God, probably I just I choose not to be a part of religion so to speak.
> Q: *Oh, sure.*
> Mitch: I don't – I don't know, it – it's probably not like atheism but not anything else either.
> Q: *Yeah, so you do believe in a God or a higher power?*
> Mitch: Well, it's not that I believe, I'm impartial, it doesn't bother me if there is or there isn't.

Mitch's worldview, like several other teens to whom we spoke, sits between the SBNR and This Worldly types. Cognisant of this, we redid our model and included this new category – Indifferent teens. They comprise 15 per cent of the teen population in Australia. Indifferent teens tend towards agnosticism with regards to religious or spiritual beliefs, and they are not as committed as This Worldly teens to a scientific worldview:

- Indifferent teens don't believe in God, but 44 per cent believe in a higher power while a further 37 per cent are unsure;
- They never or rarely attend services of worship;
- Seventy-three per cent of Indifferent teens 'maybe' believe in life after death; 44 per cent 'maybe' believe in reincarnation;
- Twenty-three per cent of Indifferent teens agree with the statement: 'The physical universe is the only thing that exists'; 46 per cent agree with the statement 'Science provides the only reliable source of knowledge about this universe'.

Taylah is one Indifferent teen we interviewed. She lives in northern Australia and when we interviewed her she'd just finished her schooling but hadn't decided on what to do next. Taylah is emblematic of the Indifferent Type. She told us that she's equivocal about God, a higher power, reincarnation and other spiritual beliefs, and consequently, there is no reason for her to go to a place of worship or perform any religious practice. She's not an unbeliever per se; instead, she's not sure and consequently just doesn't care that much. She said:

> Q: *I just wondered, would you describe yourself as a spiritual person?*
> Taylah: No.

Q:	*On what basis would you feel like no, that – that that doesn't apply to me? You don't really have a belief in things that you can't see? Or some people believe in astrology or meditation, or things like that?*
Taylah:	I wouldn't say that I'm atheist but I'm not religious, I'm just somewhere in-between, and [I] like little bits of this religion I like, little bits of that culture I like, or that belief. Yeah.
Q:	*No – no worries. But you wouldn't identify as spiritual either?*
Taylah:	No.
Q:	*And when you say, a little bit of this belief, a little bit of that, it's okay if you don't want to, but, could you give any examples of that? Like you might like something in – like you might like something in – in Buddhism or this or that, other tradition?*
Taylah:	Well I can like Buddhism and whatnot, it's like a part of like [practising] self-care.
Q:	*Yes.*
Taylah:	And I think [it helps] people in themselves to help outwardly and stuff like that.

While she appreciated the potential value of some aspects of religion, Taylah made sense of her experiences and her place in the world in terms that are grounded in the here and now, convinced that we can live ethical lives without religion. Her outlook on life is focused on caring for herself, and others. Taylah said:

> I normally make sure I have time to do things I enjoy. I make sure I have time to read and to write, and to do art and play music. I'm a very creative person; if I'm not doing those things, then I'm not happy with myself, and [I make] sure I've got time to make sure I look after myself and do those things … And I want to be able [to help others]. [If] I'm not happy I don't want to help other people, so making sure I'm happy and then [I am] able to help others.

This philosophy is indebted to her parents: 'They say, be happy enough, look after yourself so you can look after others.'

Like most of the teens we chatted to in depth, she cared about social justice. For her, this included advocating for marriage equality, and before the late 2017 Australian Marriage Law Postal Survey (which was for adults), she'd been an activist at her Catholic school: 'I was doing things [to support] marriage equality and everything … I … helped around things at school, like programs.' Her school supported this social action: 'I was in a Catholic school and they were actually very good and open to adding things to classes and stuff, especially sex education and things.' Her motivation was deeply personal: 'I've got family that are gay, and my best friend's trans.'

Taylah impresses with her openness and tolerance, which extends to cultural and religious differences. She affirmed that it is important to know about different faith traditions, saying: 'Religion is important to different people, and different religions and … the way people act.' Moreover:

> It's important. Knowing somebody's background is important, in like knowing their history, like someone's religion is like integral to a bunch of different things even if it's just workplace practices.

We also heard a familiar refrain: 'I don't mind whatever you identify as, as long as you don't try and force your beliefs upon me.' Taylah mentioned that her peer group at school was both varied and open:

> That was the main thing, and we all got along like within my own immediate close friend group, we had that variety of beliefs [secular, atheist] and religions and we all got along fine.

The theme of getting along, and how and where students learn this, are discussed at length in Chapters 7 and 8. The fact she went to a Catholic school and had exposure to general education about religion is instructive. Overall, Taylah is typical of this type, and her outlook on life is best understood as uncommitted to any point of view, tending towards secular indifference.

Explaining indifference

We have seen repeatedly in the past few chapters that the way a teen is raised is the strongest predictor of their ideas and values. The data analysis shows this is true of Indifferent teens as well. For example, teens whose parents are Nones are two and a half times more likely than teens with religious parents to be Indifferent. If religious traditions are not an integral part of a family story (as is the case with Nominally Religious teens), or an expected part of everyday life (like it is for Religiously Committed teens), then it is hard to imagine how their worldview could be anything apart from secular. Archie, an Indifferent teen, is an excellent example of this:

> Q: *And where do your parents sit in terms of their religious views and practices?*
> Archie: It's a bit of a grey area. My dad is, I think, Catholic. I suppose he'd be Catholic, and my Mum is, like [names a Christian

	sect]. I'm not sure what denomination of Christianity that is, but, yeah.
Q:	*Do they attend church?*
Archie:	No.
Q:	*No. Did they, throughout that time when you were baptised [he was baptised as an infant], then they also stopped attending church?*
Archie:	Well, they used to attend church on an occasional basis but they stopped as well. I think it was after they split up.

Overall, Indifferent teens are not as closed off as This Worldly teens to religious and spiritual possibilities. One background clue is suggestive of why this might be the case. Fifty-two per cent of Indifferent teens believed in God when they were children, compared to about a third (35 per cent) of This Worldly teens. Perhaps this 'once' belief (plus parental influence) lends itself towards having an agnostic rather than atheist worldview. Here is Archie on this:

Q:	*Now, just a few more questions now, Archie, just your history in regards to religion, spirituality, non-religion. Would you identify yourself as a religious person, as a spiritual person?*
Archie:	No, I wouldn't. I identify as agnostic.
Q:	*Was there a time when you ever did believe in, like, God or some kind of higher power?*
Archie:	Yeah. When I was a child, when I was younger because I remember that I was baptised. When I was six and I used to go to Sunday School for a few years, but then, as time went on I started to form my own opinion on these kinds of matters.
Q:	*Were there specific things that led to you changing your views or was it just a very gradual process where certain things you were being told didn't match up with conclusions you were coming to or drawing yourself? Were there particular events or issues?*
Archie:	I think it was gradual. It was a gradual progression over several years.

The fact that there is some dissonance between teens and parents (for both Indifferent and This Worldly teens) is not surprising. As we noted in Chapter 4, there is a generational shift taking place, and every generation in Australia ends up less religious than the one that came before it. As Brett Mercier and colleagues note: 'Children of each generation are raised witnessing fewer displays of religious commitment than the last, making them less likely to believe in God and less likely to expose their children to displays of commitment.'[24] This is evident in the stories of This Worldly and Indifferent teens.

Conclusion

The three previous chapters have explored the different worldviews of Australia's Gen Z teens and some of the immediate social factors that predispose a teen to follow one path and not another. Stepping back to consider the bigger picture, we noted at the outset of this book that contemporary Australian teens live in a multifaith, multicultural society. The diversity of types we discovered reflects this broader culture. Sitting between poles of strong personal religiosity and atheism, we see an interest in spirituality *without* religion, an interest in spirituality *with* religion and indifference to these kinds of matters. Some teens follow strictly scientific ways of thinking about the world, but the majority of teens have subtler and less this-worldly ways of living.

It is pertinent to ask whether these worldviews make a difference in how teens might respond to those around them. Are there differences between groups when it comes to how they view religion's place in society or attitudes to LGBTQI+ rights? Or are teens of all stripes much better than adults in the business of getting along? We explore these kinds of questions in the remaining chapters.

7

Awash but not adrift: Teen attitudes to religious diversity

Three Jewish teenage boys were recently vilified on a bus because of their religion. The perpetrators were also teens. Riding home from one of Australia's largest shopping centres in suburban Melbourne, the boys were taunted about the religious clothing they were wearing (principally a small skullcap called a kippah) and subjected to vile comments about the Holocaust. Talking later to a newspaper reporter about the incident, one of the Jewish teens said that he'd experienced anti-Semitism like this before, stating: 'I've had situations where people have yelled derogatory comments from a car going past on a Saturday as we walk to the [Synagogue].'[1] This is not an isolated incident, and there have been other recent examples of religious vilification featuring both teenage perpetrators and victims. One case was so serious that a teen was criminally charged with 'stalking, harassing and threatening to kill a bullied Jewish schoolboy and the boy's mother'.[2]

Some of the Jewish teens who were part of our focus groups described similar experiences of anti-Semitism. On occasion, the offenders were other teens. Here is one incident in particular:

P1: We went on the [names well-known school event] and there was a lot of anti-Semitism there. But it's just weird how much there was. A friend had lost his bag and we were going around to all the different schools saying 'Oh have you seen this bag?'. And this guy was like, 'Oh, do you come from the Jewish school?' And we said, 'Yeah.' And we said, 'Oh where is it [the bag]?'. This guy basically heiled [Nazi saluted] in our direction ... [saying] 'It's over there', and pointed as a heil. And we were like, 'Sorry?'. And I called them out on it.

P5: Was it just like, [a] straight [arm salute]?

P1:	Yeah, yeah, yeah.
P5:	It was obviously…
P1:	Like, it was definitely a heil. And, I called him out on it and he was embarrassed and he apologized but, like… yeah. People just don't get that it's just so offensive.
P3:	Yep, that's offensive. Lots of people died, lots of families.

Contrast these ugly scenes with the picture shown in Figure 7.1. It was drawn by a girl when she was 12. Now in her mid-teens, she's a member of the Gen Z birth cohort this book is about.

The picture was drawn casually one evening shortly before Easter. When asked about it, she noted that while Easter had traditionally been a Christian festival this made little sense to her or her friends. These days, she said, Easter was for people of all faiths *and* the nonreligious. This picture is suggestive of how most Australian teens probably feel about religious diversity. It's a fact of life, another untroubling point of difference in a world of differences. Two of the artist's best friends identify as Muslims.

Nonetheless, these recent examples of religious vilification show that it is present among teens. But how many feel this way, and who acts on these impulses? How many religious teens have experienced religious vilification?

Figure 7.1 Easter picture.

And stepping back from these extremes, how positively or negatively do teens view different religions, and how do they feel more generally about religion in society? This chapter explores teen attitudes to religious diversity. We start by examining teen views of Muslims, Hindus and Buddhists, among other faiths, and their lived experiences of religious diversity – at school and in their local communities. Next, we explore teens' overall attitudes to religion's place in society and freedom of religion. We find that most teens happily accept religious diversity and are supportive of freedom of religious expression, mostly because it is part of the everyday fabric of their lives.

In the previous few chapters, we have explored how teens think about religious, spiritual and nonreligious matters. Now, we shift our focus to the *lived experience* of religion, specifically, the lived experience of religious diversity. This brings into our analysis the idea of 'lived religion' discussed in Chapter 1, by exploring 'worldviews' in context and not as abstract 'systems of belief'. In this chapter, the context is a religiously diverse society. In subsequent chapters, this context is school.

'Oh my God, don't judge me': Teen attitudes to Australia's different religions

We begin this chapter by examining what teens think of various religious groups in Australia, of which we have many – part of a diverse cultural and religious mosaic that now characterizes contemporary Australia. Using data from the AGZ survey, Figure 7.2 shows teen attitudes to Australia's four largest religious groups (Christians, Buddhists, Muslims and Hindus).[3] Additionally, we asked about attitudes to 'Religious Nones'.

For the most part, Australian teens have positive attitudes to Buddhists, Hindus, Muslims, Christians and Nones, and only a small proportion are neutral or negative. All five groups receive overwhelming 'positive' support (which adds together 'positive' and 'very positive' answers) from Australia's teens: 85 per cent for Christians, 83 per cent for Nones, 81 per cent for Buddhists, 75 per cent for Hindus and 74 per cent for Muslims. Certainly, Australia's smaller religious groups – Hindus, Muslims and Buddhists – have less 'positive' support compared to Christians and Nones, but the overall picture is one of teens accepting of Australia's diverse religious tapestry.

A comparison with a study of Australian adults which was conducted about the same time as our survey (the Scanlon Foundation Mapping Social Cohesion

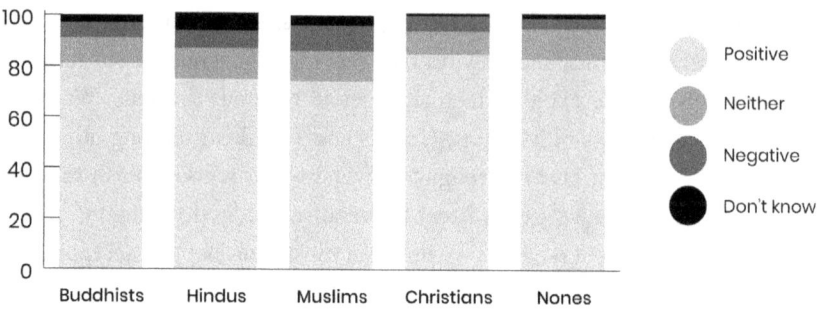

Figure 7.2 Australians aged 13–18: View of religions and Religious Nones in Australia (% of teens).

Study) shows that teens are more accepting and less prejudiced than adults when it comes to religious minorities. For example, approximately 23 per cent of Australian adults have a *negative* personal attitude towards Muslims compared to 10 per cent of teens, and similar differences emerge concerning attitudes to other religions.[4] These are notable points of intergenerational difference, consistent with international findings that show the younger age cohorts are generally more accepting of religious and cultural differences.[5]

Why are there differences when it comes to personal attitudes to different faiths? As we show below, teens are more likely than adults to have friends who are Muslim and less likely than adults to be conservative Christians (an important factor in anti-Muslim sentiment).

> **In surveys we trust?** With so many teens affirming positive attitudes, it is valuable to discuss how valid these findings are. It is well understood by survey researchers that attitudinal questions can be affected by 'social desirability bias' (SDB). This is the 'tendency of respondents to give answers they believe are more socially desirable than responses that reflect their true feelings'.[6] In our case, the teens we interviewed might have sought to appear more tolerant and accepting than is ordinarily the case in their daily lives. There are various strategies that researchers employ that theoretically reduce SDB tendencies (e.g. different survey modes, such as an anonymous mail or online surveys rather than the telephone), but according to the latest research, the *mode* (phone; online) of data collection doesn't make that much difference.[7] Question and response phrasing can also influence the types of answers people give. Ultimately, however, some level of SDB is present in all behavioural and attitudinal questions, and it is not always possible to work

out the scale of this.⁸ (And SDB is complicated phenomena in any case, as people make intricate judgements all the time about what is appropriate and not appropriate to say publicly and privately, or what they say versus what they think.) Responses to certain kinds of questions are further complicated by the fact that politically and socially engaged people tend to participate more in surveys (this is an aspect of what is called non-response bias).⁹ Consequently, there is probably *some* overstatement of positive sentiment among our teens. Overall, however, we can have confidence in the figures because of data weighting (for representativeness), the care we took with the question-phrasing, the implementation of the survey in the field and the fact that the survey answers reflect sentiments we heard expressed in the interviews and focus groups. There's every reason to think that the majority of teens do have positive attitudes to religious and cultural minorities at, or close to, the levels we have detected.

Very few Australian teens hold 'very negative' views about Islam, Buddhism and Hinduism, all of which have minority status in Australia. **There is a small proportion of teens, in the order of about 20 per cent, whose views of Hinduism, Buddhism and Islam might be classified as 'neutral' or 'negative'.** (That is, when asked about their personal view of each of these groups, the totality of their answers was some combination of 'negative', or 'very negative' or 'neutral'.) Interestingly, this group *clusters together* regarding their views of minority religions. That is, if a teen has negative to neutral views of one minority faith, there is a very high likelihood they have a negative to neutral view of the other two.¹⁰

Based on a survey alone, it is difficult to understand precisely the shades and nuances of a person's point of view. They may happily accept religious diversity (as we show below, almost every Australian teen thinks that having people of many different faiths makes Australia a better place to live) but might simultaneously be cautious about aspects of religion, or extreme expressions of that faith.

Some insight into this comes from Annie, the Nominally Religious teen we introduced in Chapter 4. She declared she had a positive view of Buddhists and Hindus but holds a 'very negative' attitude towards Muslims. Early in her interview, we asked about global events that worried her:

Annie: Yeah, so like, oh my God, don't like judge [me] or anything, but like that whole ISIS thing and stuff.

Q:	*No, no, no. When you say [that] you mean like terrorism?*
Annie:	Yeah, terrorism, yeah.
Q:	*Yeah, so that is quite a concern for you. I mean, specifically, what concerns you about that? I mean it's a very understandable concern, what element of that concerns you?*
Annie:	Because [if] people don't follow a certain religion they're just willing to kill others and stuff, so.
Q:	*So, it's kind of the ideology of it, or?*
Annie:	Yeah, yeah.
Q:	*And do you, I mean do you directly, kind of have a fear of your safety around that or is it more just that they hold those views?*
Annie:	I think it's just a view that I hold and if I was around certain people that I know follow that sort of religion, then yes, I'd be scared, but it's just like a view that I have.
Q:	*Sure, like do you have, we'll probably get into this later anyway, but do you have friends that do follow Islam, or are you saying more or less?*
Annie:	No, I don't, no I don't associate with those, sort of people.
Q:	*OK, sure.*
Annie:	Oh God.
Q:	*In regards to this issue or any issue, would you be willing to protest or takes forms of action?*
Annie:	No.

The actions of a violent, Islamist movement – one covered extensively in the media – have influenced her thoughts about this faith. Later in the interview, we asked about her view of yoga and she commented briefly on its religious heritage. This led to a further exchange about Muslims, and again, we can see how things that have happened overseas have conditioned her thoughts and feelings.

Annie:	Yeah, to be honest, I don't really have a problem with anyone's religion unless Muslamic [sic].
Q:	*Unless it's what sorry?*
Annie:	Yeah, unless it was like Muslamic-based and stuff like that.
Q:	*So that's really your main concern … just to unpack [that] a little bit, what's your main, concern or dislike if that's right [word] to use?*
Annie:	Just the beliefs and what they do to their people if they don't believe in stuff, you know.
Q:	*What's your understanding of that, if they don't believe?*

Annie:	Oh, they kill people and stuff if they don't [believe in] so Alluh [sic] and yeah.
Q:	*You feel that all people that follow the Islamic or Muslim faith have that approach?*
Annie:	Not all, but I know, well I don't know, I just think that nothing good comes from them. So, I wouldn't trust [them].
Q:	*You wouldn't trust someone of that faith?*
Annie:	No, not at all.
Q:	*Do you mind if I ask you what's, like what sort of has informed that, well it's been major influences in you coming to that?*
Annie:	Just the things that I see on the internet, on the news and my Dad works for [NAMES PARTICULAR OCCUPATION WITH OVERSEAS POSTING], so it's just like, yeah, things like that.
Q:	*Yeah, sure and has he directly encountered, has he been in places where?*
Annie:	Oh, yes, yep he has … he has.
Q:	*Do you have a concern, like do you feel that there is likely to be a major Islamic influence [from that] in Australia or do you feel like it's pretty minor?*
Annie:	I mean there has been in the past few years, like in Sydney, the Lindt siege, or like last year in Melbourne, yeah, I do. I feel like there's something bigger going to happen or something.

This is a delicate conversation to have, and we are grateful to Annie for her candour. It is hardly an expression of hatred – rather, she exhibits caution and perhaps a lack of knowledge about the contours of contemporary Islam. (Teen knowledge of religion is something we explore in greater detail in the next chapter.) Nor is there any indication that she acts out these views in public. It seems like a private set of thoughts. Her view illustrates amply some of the complicated, global, 'media-ated' factors that might condition a person's point of view and how this translates into antipathy towards Muslims. Her attitudes do not seem to arise from everyday encounters with Muslims, either at school or her neighbourhood.

This gives rise to important questions: does living amid religious diversity (having religious friends, and living near places of worship) make a difference to one's attitudes? If she had Muslim friends, would her views remain the same? We explore these questions in the next section as we look at how religious diversity is imbricated in teens' everyday lives.

'Most of my friends from like outside of school are either Italian Catholic or Greek Orthodox': Living with diversity

Some of the focus group settings we encountered were awash with diversity – religious, cultural or otherwise. Typically, this reflected the school community and the catchment area the school served. Below is an exchange we had at a private school in the inner city:

> Participant 2: It's like, it's pretty diverse there's a wide range of religions at the school not everyone is [NAMES DENOMINATION]. People come from all sorts of religions and our school respects that as well.
>
> Q1: *Yeah? So, would you say most kids are coming from a [DENOMINATION] background or not everyone else?*
>
> P2: Oh, I don't really think most.
>
> Q1: *Yeah?*
>
> P2: There's like the large portion that is, I think, there are lots of Christians at school.
>
> Q1: *And, what about – just other kinds of cultural diversity?*
>
> P2: Everyone accepts all the other cultures that we have in our school.
>
> Q1: *Yeah? Does that happen just organically because there are so many different cultures? Or does the school do stuff to kind of*
>
> P2: It just kind of happens.

At another school, with mostly Muslims students, we had this exchange:

> Q: *So how would you describe the [local] area around here in terms of diversity?*
>
> Participant 4: I think it's ... I don't know, I think it's a very diverse but like not really at the same time because it's just a weird mix of like diversity because there's like you know [NAMES A CATHOLIC SCHOOL] and then there's our school and the primary school. So, there's a very big Muslim population here and there's also a very non-big Muslim population. ... And it's close to [NAMES SHOPPING STRIP ASSOCIATED WITH MUSLIMS] so I mean, everyone goes there. So ...
>
> P1: Non-Muslims, that's an interesting category. Who's in that group?

P4:	Like everyone who's not Muslim.
P1:	Everyone who's not Muslim. Them. Oh, them.
P7:	Yeah. Most of my friends from like outside of school are either Italian Catholic or Greek Orthodox. It's very common.

How typical is this for most teens? We travelled to diverse regions and places across Australia for our focus groups. While some places were far more monocultural than the two examples above, there was still cultural and linguistic diversity evident in the participants' backgrounds and school context. This reflects contemporary Australia: one in four people are born overseas, and an even higher proportion have one or both parents born overseas.[11] *Forty-three per cent of teens in our sample had one or both parents/guardians who were born overseas.*

To formulate a national picture of teens' attitudes to religious diversity, we asked teens in the survey about the religious differences they experience in their everyday lives. In particular, we wanted to know if they had friends who followed different faiths. This is shown in Figure 7.3.

We didn't specify what we meant by 'friend' other than saying, 'Thinking about people you know; do you have friends who are …'. This figure shows that 27 per cent of teens have a friend who is a Buddhist, 28 per cent have a friend who is Hindu, 30 per cent have a friend who is Jewish and rather remarkably, 43 per cent claim to have a friend who is Muslim. Unsurprisingly, almost all (92 per cent) have a friend who is Christian. Taken together, only one-third of teens said they *didn't* have a friend who followed any of Islam, Judaism, Hinduism or Buddhism. Thus, the majority of Australia's teens are friendly with someone who is a member of a religious minority.

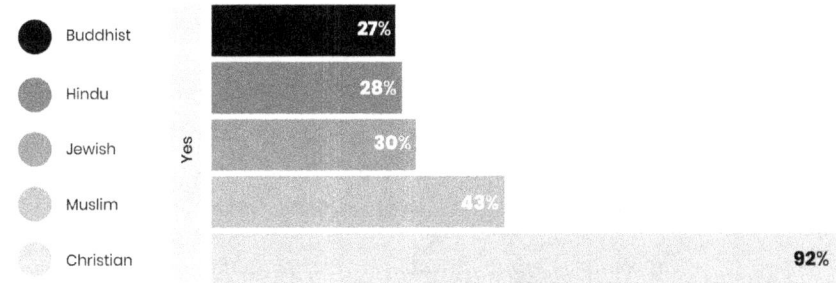

Source: AGZ Survey 2017

Figure 7.3 Australians aged 13–18: Have friends who follow a faith (% of teens).

The proportion claiming to have a Muslim friend is intriguingly high and higher than the other faiths apart from Christianity. There may be some social desirability bias influencing this figure, with survey respondents eager to seem accepting and tolerant of Muslims. Even if that were the case, it still says something interesting about their preparedness to live with and accept diversity. But we are not convinced that there is much social desirability in the answer. Teens have a far higher statistical probability than older generations of having Muslim friends: Australian Muslims are three times more likely to be Gen Zs than to be Baby Boomers. Besides, young people experience the melting pot of school, where they come into contact with a diversity of peers.[12]

One of the authors of this book (Andrew) figured he'd try and understand this a little more by talking to two of his children, both of whom are Gen Z teens. Growing up, Andrew (a member of Generation X) knew few Muslims and counted just one as a close friend. His teen children, by contrast, have many Muslim friends, at school and beyond. Their Muslim school friends openly express aspects of this identity, or are conspicuously Muslim – they wear some religious clothing, come from Muslim-majority countries or because their religious observances identify them (e.g. dietary choices, participating in Ramadan and Eid, or one case, avoiding the family dog).

> **Digging deeper:** Teens who had friends of faith were asked how often they talked with their friends about their religion. Of those with a religious friend (Christian, Buddhist, Hindu, Jewish, Muslim), 9 per cent talk 'often' to them about their religion, 29 per cent talk 'sometimes', 42 per cent talk 'rarely' and 14 per cent never talk to them about that faith; 5 per cent claimed to have no friends of any faith.

We got the sense from our qualitative data that religion, while acknowledged, was not often a topic of conversation among friends, and when it did come up, it was an uncontroversial theme, a fact of life. Samantha (Seeker worldview type), a Buddhist teen who lives in a highly diverse area, was asked about this:

Q: *In your peer group ... would have there been people that were Muslim, yourself Buddhist, others that were Christian?*
Samantha: Yeah, there were, there were ... [and] there were some Buddhists, yeah.

Q:	*And, I mean you mentioned it, briefly, before. Were people comfortable to speak about religion amongst friends, even when there were people of different religious backgrounds?*
Samantha:	Yeah, but we didn't really, even if we spoke about it we didn't really focus on the differences. We were really, we were focused on the similarities, we had kind of agreed to it. Even if there were – even if there were differences, we accepted it anyways. So Yeah.

And Andrzej (Seeker), said this of his discussion with friends:

Andrzej:	Yeah, I think it's really important just to, focus on the similarities that we all have. Because, of course, religion it teaches us the good things in life and even if there are differences you don't want to, you don't want to start any arguments because of it because they can't really change it, yeah.
Q:	*Do you have friends that are – are similar or quite different in regards to their ideas or practices about spirituality or religion?*
Andrzej:	Ah, yeah, I have friends that range from strictly atheist to much more devout, Christians and who have defined their branch as Baptist and I've got friends who are Hindu as well so.
Q:	*Yeah, right. Does that religious and spiritual diversity sit pretty comfortably amongst the friendship groups?*
Andrzej:	Most – I think, yeah, most of them, yeah. The ones that have the more strictly atheist ones it's a little bit, it's just tenser, sort of, it's trying to avoid that issue when we're in a conversation.
Q:	*So that's where you've found the most controversy along these lines rather than with devout Baptists or Hindu friends or is that –*
Andrzej:	Yeah, I think, I think having some faith, the people with some faith are a little bit more understanding than the people with – if you're willing to let me label – atheism as no faith then, no faith.
Q:	*Sure. Is there – do you feel like there's a stronger conviction for them to defend their point of view, or argue against yours or something?*
Andrzej:	Yeah, I think, the atheists, I think they have, I feel like they're trying to prove something whereas people who are – my more

religious friends are more accepting of people despite having different religions or different beliefs.

Another aspect of living with diversity we wanted to explore was whether teens lived near a mosque (Islamic), a Buddhist temple, a synagogue (Jewish) or a Hindu temple. Some scholars argue that proximity to difference is an important factor in producing more tolerant and accepting attitudes.[13] This is reported in the next chart, Figure 7.4.

We left it up to the respondents to decide what constitutes their local area. Most respondents don't live near a place of worship, with less than 10 per cent living near a Buddhist or Hindu temple or synagogue. Sixteen per cent indicated that they lived near a mosque. Interestingly, almost one in ten teens said they had no idea if they did or didn't live near one of these places of worship.

> **Digging deeper:** Teens who live near a place of worship were asked if they thought the presence of that place made their area a better place to live, neither, or a worse place to live. Only a tiny number of survey respondents – a handful of people – thought such places made the area a worse place to live. About two-thirds thought such places made no difference and about a third to a quarter felt various places of worship made their area a better place to live.

In the previous section, we saw that approximately 20 per cent of Australian teens have a negative to a neutral view of Hinduism, Buddhism and Islam. Is there a relationship between this point of view and whether or not a teen has

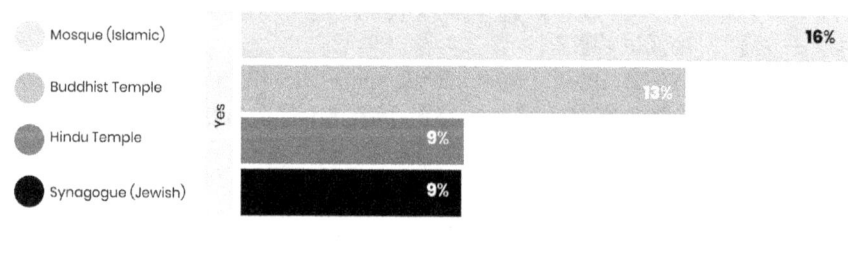

Source: AGZ Survey 2017

Figure 7.4 Australians aged 13–18: Person lives near a place of worship (% of teens).

friends of these faiths, or lives in a religiously diverse area? Or do other factors lend themselves to that attitude, like gender or the type of school a person goes to? In the previous chapters, we have used some statistical methods to weigh the relative influence of different sociocultural factors. This is what we can say about those who have a neutral or negative attitude towards people who are Muslim, Hindu and Buddhist.

Worldview type. Teens who are Religiously Committed are twice as likely as This Worldly teens to have negative or neutral attitudes towards people who are Muslim, Hindu and Buddhist. Most of the Religiously Committed teens in our sample are members of conservative Protestant churches (e.g. Pentecostal or evangelical). These churches tend to adhere to a far narrower view of which religion is the 'true' religion (religious exclusivity), especially when compared to some of the more liberal or mainline denominations (e.g. Uniting and Catholic Churches). This may result in ambivalent or negative attitudes towards religions apart from their own.

School type. Teens who attend independent schools are twice as likely as teens who attend Catholic schools to have negative or neutral attitudes towards people who are Muslim, Hindu and Buddhist. In part, this finding is probably due to Catholic students' greater exposure to *general religious education* than students in independent schools (something we discuss in the next chapter). But it has to be about more than that too, given that a lot of government schools *also* don't offer education about religion. (Additionally, the statistical procedure we have used looks for distinct sources of influence, rather than reduplicating different measures of the same thing.) The main reason for this finding is likely the 'tolerant-of-*all*-religions' ethos openly expressed in most Catholic schools and the fact that a proportion of independent private schools in Australia are 'Christian' schools affiliated with conservative Christian traditions that tend towards religious exclusivism.

Friends. Teens who have no friends of a minority faith are twice as likely as teens who have friends of a minority faith to have negative or neutral attitudes towards people who are Muslim, Hindu and Buddhist. Having friends of other faiths means that a teen is probably not bothered by such religious differences.

Place of residence. Teens who live in more socio-economically disadvantaged areas rather than socially advantaged areas tend to have more negative or neutral attitudes towards people who are Muslim, Hindu and Buddhist. It may be that there is less diversity in such locations, or it might be that the negative identity politics propagated by some politicians get a better run in these areas.

General religious education (GRE). Teens who have had *no general education about religion* (GRE) at secondary school are somewhat more likely than those who have had GRE to have more negative or neutral views of Australia's minority religions. In the next chapter, we explore the value of education about religion and how it can contribute to improved tolerance of religious differences.

As we have argued in this section, Australian teens are not, for the most part, the agents of religious discrimination and intolerance in contemporary Australia. For the most part, they get on well with, or tolerate, those who are different from themselves. This echoes themes we raised in the introduction of this book.

The dark side of diversity: Religious discrimination, vilification and hatred

This chapter started with a description of religious vilification perpetrated by teens, alongside a story of acceptance and harmony. In the process of conducting this research, we found teens getting along, happily accepting differences between each other. Take this focus group exchange for example:

Q1:	*And what type of cultures and religions are your classmates?*
Participant 4:	Muslim.
P6:	Most are Catholic.
P4:	Yeah. There's a lot of just like Christian students [here] like Catholic.
Q2:	*How do you get on with them?*
P4:	Very well.
Q2:	*Very well?*
P4:	There are not any clashes really.
Q2:	*So, with the difference, it doesn't make any difference?*
P4:	No, no. Not really.
Q1:	*Do you talk about your religions, or your cultures, much at school?*
P4:	Yeah. Sometimes we might if it's brought up.
P8:	Yeah, yeah.
Q2:	*What might bring it up?*
P4:	I don't know, maybe if we're talking about what we did on the weekends.

There was also consensus that Australian is comparatively free of religious vilification. Here's a group of Muslim teens talking about this:

Participant 7: In Australia … there's not much hate and prejudice.
P5: Yeah.
P7: Compared to other places in the world. We're like – we're pretty good in Australia. We're not as bad. People are free to express their views. They disagree with Islam, fair enough I don't care to be honest but compared to other countries they're very, there's a lot more hate and prejudice compared [there] to what's going on here. I mean here it's most likely, it's mostly through social media, where a lot of, there's a lot of hate and there's a lot of people that try to express their opinions 'cos they're behind the screen. They wouldn't probably do the same thing if it was in real life.
P4: Yeah.
P3: Yeah.
P2: I feel like especially when we're blessed to be in Australia, where everyone's accepting but there are some things like the internet, like other platforms people use, like Pauline Hanson, who have negatively expressed their opinion.
P6: Because Australia's like so accepting. Like I have family friends that live in France and they're not allowed to wear their headscarf.

That said, Muslim, Jewish and Hindu students who took part in the focus groups and interviews described specific instances of religious vilification, referred to as Islamophobia and anti-Semitism. Below is an example told to us by a group of Muslim teens:

Participant 8: I was walking down the street, it's not that easy for a guy to be identified, oh he's a Muslim, but, girls, females, you know they can – 'cos of their headscarf it's easy to identify Muslim, so it's easier for them if they're with their friends or whatever, it's easy for them to target them and stuff.
P2: Yeah. No. I wear the headscarf outside of school. So, I'm kind of like a target for attacks and stuff. I've been yelled at a few times, across the street.
P4: Yes.

P2:	Walking up and down and it's really scary [when they are abused], 'cos it's like, I've got a cloth on my head, why are you attacking me? I was walking down the street and this person in a car, started yelling at me, 'Take off your scarf', and stuff and it was really scary, 'cos it's like – it's – it's not bothering you, you know… it was around here [the inner-city area we did the focus group]
P5:	Yeah. Same with me, someone screamed, 'Go back to your country.'
P4:	Yeah. I was born here!
P5:	Like at the beach. I was just walking back to my car and someone's like, they were driving and as they were driving they wound down the window and said, 'Go back to your country.'

This draws us to our survey and what this tells us about the prevalence of these kinds of incidents. We asked the Muslim, Hindu, Buddhist, Jewish and Sikh survey respondents to tell us about their experiences. Because their numbers are low, we can't make strong statistical inferences from these data. Rather, these provide *qualitative* insight into the preponderance and location of religious discrimination.

A third of Muslim, Hindu, Buddhist, Jewish and Sikh said yes to the question: 'Now, thinking about your own life, have you experienced discrimination, been teased or abused because of your religion over the last 12 months?' We were also able to ask where this had taken place (Table 7.1):

This table shows where the incidents of religious discrimination took place. (Respondents could nominate more than one location.) Forty-one per cent of

Table 7.1 Reported instances of religious discrimination of Buddhist, Hindu, Sikh, Muslim and Jewish teens

Where did the discrimination or abuse take place?	% reporting this as a place where vilified
School	41
In public e.g. on the street or at the beach	19
Public transport	19
Social media	15
Other	7

Note: Does not add to 100 per cent because respondents could nominate more than one location.
Source: AGZ Survey 2017.

vilified teens said they had experienced discrimination at school; 19 per cent had experienced it at the beach or on public transport. Fewer reported it happening to them on social media or other places. These data are only indicative given the tiny numbers in our sample, but it is instructive that the most commonly reported site of discrimination was school.

Two of our Muslim interviewees talked about religious abuse at school. Ferazia (Seeker worldview type), a Lebanese-Australian Muslim, said this when asked about religious discrimination:

Ferazia:	Not really because I like I don't like, wear a headscarf, or do that but I know people who do that, they have.
Q:	*Yeah, sorry, people that do have then experienced?*
Ferazia:	Like wear a headscarf, yeah.
Q:	*Yeah.*
Ferazia:	They will get funny looks and stuff.
Q:	*Yeah, and was that at school or just in the general public?*
Ferazia:	Yeah, at school, at school as well, yeah.
Q:	*And again, is that in a highly diverse area or is it in an area where maybe there wasn't …*
Ferazia:	No, like school was pretty diverse but not in terms of Arabs and Muslims. It's diverse in like Asian communities or Greeks.

Deniz (Religiously Committed) said this when asked about religious vilification:

Deniz:	Not really, no. I was the person who bullied the bully, so.
Q:	*Did you say you bullied the bully?*
Deniz:	Correct.
Q:	*OK. What sort of bullying was the bully doing?*
Deniz:	Oh, just like mentally.
Q:	*What, were they teasing people based on their religion or just generally?*
Deniz:	They would argue over stupid stuff and say, 'You're Muslim. You stone people to death' or whatever.
Q:	*Oh OK.*
Deniz:	I used to say that you do consider yourself as perfect, do you, and all that, you know?

While we were told in the focus groups and interviews that schools are generally harmonious places when it comes to the management of religious diversity, discrimination or abuse still happens.

In the next chapter, we explore the effectiveness of strategies that schools employ to improve intercultural understanding. Thus far, we have shown that teens are extremely tolerant of Australia's religious minorities and generally have positive everyday encounters. How do they feel more generally about religion's place in society and the right of religious people to practise their faith freely? This has been a topic of much recent public debate and discussion in Australia. Shadowing our data collection was the 2017–18 *Religious Freedom Review*, which comprised an expert panel which heard public submissions, all designed to explore 'the intersections between the enjoyment of the freedom of religion and other human rights'.[14] Our research was the only one that described what Australia's teens have to say about these topics.

'Let the follower of the religion do what they want to do': Attitudes to religious diversity

Residents in the regional Victorian city of Bendigo endured a bitter fight a few years ago about the building of a mosque on the outskirts of town. This case eventually went to the High Court of Australia, which decided that the local Muslim community had the right to have a mosque, where it would fit in alongside Bendigo's churches and temples.[15] In 2018, two years after the High Court ruling about the Bendigo Mosque, One Nation leader Pauline Hanson put a motion to the Australian Senate seeking to ban burqas and niqabs – religious clothing worn by a tiny minority of Australia's Muslims.[16] The dissenters lost the vote 43–4. Curiously, among them was a self-described libertarian (David Leyonhjelm), a political stance that would usually oppose any attempt to curtail religious liberties.

As we show in this section, however, there is little support among teens for this kind of religious regulation or discrimination. The abiding theme among teens is that people should be free to practise their religion – so long as that then doesn't infringe on the personal liberties of others.

We asked a large number of questions about religious liberty and religion's place in society in our survey, what we will call 'Freedom of Religious Expression' for short. By this, we mean *supporting or not supporting* the right of religious groups to freely practise their religion, whatever form that takes (like being allowed to wear religious clothing or build temples, churches and mosques). This is different to a religiously conservative understanding of religious freedom, where 'freedom' includes the right of religious groups to 'discriminate against those of whom they disapprove or over whom they wish to exert power'.[17] An example of this would be a religious school refusing to hire LGBTQI+ teachers. Table 7.2 shows teen attitudes to various forms of freedom of religious expression, according to our six different types.

Looking down the column on the right, and the last three items, we see that teens overwhelmingly endorse the right of others to freely practise their religion (so long as they don't impinge on others' rights) and support religion having a place in society. For example, 93 per cent think that having people of many different faiths made Australia a better place to live; 90 per cent agree that students should be allowed to wear religious clothes or jewellery to school; 89 per cent think that all religious groups in Australia should be free to practise their religion the way they want to.

These sentiments were heard commonly in our focus groups. Deniz (Religiously Committed), a Muslim born overseas said:

> Considering how much freedom we have, there is a pretty open space for themselves [religious people] to practise who they are. Even some schools have their own time to pray, not just for Muslim but also Christians. So, they have their own time where they can practice the Bible and everything. So, I believe that everyone has their own time to do what they want to do.

Two items in the table draw a larger group of dissenters: the questions about banning religious clothing that covers the face and the construction of mosques and temples. These statements implicitly refer to Muslims rather than other religious groups, and we have already seen that there is more ambivalence about them compared to other minority religions. Twenty-four per cent of teens agree that 'the government should ban any religious clothing that covers a person's entire face', and 33 per cent agree with the proposition that 'local communities should be able to prevent the construction of mosques or temples in their area if they don't want them'.

Interestingly, Table 7.2 shows that the *least religious* teens (This Worldly teens) are not leading the way when it comes to opposing these two religious freedoms. *No one type* is more or less opposed to a ban on religious clothing that covers the face or the construction of mosques and temples (i.e. any differences shown in the table are not large enough to be statistically significant or consequential). Other factors, beyond a latent religious or spiritual orientation, are at play here.

To summarize what the survey tells us about teens' overall attitudes to 'freedom of religious expression', we dug deeper into the data, and using a data-reduction technique (factor analysis), we discovered that these five items are effectively

Table 7.2 Australians aged 13–18: Attitudes to the freedom of religious expression by worldview type (% of type)

Item	Response	Worldview type (%)							Total for all teens (13-18)
		This Worldly	Indifferent	SBNR	Seekers	Nominally Religious	Religiously Committed		
The government should ban any religious clothing that covers a person's entire face	Disagree/strongly disagree	77	74	72	78	64	71		72
	Neither	3	7	4	1	5	4		4
	Agree/strongly agree	20	19	24	20	31	25		24
Local communities should be able to prevent the construction of mosques or temples in their area if they don't want them	Disagree/strongly disagree	66	69	55	70	62	53		62
	Neither	6	7	3	4	6	6		5
	Agree/strongly agree	29	24	42	26	33	41		33
Students should be allowed to wear religious clothes or jewellery to school	Disagree/strongly disagree	9	4	6	10	10	13		9
	Neither	3	1	2	0	1	1		1
	Agree/strongly agree	88	95	92	90	89	86		90
All religious groups in Australia should be free to practise their religion the way they want to	Disagree/strongly disagree	11	6	10	5	8	11		9
	Neither	3	3	2	0	1	4		2
	Agree/strongly agree	85	92	88	95	92	85		89
Having people of many different faiths makes Australia a better place to live	Disagree/strongly disagree	7	2	5	4	4	8		5
	Neither	3	3	2	0	2	1		2
	Agree/strongly agree	90	95	93	96	94	91		93

Source: AGZ Survey 2017.
Note: May not add up to 100 per cent due to rounding or because small numbers of 'don't know' responses have been omitted.

measuring a broader, latent point of view regarding the right to freedom of religious expression.[18] The factor analysis reveals that only a tiny proportion of teens are deeply opposed to the broader ideas of freedom of religious expression. A larger minority, about a third of teens, are ambivalent about these freedoms. *The rest, about seven out of ten teens, endorse the notion that devotees of different religious traditions in Australia should be allowed to follow their faith without interference.*

That said, for all the general support for the right to freely express one's religion, opinion is divided when it seems that religion might impinge on the rights of others. This is expressed in the next table, Table 7.3, which explores the role of religion in society.

Looking down the columns on the right: most teens (85 per cent) agree with the proposition that there is religious discrimination and abuse in Australia. They know it is present in society, even though few admit to being perpetrators themselves.

The next few items tell us something different: 45 per cent of teens think that religion causes more problems in society than it solved; 50 per cent think that people with very strong religious beliefs are often too intolerant of others, and 34 per cent think that religion should have no place in our parliament or official ceremonies. (The item about religious people being more intolerant than others is interesting – our survey was in the field at the same time as the Marriage Equality Postal vote, and teens could observe active expressions of religious intolerance. We discuss this more in Chapter 9.)

The results in Table 7.3 demonstrate that This Worldly teens are most likely to think that religion causes problems in society, or that religious people are more intolerant. However, most of the differences between the various types are not large enough to be statistically reliable. The only robust differences are between This Worldly teens and the Nominally Religious and the Religiously Committed. That makes sense given these questions are not so much about the right to express one's religious preferences; rather, they are about how religion is enacted in the public sphere.

It was clear from the interviews and focus groups that teens are relaxed about religious expression, so long as it does not infringe their rights. Here are two interesting exchanges from different focus groups. The first flowed from a discussion about a well-known Pentecostal congregation:

Participant 2:   Didn't they – weren't they in the news a couple like, a little while ago about the fact that they were, people thought

Table 7.3 Australians aged 13–18: Views about religion in society (% of type)

Item	Response	Worldview type (%)						Total for all teens (13–18)
		This Worldly	Indifferent	SBNR	Seekers	Nominally Religious	Religiously Committed	
People of different faiths experience discrimination or abuse because of their religion	Disagree/strongly disagree	14	9	15	24	12	12	14
	Neither	1	5	2	1	2	1	2
	Agree/strongly agree	85	87	83	75	86	87	85
People with very strong religious beliefs are often too intolerant of others	Disagree/strongly disagree	31	34	40	45	45	50	40
	Neither	5	12	4	5	6	8	6
	Agree/strongly agree	64	54	56	50	49	42	53
Religion should have no place in our parliament or official ceremonies	Disagree/strongly disagree	42	57	68	76	69	75	62
	Neither	4	5	4	1	2	3	3
	Agree/strongly agree	55	38	27	23	28	22	34
Religion causes more problems in society than it solves	Disagree/strongly disagree	39	41	44	51	59	67	50
	Neither	5	16	2	3	3	2	5
	Agree/strongly agree	55	43	54	46	38	31	45

Source: AGZ Survey 2017.
Note: May not add up to 100 per cent due to rounding or because small numbers of 'don't know' responses have been omitted.

	they were just trying to scam people for money? But I'm like, well if that is the religion keep it. Leave them alone. [Laughter] Let them do what they want to do. And let the follower of the religion do what they want to do.
Q1:	*Do you guys agree with that?*
P2:	Yeah.
P1:	As long as it doesn't affect like …
P2:	Yeah, it doesn't affect …
P5:	Like laws. If it doesn't infringe on laws or human rights, then go ahead.
P1:	Yeah.
P1:	Or if it's like…
P2:	Because isn't one of the human rights to have a religion?
P5:	Yep.

Similar views were expressed by another group of teens in the exchange below. Among them was the Pastafarian-following (the spoof religion) teen we met in Chapter 6:

P1:	So, I think a big thing about it [Pastafarianism] is with – how we view religion can be in a sense altered by how much we're willing to be open to it because with religion there's this big thing like, oh, this religion was discovered then and then all these people believe in it. But to an extent, some people believe that the first religion has to be the right one and that all others are just either branches or like people that didn't like that religion.
P2:	I've only really disagreed with people about things, such as like I guess you could kind of call it a political view or something or people who are like homophobic or something, which I guess comes a little bit more into play when you, it comes to a person either where you know somebody who like I guess is openly homosexual and then like …
P3:	Well, I only have an issue with it if – I don't generally care what – what a person believes, as long as they don't try and implement the way they think on the way I think.
P2:	Yeah, or as long as they are not making specific reference or offending people with like their views.

This exchange illustrates that many teens have interesting, thoughtful views about religion, diversity and co-existence. It's part of their everyday lifeworlds, and their views on it are quite considered.

Conclusion

The findings presented in this chapter suggest that while many young Australians have a largely positive view of religion and accept religious diversity, an appreciable minority think religion causes more harm than good, are against the construction of mosques and temples and think religion has no place in Parliament. We also found that many young Australians are aware of tensions between religious rights and other human rights and that the latter should be respected. The next chapter explores what teens have been taught about religion at school and how this impacts on their attitudes to religious diversity.

8

Taking it to school: Worldviews and religious education

Q: *How would you describe the diversity [in your school]? … Like what does that look like to you?*
P5: Like a pizza but with all the toppings on it [Laughter].

Many of the teens who participated in the study experienced their school as a place of cultural and religious diversity, and this was implicitly accepted as a good thing. One student noted: 'It just kind of happens,' and another explained: 'I feel like [people who identify as religious are] respected [at the school] because, like, since we're [such] diverse people – heaps of people have different religions – so we've all, kind of, learnt to co-exist together.' That said, teens weren't naïve and were cognisant that schools could be sites of religious vilification. Students at a government school in one of their state's most culturally diverse neighbourhoods had this exchange:

P5: It's pretty fair here. Like you know.
P2: Especially at this school, well, not [at] other schools. It's not necessarily…
P5: Oh yeah.
P2: But here definitely. Yeah.

Elsewhere, students at a different government school described how one of their Muslim classmates gave a presentation about her experiences of discrimination:

P2: This girl did a speech … and she spoke about how she's discriminated against.
Q1: *Based on her –?*
P2: Religion.
P1: But that was less about being like discriminated at school and more about just the fact that …

P2: Society.
P1: About terrorism right now and because she's Muslim, people for some reason …
P2: Make ignorant comments.
P1: And relate Muslims to terrorism. So things about like the typical Australian, 'Get out of my country'.

In the previous chapter, we explored teen attitudes to diversity and the factors that inform these attitudes, including families, peers and communities. But what about schools and the kind of education students receive there? What have students learned *about* religion at school, and what do teens think of what they have been taught? What role does religious education play in shaping attitudes to religious diversity? Can education about diverse worldviews improve inter-religious understanding, and if so, how?

This chapter begins by briefly recapping the ways religion is taught in Australian schools. From there, we examine how much Australian teens know about diverse religions. Next, we explore who has received what kind of education about religion and assess the impact this has on their attitudes to religious diversity.

Why school-based education? We have a specific focus on education in the remainder of this book because school takes up such a large part of a teen's life and is a context where personal worldviews are 'lived out', yet it is adults who determine what gets taught about any given topic. We are interested in the extent to which school curricula on diversity topics (in this case, religion, gender and sexuality) aligns with the broader sweep of teen worldviews and whether it can be improved to better accommodate their points of view. We do not explore in great detail whether the six different teen worldview types have different attitudes to education about religion or LGBTQI+ issues per se, except where it is especially pronounced. Rather, we show more broadly the kinds of investments and interests teens have in what they get taught. We should add that in focusing on religion, gender and sexuality, we are not suggesting that these things are what matters most to teens (any more than relationships, friendships, politics, the economy or the environment), but they are an important and intertwined part of their everyday lives nonetheless.

A hot topic!

The place of religion in Australia's government schools has long been a hot topic. The terrorist attacks of 11 September 2001 and early 2000s London and Bali bombings amplified negative media reporting about Islam and Muslims. Fears of homegrown terrorism ignited parochial 'values' debates, with some in the West calling for values education that would promote Western, Judaeo-Christian, European, British and/or Australian values. By contrast, others argued that it was preferable to teach about diverse religions and worldviews at school, to build religious literacy, counter negative perceptions of religious minorities and promote respect for religious diversity.[1]

In Chapter 1, we described the two major ways religion is taught in Australian schools, which we will reprise here briefly. First, there is 'confessional' Religious Instruction or Religious Education, known colloquially as RI, RE or SRI (where 'S' stands for 'special'). This is defined as 'instruction provided by churches and other religious groups and based on distinctive religious tenets and beliefs'.[2] SRI is not offered at any Australian government secondary schools. However, most Australian states allow volunteers from religious organizations to provide SRI to *primary school* students in the government sector.[3] In recent years, this has been a controversial practice. There have been organized and impassioned efforts by parents, as well as secular and religious lobby groups, to either stop or retain SRI.[4]

Catholic RE (commonly called RE, rather than SRI or RI) is taught at Catholic primary and secondary schools. The independent school sector is mixed. Many of these schools are faith-based schools and provide SRI in their faith tradition, particularly at the primary school levels.

The second way religion is taught in schools is through non-doctrinal general religious education (GRE), defined as 'education about major forms of religious thought and expression characteristic of Australian society and other societies in the world'.[5] The Australian Curriculum, which was developed in the late 2000s, includes an emphasis on respect for religious diversity in its guiding framework but has provided limited opportunities for GRE to be taught as a discrete subject.[6] Thus, GRE at primary and early secondary levels tends to be incorporated into other social studies subjects. That said, most states offer a dedicated subject (called 'Studies on Religion' or similar) in Years 11–12 that focuses on diverse religions and ethics.[7] Yet, very few government schools offer this subject and it is mainly taught in Catholic or independent schools.

More recently, and following a global trend, there has been a push to include Worldviews Education (WE) in Australian schools, instead of GRE, as it incorporates both nonreligious and religious worldviews.[8] As a result, in 2015 the state of Victoria introduced two dedicated sections on worldviews and religions in its iteration of the national curriculum at Kindergarten–Year 10 levels. It is the only Australian state to have done so.

As part of our research, we were interested in how different types of education influenced young people's views about religious diversity, so we investigated this in our focus groups, national survey and follow-up interviews. However, it is useful to first explore precisely what teens know about faiths and traditions apart from their own.

What do teens know about religion and spirituality?

One early objective in the AGZ project design was to ascertain how much Australian teens know about religion – their level of 'religious literacy'. This is a very difficult thing to measure. Following an American research project, our initial plan was to include in our national survey questions that tested knowledge about religion.[9] We drafted survey questions like: 'Which [of these] religions aim at nirvana, the state of being free from suffering?', and 'When does the Jewish Sabbath begin? Does it begin on …?'. We planned to ask about eight questions of this kind. After consideration, we decided not to use this approach, as we felt that survey respondents might be alienated by questions that seemed like a school 'pop quiz' and consequently might stop responding if they were not getting the right answers. (It would also use up expensive survey time if the interviewer had to say whether the answer was correct or not.)

Instead, we decided that we would get a qualitative handle on religious literacy by understanding how *conversant* they were in talking about religion's place in society and their appreciation of religious difference and diversity. We can say that for the most part, teens did not struggle to answer the survey questions or address these matters in the focus groups and interviews. Further, we asked our survey participants about whether they had received general education about religion at school (see sections below), and we assume that those who have had this education will, for the most part, be better informed and knowledgeable about religion than those who have not.

On the matter of how familiar teens were with religious topics, to start the focus groups, we showed the participants images of religious, spiritual and atheist figures, as well as symbols and places, to see if they recognized them and what, if anything, they could say about these pictures. This activity was designed as a conversation starter. However, the discussion about the pictures gives us some additional insight into how conversant they were about different religions and faiths. Pictures of Uluru, Pope Francis, Mary Mackillop, the Dalai Lama, a yogi and a Buddhist statue had the highest level of recognition. Other images, of cathedrals, and specific atheist, Muslim and Jewish people seemed less familiar. Most teens couldn't properly name (or didn't know) the Anglican Cathedral in their state capital city, Hillsong Church, the Wailing Wall, Yassmin Abdel-Magied (a young Australian Muslim public intellectual) and Richard Dawkins (renowned atheist), while no teens recognized the image of Anne Aly (a Muslim federal parliamentarian) or an atheist symbol.

Many of our focus group participants identified with a religious tradition, and for the most part, these teens displayed familiarity with and knowledge of images from their tradition. For example, some teens who identified with a Christian tradition recognized easily images of Mary MacKillop and Pope Francis, and Buddhist teens recognized images of the Dalai Lama. Some Jewish and Muslim teens seemed to know most about the other images. Below, we note specific reactions to these pictures. This discussion is not intended in any way as a definitive conclusion about levels of religious literacy; rather, we include it to illustrate what we encountered in the focus groups.

Uluru image [Indigenous sacred site]

Many teens recognized the image as Uluru, the Indigenous name for Australia's best-known sacred place, and many also said it was 'Ayers Rock' (its Anglicized name). One student described it as 'an Aboriginal sacred space', and a second said: 'It's acknowledging the Aboriginal culture. That's their sacred site.' Another reflected on their experience of awe and wonder when they visited Uluru, saying:

> It was just a nice place to go to and the sunsets there were just beautiful, and everyone was like sitting there watching it, it's really big too, like, in photos it's just a rock, but then you go and see it, and it's like, oh my gosh, it's so big and it's just red and it's really pretty … there was some … designs, Aboriginal paintings on it as well. Some of us were like, it's just a nice place to go and it had a spiritual feeling to it.

Teens also associated the image with 'Australian culture' and 'Aboriginal religious culture. The Aboriginals. Dreamtime. All that sort of stuff'. One student described it as 'a famous Australian landmark' and some other teens couldn't identify the image but associated it with 'Australia', 'mountains' and 'a mining site'. Other teens also didn't name the image but said it was linked to 'Aboriginal' and 'Indigenous people's … history and religion' and 'where they were from'.

Pope Francis image

Many teens recognized the image of Pope Francis by name, while others simply referred to him as 'The Pope' and associated him with the 'Catholic Church', 'Christianity' and 'Jesus Christ'. Several noted that Pope Francis was popular, 'a leader for billions of people' and a 'strong figure influential to religion'.

Dalai Lama image

The Dalai Lama's image was greeted with widespread recognition. When pressed a little further on what the teens knew about him, some seemed to know very little. One student remarked he was 'famous' but did not know why. Another student asked: 'Is he an authority figure, because I don't know.' One discussion went like this:

> Q1: *So does anyone know who the Dalai Lama is?*
> P1: Well, we kind of, we don't know very much about it.
> P3: I've heard of him before.
> P2: I don't know what the Dalai Lama does, is he like the Pope of his religion?
> P1: I think that's a good way of describing it, yeah.
> P2: He is. I reckon that's a good call. Yeah. Of Buddhism.

Those that did recognize him also described him as 'Buddhist', 'a Buddha', 'a monk' and as a 'leader' and 'representative' and the 'Pope for Buddhism'. One non-Buddhist student from a select-entry class at a government school gave an enthusiastic and relatively well-informed response:

> He's adorable. He's the spiritual leader of the Tibetan people. Ah, I believe – I'm pretty sure it's Buddhism. He's the leader of the Buddhist movement. He's the fifteenth Dalai Lama I think. This is just from, ah, I read somewhere. That's about all I know.

He is the fourteenth Dalai Lama, she was very close. One student mistook him for a 'Hindu monk'.

Anglican Church image

Only two out of the ninety-four focus group participants correctly recognized this image (we used an image of the Anglican Cathedral in their state's capital city). Most mistook it for a Catholic Cathedral. It was also simply described as a 'church' or 'Cathedral' by many and even mistaken as an Indian or Sikh temple due to its elaborate arches.

Hillsong image (Australian Pentecostal movement)

Two Pentecostal teens and one Muslim were the only ones who recognized the image specifically as Hillsong Church. Others described the image as a 'concert', 'church group concert', a 'conference', a 'festival', as 'Evangelical' and 'Pentecostal' worship, as 'Jesus Christian rock or something, they're like a Christian band but they're metal at the same time, pretty strange'.

Yassmin Abdel-Magied image (Prominent Australian Muslim public intellectual)

While most teens didn't recognize the image of Yassmin Abdel-Magied, one student, who was Hindu, named her simply as 'Yassmin' and was aware of who she was. There was some recognition of her from her appearance on the TV show *Q&A*, yet most couldn't identify her by name.

Wailing Wall image

Apart from some Jewish teens with whom we spoke, only one student correctly recognized the image as the Wailing Wall. Others noted the image was associated with 'Judaism', 'Jews', 'praying Jews', 'Israel', 'the Jewish wall'. One student incorrectly identified the image with Islam.

Evolve symbol image

The 'evolve' symbol is a parody of the Christian 'fish' car sticker. The evolve version shows the fish with legs and the word 'evolve' in it. Many were not familiar with this image. Some said that it was linked to 'Charles Darwin', 'Darwinism' and 'evolution'.

Richard Dawkins image

Only one student identified the photo of prominent atheist author Richard Dawkins. Another didn't recognize his picture but after the researcher named him, stated: 'I have heard of Richard Dawkins. I've read his book, *The God*

Delusion. That's a really good book.' Another knew Dawkins was 'quite strong on … ideas about evolution' and had 'written a lot of books'. Many of the responses were humorous: one said that Dawkins was 'a pastor' and another as 'the head of the Catholic Education Department'. Others thought he was 'a politician', an 'actor', an 'author', a 'celebrity', a 'Scientologist' and as someone from the 'Save the Flamingos Foundation', given his flamingo tie. Many hadn't heard of him at all.

Our focus group sample is not representative of the teen population in Australia, but it was socially, culturally, economically, geographically and religiously diverse. Overall, *in this limited, non-scientific exercise*, the participants demonstrated moderate levels of recognition and were reasonably conversant with the images. At least one person recognized any given image, while other pictures were more widely recognized. It is interesting to note that even when the participants mistook an image they had a wide religious and spiritual vocabulary to draw upon to make educated guesses. If we had to make an educated guess ourselves about how conversant Australian teens are with the doctrines and teachings of different religions, we'd say that few have an especially deep knowledge of religious traditions *apart from their own*. This is probably the case with the broader Australian population too.[10]

There was some humour evident in some of their responses. A recent study of the way religion is depicted in the Australian media shows that humour is often applied when discussing Christianity and also occasionally Islam.[11] This could perhaps reflect a sense of laconic ease, gained with growing familiarity. On the other hand, the use of humour when discussing religion remains a sensitive issue for some, and could also be a sign of underlying prejudices in some cases.

Religion and education in Australian schools: SRI and GRE

In this section, we examine how teens have been taught about religion at school. Table 8.1 shows the kinds of education about religion Australian teens receive at secondary schools.[12]

The survey data show that approximately 27 per cent of Australian secondary school students have received both GRE and SRI. Approximately the same proportion (28 per cent) have received GRE only. Taken together, this means that at least half (55 per cent) of Australian secondary school students have had

Table 8.1 Australians aged 13–18: Education and religion at secondary school (% of school type)

Type of education received at secondary school	School type (%)			
	Catholic	Private	Government	Total for all teens (13-18)
GRE and SRI	81	37	0	27
SRI only	10	9	0	4
GRE only	8	12	44	28
Nothing	2	42	56	41
Total	100	100	100	100

Source: AGZ Survey 2017.
Note: Percentages have been rounded and may not add up to 100 per cent. Missing responses have been excluded from the table.

some form of GRE. By contrast, 41 per cent claimed to have had no 'lessons or information' on religion at all, and only 4 per cent claimed to have SRI only.

The kind of school a person attends influences the kind of education they receive. Consequently, we see that 56 per cent of students attending schools in the government sector claim to have received no lessons or information about the major religions of the world, while 42 per cent of those attending independent schools claimed to have no lessons or information about the major religions of the world. Only 2 per cent of Catholic students claimed to have had no SRI or GRE. This is possible if the student arrives in a school in the senior years, when SRI and GRE may not be part of the senior curriculum. By contrast, SRI is routinely offered in Catholic schools. For the most part, our data show that Catholic schools teach SRI in conjunction with GRE: 81 per cent of Catholic students claim to have been taught both, compared to 37 per cent of students in the independent system. In the next two sections, we explore students' experiences of SRI and GRE.

Experiencing Special Religious Education (SRI)

Only a minority of Australian students (31 per cent) have encountered SRI at secondary school, and generally, this has been in conjunction with GRE. There are fewer restrictions on offering SRI at primary school (see above); consequently, we were unsurprised to discover that 61 per cent of Australian teens had received some SRI at primary school (whether that be at a Catholic, independent or government school).

Only a few teens in the focus groups and post-survey interviews talked about their SRI experiences, and it did not seem overly important to them. While some teens accepted that there was a place for SRI in Christian secondary schools, others thought that a Christian focus was problematic given the religious diversity within most school communities. One felt that as though they had been 'learning about Christianity ... for like our whole lives ... in [Christian] schools. We're kind of going to [just] see the Christian side of things'. Only one person attending a state school spoke of the controversy surrounding SRI (which is called 'Scripture' in NSW):

> Yeah, in some of the primary schools ... we used to have Scripture [SRI] and there was a huge argument between the parents and the Scripture teachers because the parents didn't want their children learning about it, whereas the Scripture people were there to teach it so then they sort of banned it in some schools.

Beyond SRI classes, students attending some Christian schools participated in daily morning prayers led by teachers and students, and whole-school services. Non-Christian students attending these schools were expected to take part in these activities, and some students in our focus groups also expressed concerns about this. For example, one commented that:

> Yeah, my best friend is Vietnamese and she's Buddhist ... she keeps it to herself unless you ask about it ... she speaks about the religion tests that we have, which are obviously [Christian], and she doesn't understand it that well because she hasn't grown up with that religion or learnt much about it, so it's hard for her to complete it.

Another student recalled how there was a 'blessing night' at their Pentecostal school instead of a school dance, and how this made a Buddhist student feel left out:

> It's, like, us going from being a girl to women or boy to a man and it's next Friday. And I was talking about his suit, and I said something about, 'Oh is your Pastor coming or something?' And he's like, 'No I don't go to Church'. And I was like, 'Oh, why?' Because I thought he was [Christian]. And he was, like, 'Oh I'm Buddhist'. And he ... was like, 'Oh is that bad?' I'm like, 'No'.

One Hindu student recalled a disturbing incident that happened to a fellow Hindu student in a Christian school:

> I know someone that ... used to go to [a Christian] school, he's Hindu, and his teacher was, you know, saying something about how Hinduism was all just made up and everything, and when we went and showed proof ... the teacher was just like, nuh, you're ... just lying.

Some students in the denominational independent schools we visited felt the way that Christianity was taught was out of touch and too prescriptive, and that this alienated many students. Others, particularly those who were religious themselves, were less fussed and remained committed to doing well in these classes:

P1: It was all very set, it wasn't like, how we interpret religion today, it was about what we have to know from the past kind of thing. It's about what was socially acceptable back then, but it doesn't matter what's acceptable now. So it's very, you know, one-sided towards what we learn. And religion is, you know, a forced subject, we don't get to like pick and choose. So people who don't like religion or don't believe in being [Christian], don't have a choice not to do it. They'll be like, 'Religion [SRI class] today, I can't believe we have to go into religion, I hate religion [that] kind of thing'. I don't mind it. But most people don't enjoy religion.

P3: Like, whenever we have a test, you'll get the couple of people who will just kind of walk in and go, I don't care what I get because it's just Religion [SRI], and like I don't believe in it all, and my parents don't care what I get. But then other people can be fixed on wanting to get good grades in religion, because it's like a [Christian] school and their parents are [Christian] and all that.

In general, most teens in the focus groups and interviews were far more interested in GRE than they were in SRI.

Experiencing General Religious Education (GRE)

Where GRE was present in government schools, participants explained that it was most often included in humanities classes. It was also sometimes mentioned in classes on Indigenous Australian culture, studies of Asian societies, Japanese and Indonesian language lessons, and annual Harmony Day/Week celebrations.

Students in a select-entry stream at a government school had received Worldviews Education (WE), spanning diverse religious and nonreligious worldviews (humanism, Marxism and feminism), as part of their humanities and ethics classes.

Interviewees who were at Christian denominational schools (Catholic and Protestant), or from Jewish or Muslim schools, also had varied experiences: some received GRE as part of other subjects, others were taught about other religions during SRI classes and some received comprehensive programs focused on religions and ethics. Dedicated Years 11 and 12 senior school subjects on religion (which some students were allowed to study in Year 10) were reported as providing the most comprehensive education about diverse religions. As noted above, these subjects are offered mainly in Catholic and independent schools.

Overall, students' qualitative comments about GRE in Australian schools reflected the survey findings: that it is variously taught in dedicated religion subjects at the senior levels, special programs (e.g. Harmony Week) or nested in other units of study. And, as we noted above, a substantial number of students indicated in the survey that they had not had any information or lessons at school about the world's diverse religions.

Other sources of information about religion

Outside of school, there are other notable ways in which young people are developing their religious literacy. Table 8.2 examines these other sources of information. Survey participants were asked, 'From the time when you started secondary school, have any of the following been helpful sources of information about the world's religions?' and were offered a range of responses.

These results show that Australian teenagers are interested in sourcing information on religion from a range of places. Direct religious experience, such as attending a service, is the least common source of religious information (47 per cent). We note too that discussion with family members is a major source of information (75 per cent). A lot of what teens know reflects the family's pattern and social and economic circumstances, and school is just one source of knowledge.

Benefits and challenges of GRE

Thus far, we have talked about the prevalence of education about religion at school. Is GRE effective? What is it teaching teens? In the remainder of this

Table 8.2 Australians aged 13–18: Sources of information about the world's religions (% of teens)

Source of information	% of teens (13–18)
Talking to people who follow a particular faith, including at school	78
Discussion with family members	75
Looking up Wikipedia or another website	69
School activities, like Harmony Week or an excursion	65
Exploring a religion, for example by reading their texts, going to a worship service, or taking part in a ritual or practice session	47

Source: AGZ Survey 2017.
Note: Respondents could choose more than one answer, so percentages add to more than 100. Missing responses have been excluded from the table.

chapter, we discuss the benefits and challenges of offering GRE at school. Based on what the students told us, this is predominantly the GRE encountered in the social studies units, and special programs, like Harmony Week, rather than the Year 11–12 unit on religious studies. (The latter is rare.)

In our survey, we asked what teens they thought about GRE, whether they thought it could promote inter-religious understanding and tolerance of religious diversity, and if it should be taught in Australian schools. Students who had experienced GRE overwhelmingly endorsed its benefits: 93 per cent agreed or strongly agreed that it helped develop an understanding of other people's religions; 86 per cent agreed or strongly agreed that GRE helped make them more tolerant of other people's religions; 82 per cent agreed or strongly agreed with the proposition that GRE was something important to study. This applied to students across all three school sectors, with no notable differences between any sector. This aligns with the findings of international and local research.[13]

Also, the large majority of students who hadn't had any GRE indicated in the survey that they were interested to receive lessons about the world's religions. Most of these non-GRE students were also interested to have lessons on nonreligious perspectives and values, including ethics, humanism and rationalism.

GRE and attitudes to religious diversity

Notwithstanding what teens told us, does education *about* religion improve attitudes to religious diversity? It is valuable to consider the relationship between the types of education about religion young people have received and their broader attitudes to religion in society. In Chapter 7, we noted that approximately 20 per cent of Australian teens have a negative to a neutral view of Hinduism, Buddhism and Islam. We explored a range of factors that were associated with these negative attitudes.

Among those findings, we discovered that young people who have had GRE tend to exhibit stronger positive attitudes to religious minorities than those who have had no general religious education. Moreover, students who have had no GRE are *somewhat* more likely than those who have had GRE (whether on its own or with SRI) to hold negative or neutral views towards Australia's religious minorities, even when controlling for gender, age, religious identity, socio-economic status, having religious friends, parental place of birth, living near a place of worship and school type.[14]

Thus, our data suggest that GRE (as we defined it in the survey) is associated with reduced negative perceptions of religious minorities and that GRE can play a helpful role in promoting inter-religious understanding. Perhaps having SRI only may entrench existing attitudes of religious superiority and exclusion, as it does not offer young people the opportunity to broaden their understanding of other faith traditions. The qualitative data tended to align with our survey findings. Below, we discuss what teens told us regarding the benefits – and challenges – of offering GRE.

Intercultural contact

Mariella (Seeker worldview type), described how it could foster greater understanding and acceptance of people from diverse backgrounds:

> I think it is an important aspect of schooling, just because we live in a world where there are different cultures and different environments and diversity is a major aspect of being alive. You have to interact with other people.

Countering negative stereotypes

Many of the teens we spoke to raised concerns about media and populist political figures perpetuating a link between Islam and terrorism. They recognized that education about Islam could play a role in countering this kind of prejudice. Several of the focus groups explained how GRE had assisted them and their peers in this way. For example, students in a select-entry class at government high school explained:

P1: As we're coming into this new generation because there's so much on the news that we are slightly scared of this idea of terrorism. But I think with the things we're learning at school we're starting to [become] …

P2: More accepting.

P1: … [and] more open-minded to how [Islam] might not be related to terrorism specifically.

P2: Yeah.

Q1: *So that's kind of something that you all understand?*

P1: Yeah.

P2: Yeah.

A group at a different school described how they had recently discussed in class how terrorism wasn't an exclusively Muslim phenomenon:

P2: We had a lesson about a week ago in humanities about terrorism and we were told to describe a terrorist and to not … hold back … anything you think, that you put on the paper, and it came up with like a lot of people thought it was Islamic extremists, like Muslim stuff like that, and then we learnt about it doesn't have to be, like there was a white female who tried to bomb, like 20 or so cars, in 1980, something.

Q: *Do you think that most of the students hearing that, already kind of understood?*

P2: Yeah, like they knew it could be anybody, but it's just the way the media interprets terrorists as Islamic extremists …

P2: The lesson was meant to be about terrorism and it was. It ended up being like, sort of a lesson about how terrorists don't have to be of one religion of one race. People can come in any shape and size and they can think however they want … someone of a certain religion doesn't just think hell-bent, I'm going to kill somebody to get my point across. Like, they could be a Christian extremist, who goes to a country like Iran and just starts killing people because they don't believe in Christianity.

In like manner, several of the interviewees described how GRE was a good way of countering misinformation, racism and ignorance. For example, Elizabeth (Seeker worldview type) said:

[A school excursion to a mosque] opened my eyes saying that all the stigma we hear on social media isn't all true, for example, the Islamic race [sic] is not just trying to take over the world and everything like that. They're just another religion and, of course, you've got an extremist like every religion we can have extremists but they only hear about the bad.

Madison (Indifferent worldview type) echoed these sentiments too:

I think that there definitely should be [GRE] … not just in, like, religious-based schools, but in all schools, because I think that not knowing creates the unacceptance [sic] of other cultures. If you learn about it in an educational environment, you learn about the cultures and the traditions and everything that goes into a religion, rather than what you hear on the news, the media sort of grouping certain religions by their, sort of, extremist groups. That's what, sort of, the general public that hasn't been educated about religions assumes, and that's a massive problem so I think that everyone should be educated about different global religions.

Jade (Seeker worldview type), who grew up in a Buddhist family and who hadn't had GRE at school, also described how it was particularly important for young people raised in religious households to learn about other traditions:

I feel like some children have been in households [that] are just Christian or Buddhist or Muslim or something like that and they, kind of, have these firm beliefs that what they believe is right. Yep. It could [be] because they've been taught by the parents and that they go to church or stuff like that and sometimes they'll be a bit closed-minded they'll be, like, 'what I believe is right' and I feel like if they learn about others religions they might not feel so other religions they're wrong and they'll be more willing to accept [others].

Opening your mind

Others affirmed that GRE could open people's mind to religious and spiritual diversity. Rose (Seeker worldview type) said:

I think it's – I thought it was an interesting topic because they're inclined to learn more about other people and how they see the world and things like that … it is a good choice to have and I think it would open – it kind of opens people's minds a bit more.

Fears of discussing religion

As well as the benefits, we also heard about some of the complications that can arise from teaching GRE. Some study participants thought that their teachers avoided teaching about religion as it could be a controversial topic, or because they felt ill-equipped to teach it. This was said in one focus group:

> I think they're trying to steer off that because they don't want to have like someone who has a strong belief or a specific point of view you know starting ... erupting something during class or something. Disrupting the class. They want to stay neutral on the topic. So everyone can have their ideas about it... [If they] ever tried to teach a class about a specific religion you might end up like offending someone in the class by accident if they've got a – like an extreme point of view on the subject so they try and stay as neutral as possible and just focus on academic learning pretty much.

Another focus group agreed that religion can be a difficult topic to discuss with their peers at school because of potential disagreements:

> P6: If we had, like, if there was something we learnt and we had a textbook about religion for example at this age and then there'll be facts there that people from other religions they'd be, like, it's not logic. They wouldn't believe in it and then they'll start, like, hating on people that believe in that religion and that can just, like, cause arguments and... because I've experienced that – not everyone believes in ... I've had talks about people, like, good people about religion ... and, like, when you're talking about your religion and you say something, there's going to be people that are just, like, 'Why would you believe in that, like, how does that even make sense?'
>
> P1: Yeah, same ...
>
> P6: Yeah.
>
> P1: Like, the Bible, I've had a friend that she didn't want anything to do with the Bible, that she would only respect, like, her religion.

Notwithstanding these specific pedagogical challenges, both the survey and interview participants affirmed the general benefits of GRE, and as we have found, it is associated with better attitudes towards Australia's religious minorities.

Australian teens' ideal GRE/WE

As the foregoing discussion and our survey data demonstrate, most teens agree that GRE (and WE) can help build greater appreciation and understanding of diversity in Australia and that there should be more opportunities for GRE/WE in all schools sectors. One of our explicit intentions with this research was to allow students' voices to be heard – specifically, how they want to be taught difficult and controversial topics, like religion, sexuality and gender. This might usefully inform any future curriculum design.

Most agreed that GRE/WE should be taught inclusively, covering a broad range of religious *and* nonreligious worldviews. For example, Tim said:

> Well, if – if there was a chance for it to be taught, it'd be taught in a way that is respectful to each religion ... taught respectfully, so that it doesn't signify any religion as being a better religion.

Some thought that the best way of delivering GRE/WE programs at school was through dedicated subjects taught by teachers using a critical and social scientific approach, whereas others thought it should be embedded in the humanities. There was no particular consensus on this point.

Many called for opportunities for direct encounters: representatives of religions visiting classrooms and students making site visits to places of worship. Jade (This Worldly worldview type) said:

> Definitely [site visits] that, like, it's always good to experience things because ... my textbooks they don't feel it as much. It seems a bit tedious, they don't want to accept it but when you see and experience things, you get more open towards, yeah, and appreciate stuff more.

Elizabeth (Seeker worldview type) went to a Catholic school and spoke appreciatively of site visits:

> We did quite a lot and, like, we went to all of those temples like I went to a Hindu temple and we spent a day being in the Hindu temple and we got to do all of their normal practices and they're praying and everything so [it] did open our eyes to the world.

And finally, while a lot of Australian primary schools offer SRI, many teens, including Vivien (Seeker worldview type), thought GRE should be first implemented at that level too:

> I do think that should be something that needs to be covered by all schools if possible. Because especially at that young age where your mind is so malleable and more open ... I think it's pretty important especially when you are at that young age ... to have the whole – a good grasp of you know, even just like a basic level of understanding of the diversity that we have out there.

Conclusion

The place of religion in Australian schools continues to be a controversial topic for many reasons. Australia has been slow to introduce comprehensive GRE/WE programs across the states, although some notable progress has been made in Victoria with dedicated sections on learning about worldviews and religions being included in the curriculum in 2015. Not surprisingly then, our research indicates a moderate, broad, but ultimately shallow level of religious literacy among Australian teens.

Regarding the controversial practice of SRI, teens' experiences of SRI classes were varied. Those who'd had it at secondary school noted that (Christian) SRI was out of step with their contemporary reality and the diversity of their classrooms. Teens also reported that those of minority faiths felt excluded by Christian SRI.

When it came to GRE, our research demonstrates that GRE programs can counteract stereotypes, prejudices and discrimination against religious minorities. (Recognizing too that for the most part, teens are already very accepting of religious diversity.) However, we found that opportunities for GRE in Australia's government schools are limited and most often included in the humanities subjects and during activities like Harmony Week. GRE in independent schools was varied and focused mainly on Christianity, Islam and Judaism, depending on the type of school it was. Some schools sometimes included opportunities for site visits and to learn from representatives of diverse faith traditions. Some Catholic schools provided much broader GRE courses that included diverse spiritualities and New Age traditions.

Many teens think that GRE programs are important in helping improving religious literacy and in countering negative stereotypes. Students strongly believed that GRE can help build a greater appreciation of religious and nonreligious diversity and inter-religious understanding in Australia and that there should be more GRE in all Australian schools. Students think GRE/WE should be taught by qualified teachers and from the earliest years of schooling. Barriers to GRE/WE included fears among teachers and students that discussions involving religion could be divisive and cause offence. In the next chapter, we continue our focus on education as we explore the relationship between gender, sexuality, religion and schooling.

9

Harry Potter, homophobia and human rights: Teens talk about sexuality education, religious exemptions and gay rights

> *Yeah, I think that sexuality should be taught in schools ... And attending a high school that was open to that and willing to accept it and even embrace it ... [It] allowed people to not have to hide and just be themselves. I thought that was really cool*
>
> Mariella (Seeker worldview type)

Like Mariella, teens in our study were vocal about issues related to the free expression of sexuality and gender at school and generally embraced difference. But people still ask us why we focus on LGBTQI+ issues in a book on young people's worldviews. We were refused permission by some school administrators when we indicated that we wanted to talk to young people about these issues *while at school* when conducting the focus groups before the survey. Using the survey meant that we were able to connect with young people in private, having first gained parental permission to talk to them. And, as is clear from this chapter, teens had strong opinions about gender and sexual diversity, and sexuality education.

Schools' reluctance to participate in such research was not surprising to us because numerous Australian politicians have weighed in on topics related to gender and sexuality. Prime Ministers Gillard, Turnbull and Abbott all politicized same-sex marriage. Prime Minister Morrison tweeted his opposition to teaching related to transgender issues in primary education in his first weeks in office in September 2018.[1] Controversy continues in Australia over independent schools' capacity to discriminate against LGBTQI+ teachers and students. Advocacy groups and religious leaders have expressed firm opinions on what sort of education young people need about gender and sexuality via submissions to numerous reviews on religious freedom.² In October 2018, leading up to the Wentworth by-election, Prime Minister Morrison announced that he would introduce laws ensuring students could no longer be expelled based on their sexual or gender identity – but teachers were not included in this change of heart.³ We are yet to see reform in this area, despite Prime Minister Morrison's partial about-face on the subject. Here we can see that what people think about marriage, families, sexuality and gender is not just influenced by their worldviews but also by recent changes in Australian public and political discourse about the topic of freedom for LGBTQI+ people.

As is evident, we were researching this book when debates about marriage equality were very much in the news. While studies of religion and young people might routinely ask about students' cultural background and ethnicity, they are less likely to be asked questions about gender and sexuality. Given how religion, faith, gender and sexuality have become entangled in public and political debates, we were particularly interested in *how young people thought about this intersection* in their own lives.

Studies of Australian youth typically separate their understandings of religion from their understandings of gender and sexuality. Researchers have studied select communities of young people who are religious or explicitly engaged in religious or ethics education to determine how this might influence their worldviews but have not considered how gender and sexual identity is mediated by religiosity. We have taken a different approach in our study, one that deliberately draws on a random, representative sample of teens. This means we have not selected young people because they identify with any particular point of viewpoint – religion or sexual or gender identity.

Our work will demonstrate that all Australian young people are influenced by debates about religion, gender and sexuality, even if they do not identify as religious or gender and sexually diverse. To put it another way, religion, gender and sexuality are of interest to all young people, regardless of how they identify or where they attend school.

The approach we used in the study reflected this understanding and distinguishes our work from those studies that directly recruit participants from LGBTQI+ communities. While we were able to survey a significant proportion of teens who identified as non-heterosexual and some who were gender diverse,⁴ we did not aim to recruit post-survey interview participants who would speak on behalf of LGBTQI+ young people or as a representative of a particular subgroup per se. One of the young people we interviewed who identified as gay in the survey did not talk about this openly in his follow-up interview, possibly because of the challenges he perceived in discussing this issue while situated in the family home. Or, maybe it was because he did not feel the need to come out to us during the interview.

We recognize that surveying young people about their worldviews, and about gender and sexuality, requires an approach that is sensitive to their age and location. Our survey and interview design enabled them to answer questions so they weren't overheard when talking about how they identified. For instance, they could answer questions by listening to an extensive range of choices and answering 'A', 'B', 'C' or 'D' and so on, rather than having to state their sexual or gender identification aloud.[5] This is a recognition that teens, like adults, may not always feel they can speak freely about this part of themselves. This is especially the case concerning sexuality and gender, where coming out could place teens at risk of alienation and abuse in the home.

Against this background, this chapter examines the gender and sexual identity of Australian teens, and their views about how this should be taught and expressed at school. Importantly, we explore how this intersects with their worldviews in ways not done previously in Australian research. We conclude the chapter by discussing the implications of our findings school education policy.

The gender and sexual identity of Australian teens

Gender refers to people's understanding of themselves concerning masculinity and femininity, while sexuality relates to people's sexual attractions. When asked how they identified in relation to sexuality, 86 per cent of the Australian teens we surveyed said that they identified as straight (heterosexual), while approximately 14 per cent said they said they identified as something other than straight (see breakout box).

It is also worth noting that the percentage of teens who identified as LGBTQI+ in our study was fairly evenly distributed across the three schooling systems. Teens who attended Catholic schools (13 per cent) are as likely as teens at government schools (15 per cent) to identify as something other than straight (there is no statistically significant difference between them). Teens who attend independent schools (10 per cent) are just a little less likely than teens at Catholic or government schools to identify as LGBTQI+. This underscores the necessity for school systems to develop policies that are inclusive of their diverse students; failing to do so will impact a significant minority of the student population *across all schools*.

Digging Deeper: Eighty-six per cent of the Australian teens told us they were straight; 2 per cent identified as lesbian, homosexual or gay; 7 per cent said they were bisexual and 4 per cent were questioning. About 1 per cent said queer or something else, and 1 per cent said they didn't know. (Does not add to 100 per cent because of rounding.)

The proportion of young people in this study not identifying as heterosexual is higher than estimates of the adult population (18+) in Australia. Wilson and Shalley estimate that about 3.2 per cent of adults identify as non-heterosexual, although their method of estimation is different from ours.[6] Their research finds that the percentage of people identifying as non-heterosexual is higher among younger rather than older age groups, with the age gradient being more pronounced for females.[7]

Notably, our study indicates a higher proportion of young people are not identifying as heterosexual compared to adults – 14 per cent compared to 3.2 per cent. This is a seemingly watershed generational difference. Our findings are also significant because it shows that research that only asks young people if they are gay, lesbian or straight invariably misses out on counting a significant proportion of young people who are questioning or refusing fixed gender and sexual identity categories. Given such diversity among teens, it is pertinent to see what they have to say about how this is taught at school.

Lessons on LGBTQI+ people at school

I don't think, at my school, I received any information about the LGBTQI+ thing.

Alice (This Worldly worldview type)

Digging Deeper: We asked students: Have you had any lessons at school about LGBTQI+ people? Thirty-two per cent said yes and 66 per cent said no. Differences between school types: 29 per cent of Catholic students had received lessons about LGBTQI+ people, compared to 29 per cent of students at independent schools and 36 per cent at government schools.

Many young people in our study – 66 per cent of teens – reported not receiving education about (LGBTQI+) issues. These issues are not only excluded in the official curriculum but are also excluded via the hidden curriculum.[8] Young people notice materials around schools that are supportive of diverse sexual and gender identities. Like Alice, they also register the absence of content related to LGBTQI+ issues. They take note when peers and teachers bring same-sex partners to social events like school formals.

The national curriculum places sexuality education in subjects like Health and Physical Education, while some religious schools incorporate sexuality education as part of religious education. Such decisions send quite specific signals to young people about how they should think about sexuality. They signal that sexuality is primarily about physical health and wellbeing or about understanding the human body, while locating education about sexuality in religious instruction sends a clear message that sexuality education is primarily related to morality and ethics.

In devising our survey questions on sexuality education at school (see Table 9.1 below) we wanted to explore many interconnected themes. Do young people want to learn about LGBTQI+ people in the curriculum? This question investigates whether young people will have an interest in learning about LGBTQI+ people, as opposed to seeing LGBTQI+ issues as only relevant to young people who identify as LGBTQI+. We also wanted to know whether young people had sought information about how different religions teach about sexuality. Beyond what is taught in the classroom, we also wanted to know how young people felt about students being 'out' at school. Did young people think that their peers should be able to openly express any sexual or gender orientation while at secondary school? We hope that by knowing more about young people's perspectives on these issues we might better inform educational responses related to gender and sexuality and sex and relationships education.

Unsurprisingly, as shown in Table 9.1, participants were overwhelmingly in support of sexuality education – both general sexuality education and education that focused on LGBTQI+ issues. We explore responses according to the type of school a person attends.

(We have decided to not present a table that shows the relationship between attitudes towards sexuality education and our worldview types because the differences are not especially great. There is large majority support for LGBTQI+ people and education *across five types: This Worldly, Indifferent, Seekers, SNBR and Nominally Religious*. Only a large minority of Religiously Committed

Table 9.1 Australians aged 13–18: Attitudes towards education on sexuality by school type (% of school type)

Item	Response	School type (%)			Total for all teens (13–18)
		Catholic	Private	Government	
Secondary school students should have the right to learn about LGBTQI people	Disagree/strongly disagree	10	14	8	10
	Neither	3	1	1	2
	Agree/strongly agree	85	81	89	86
Secondary schools should allow students to openly express any sexual or gender orientation	Disagree/strongly disagree	11	16	9	11
	Neither	1	1	2	2
	Agree/strongly agree	87	77	87	84
School is not the place to discuss issues related to sexuality	Disagree/strongly disagree	72	69	74	72
	Neither	7	5	3	4
	Agree/strongly agree	20	25	19	21
Sexuality education at school should include information that is relevant to LGBTQI people	Disagree/strongly disagree	15	21	11	14
	Neither	5	2	1	2
	Agree/strongly agree	79	73	85	81
It is important for young people to learn what religions teach about gender and sexuality	Disagree/strongly disagree	18	15	22	19
	Neither	5	3	5	5
	Agree/strongly agree	77	79	69	73

Source: AGZ Survey 2017.
Note: May not add up to 100 per cent due to rounding or because small numbers of 'Don't know' responses have been omitted.

teens – 40 per cent of that group – are resistant to or ambivalent about LGBTQI+ rights and education. Otherwise, *the majority of Religiously Committed teens are supportive*. In other words, most teens – no matter their worldview type – support LGBTQI+ rights and education at school.)

Looking at totals in the right-hand column, we can see 86 per cent of survey participants support secondary school students' right to learn about LGBTQI+ people as part of their schooling, while 84 per cent support students' right to identify publicly according to their sexual or gender identity. Eighty-one per cent of students think that sexuality education at school should include information that is relevant to LGBTQI+ people. In the main, Australian teens strongly support LGBTQI+ rights and education in the school context.

There are some modest differences between school systems. Across all the items, students in government schools are somewhat more likely than students in independent or Catholic schools to support LGBTQI+ education and rights. Much of the resistance to LGBTQI+ rights and education in Australia is due to the standpoint of some conservative religious traditions. We think the differences between school types thus reflect the religious commitments of *some* fee-paying schools and parents and students within those schools. As noted above, the *small pocket* of resistance or ambivalence to LGBTQI+ rights and education among teens is found mainly within the Religiously Committed worldview type.

That said, in our follow-up interviews, not a single participant spoke unequivocally against sexuality education that supports LGBTQI+ people. However, three participants expressed some concern about how that education might be presented. The reasons participants gave for supporting sexuality education are presented below, followed by comments from those who express concerns or ambivalent support.

In her response to a question about social concerns that interested her, Mariella (Seeker) raised the issue of bullying and related this back to education about diversity:

> I've been to two schools ... the first school that I attended was not nice and just the environment was just not a good learning environment.

Mariella spoke about the positive impact that comes from a school that places a strong emphasis on accepting sexual, cultural and religious diversity. She saw this as central to the non-existence of bullying at her second school. As an example she discussed was her peers' acceptance of a trans student:

> Someone in my year transitioned during Year 12, which I thought was a pretty bold thing to do. And I was so surprised that everyone was very accepting.

Madison (This Worldly) felt that avoiding sexuality education at school and particularly education around diverse sexualities reflected an 'underlying intolerance for that sort of thing'. She highlighted the desirability of education about LGBTQI+ issues happening at school and not just online:

> I think it's so important because, I don't know, if kids are questioning these sorts of things or confused about these sorts of things, they're going to go – they're not going to go to someone they know, they're not going to go to someone in their school, they're going to go online and try and work out what's going on there, and I just don't think that that's the best way for them to work it out, because there's so much intolerance in our society about those sorts of things ... and I think that the basis of that is built into the education system because it's not included and it's not, like – it's a normal thing and it should be included.

For Madison, the requirement for sexuality education to be taught at school was that it might act as a counterpoint to what she perceives as widespread intolerance. She attributes this intolerance to the education system and its failure to normalize diverse genders and sexualities through their inclusion in the curriculum.

Madelyn (Religiously Committed) highlights the value of people being informed about the appropriate terminology to reduce offence:

> I do think that because there are a lot of kids now who get confused by all the different terms and they do need to know them so they're not insulting anyone who's around them or who has a family member or a friend who is going through that and, you know, that transition as well because everyone is sort of evolving through their different times in their life and to not feel as though like they can't say particular things. We should already be the first person making the step forward and to go, okay, that's not okay or this is the correct term or, you know.

Fabian (This Worldly), also places a lot of faith in the power of education on LGBTQI+ issues: 'I think it will stop the stereotypes and the false accusations on that group of people.' Alice (This Worldly) also wants schools to educate young people above diverse sexualities and genders. She also qualifies this support by suggesting that teachers need to cultivate a neutral and open environment:

> I don't think, at my school, I received any information about the LGBTQI+ thing at my school. I think, definitely if it's something that people want to discuss to do at school ... the teachers have to be open-minded to do it and accept that there will be students who will support or not support it, and they just have to make sure it stays in a good environment and it's not something that's sort of already

pitched to the students in a certain way, of like, oh it's bad or it's really good you know, it's got to be quite neutral in that way.

Self-identifying as an atheist like her father, Alice also sees herself as more tolerant of religious diversity than him. One way in which this worldview is apparent is in Alice's desire for more education about LGBTQI+ issues, but not in a way that insists upon legislating tolerance through curriculum design.

Given such comments, we wonder what a neutral curriculum would look on this topic. History tells us that education about sexuality, especially LGBTQI+ issues, is never neutral. Is 'neutral' here a stand-in for evidence-based curriculum? Or do these young people have something else in mind when they invoke neutrality?

A minority of young people had reservations about supporting a more inclusive sexuality education, and, consistent with our approach of understanding the relationship between religion and sexuality, we were keen to know how their worldviews informed their position. Twenty-one per cent of students were unsure whether a school was an appropriate place to discuss issues related to sexuality. Our survey data suggest that this resistance comes mainly from a small group of Religiously Committed teens. Religious commitments, especially participation in conservative religious traditions, are an important influence on teens' response to LGBTQI+ issues.

This is not the only point of difference. Much earlier in this book, we noted major generational differences between Gen Z and Baby Boomers (their parents' generation) concerning religion and spirituality. It was clear from the interviews that teens' receptiveness to LGBTQI+ education seemingly places them at odds with how they perceive older generations, something we explore in the next section.

Teens' accounts of generational differences related to gender and sexuality

Baby Boomers ... [their] generation is much more intolerant of sexual diversity than our generation

Madison (This Worldly)

As we indicated in Chapter 2, 52 per cent of young people aged 13–18 declare themselves as having no religious affiliation. Though increasing numbers of young people identify as having no religion, there continues to be a strong community and governmental support for faith-based schools, and public funding of those schools. But listening to young people in our study, it is clear that support for faith-based schools does not translate into a desire for curricula that refuses to be inclusive of LGBTQI+ young people.

There is a massive disconnect here between the curriculum schools offer and young people's worldviews. The majority of young Australians in our study are immersed in peer cultures where sexual and gender diversity is no longer controversial.[9] Moreover, they see older generations as out of touch yet paradoxically formulating education about this issue.

Lucinda (SBNR) is an example, having received extensive sexuality education at school. After observing backlash from other parents about sexuality education on offer in her school, she argues it is important to educate older generations about sexuality:

> I think if there's better education across the board not just in schools as well as educating children to – educate their parents almost, like, just continuing it so it doesn't just stop with us learning about stuff and then our parents not knowing or our grandparents.

Generational differences played out in several ways. For Lucinda, education about sexual and gender diversity needs to go beyond the school – and she perceives young people as potentially well placed to shift thinking across generations. Madison (This Worldly), like Lucinda, perceives older generations as more likely to be intolerant of 'sexual diversity':

> It's hard to put an umbrella over a whole group of Christians, but I would say that most religions these days they're all run by older generations, Baby Boomers, those sorts of people, and in general that generation is much more intolerant of sexual diversity than our generation. I think that as our generation shifts over to be the ones in charge, the perspective will change but, in any extreme religion, they're always going to believe what they've believed from the very start.

This perception of older generations as intolerant was also expressed by young people who we identified as Religiously Committed. Quite a few young people in this category who agreed to be interviewed sought to distinguish themselves from what they perceived as the overt homophobia of their parents' generation. But they also expressed worries about when it was appropriate to teach sexuality education. They did not believe that 'religious freedom' would be compromised by education about LGBTQI+ issues in schools but recognized that others in their communities might not share their perspectives.

Ashleigh (Religiously Committed) wrestles with the question of when education about LGBTQI+ issues might be appropriate in a school context:

> So I think it will create something that doesn't need to be addressed right now, like yes in maybe their last years of high school, but not like earlier than that. Because I feel like there are certain things that just like a child doesn't need to know because it's just going to corrupt their childhood and make them think about things they don't have to worry about right now. Like they are not going to vote on gay marriage, are they? It's good to know that it's out there, but to – they need to be taught how to respect those kinds of people and treat them as normal people, so that – it's just something they need to learn not to treat them as different people.

Ashleigh is ambivalent about the inclusion of LGBTQI+ issues in the school curriculum and invokes discourses of 'childhood innocence' to explain her ambivalence about when young people should be educated about these issues. Liberal Prime Minister Scott Morrison invoked similar sentiments when he became PM, tweeting: 'We do not need "gender whisperers" in our schools. Let kids be kids.'[10]

Both Ashleigh and Morrison identify as committed Christians, but they don't use this worldview to explicitly justify their worries regarding gender and sexuality in education. Both invoke the vulnerability of children. Religiously committed people, at least in these instances, don't publicly articulate a religious objection to more inclusive education. Arguably, concerns about childhood innocence invoke a more secular worldview, one that perceives all children as particularly vulnerable to early exposure of information related to non-normative gender and sexuality.

While Ashleigh echoes Prime Minister Morrison's sentiments, she is keen to be seen as more progressive than people of her father's generation. She sees her father as having been strongly influenced in his homophobic attitudes to sexuality via his exposure to negative public discourse at the peak of the HIV/AIDS epidemic. She said:

> It's like my father doesn't want to hear about gay rights because ... his generation was taught that, it was in a time that like AIDS and stuff was around, so he is secretly afraid of gay people because he thinks they're disease-ridden. By letting a child just see the person for who they are, a child would just acknowledge them as a normal person. Daniel Radcliffe [who played Harry Potter] is a person that

supports gay marriage, and he says it's because he never saw them as different people. He was brought up with a family [whose] best friends were a gay couple.

Ashleigh rejects her father's homophobia, seeing it as symptomatic of a particular era – she invokes influential figures in her own life, like *Harry Potter* actor Daniel Radcliffe, who have been outspoken against homophobia. But she still worries that education about LGBTQI+ issues can lead to 'corruption' (her word), especially at primary school. Ashleigh understands the power of public discourse in shaping worldviews, for good and ill. She also believes that familial proximity to gay people promotes support for differences. This suggests that for Ashleigh, exposure to gay people outside school is an acceptable part of growing up, but exposure at school – outside the family context – appears to be a step too far.

The sensitivities of addressing LGBTQI+ issues at school are certainly not lost on the young people we interviewed. Samantha's (Religiously Committed) friendship group is highly diverse – she lives in one of the most religiously and culturally diverse parts of Australia. When asked, Samantha expressed support for LGBTQI+ issues being taught at school. Speaking about how her friendship group chooses to manage diversity, Samantha talks about their propensity to focus on similarities rather than differences. She describes a couple of Christian friends of hers who were not in favour of hearing about LGBTQI+ issues at school. Below she talks about her desire to avoid conflict on the issue:

Samantha:	I had a couple of Christian friends and they were really against it but I didn't say anything about it because maybe that's just the way – the way that they were taught about what was right and what was wrong, so …
Q:	*Yeah. So it came up but, you didn't sit there and explore that in-depth because that would be quite awkward, yeah?*
Samantha:	Yeah.

Samantha doesn't attribute her peers' opposition to LGBTQI+ curriculum to a lack of knowledge but to how her friends are raised. Maybe this is why she is reticent to explore their objection? If these views opposing inclusion had been expressed inside the classroom, what might be the outcome? Should teachers/peers probe in such situations or follow Samantha's example and maintain silence? To put this another way, could Samantha's silence be read as empathizing with her peers rather than feeling awkward? For students/teachers who identify as LGBTQI+, silence may not be a viable option in such exchanges. If young people are opposed to learning about LGBTQI+ issues in schools, and it appears a minority of them are, what is the best response? Are students and teachers equipped to have complex conversations about sexual and gender identity that allow for different perspectives?

Another young person, Vincent (Religiously Committed and identifies as gay), spoke in favour of learning about LGBTQI+ issues in sexuality education and attributed this directly to the new law supporting marriage equality. He thinks it is good 'for children to learn about these things', as long as it is not 'enforced'. Madelyn (Religiously Committed) captures the tensions between her strong religious convictions and her total support for sexual freedom. She supported LGBTQI+ peers during the marriage equality postal vote (more on this below) and passionately defends sexual and gender diversity. In speaking about tensions that might arise between her strong support for diversity and her deep religious involvement/commitment she says:

> Many people in the church have different views and opinions about that but personally, for me, I am fully accepting of them. And, you know, I've got so many friends that I've met who I still have now who identify themselves as gay or, you know, transgender and I think like they're very brave to tell their family and to tell friends so I think that's very empowering of them.

Overall, our research demonstrates high levels of consensus among Australian young people for education that is inclusive of sexual and gender diversity, regardless of their religious affiliation.

At the same time that we were collecting our data, the *Religious Freedom Review* was conducted by a government-appointed expert panel led by former Liberal minister Philip Ruddock. This review was designed to make recommendations to the government about legislative protections for 'religious freedom'. The panel received more than 15,500 public submissions. Frank Brennan, a Jesuit priest, legal expert and a member of the Ruddock panel was cited in a submission lodged by the Association of Heads of Independent Schools of Australasia (AHISA):

> Under the Sex Discrimination Act, religious educators can discriminate in good faith against teachers and other staff, or even against prospective students, on the ground of their sexual orientation, gender identity, marital or relationship status 'in order to avoid injury to the religious susceptibilities of adherents of that religion or creed' *But what if it can be demonstrated that the adherents of the particular religion or creed voted overwhelmingly in support of same-sex marriage?* [AHISA's emphasis][11]

AHISA is recognizing that claims to freedom, oriented around religious traditions, might not reflect the views of many – probably the majority – of adherents of a particular faith. Or, for our purposes, young people who attend religious schools. To put it another way, how should the state measure protections for a particular creed or religion *when the adherents demonstrably are at odds with that creed*?

So if the vast majority of young Australian Catholic teens support marriage equality (our survey shows that 85 per cent of them do, see the next section), it seems that adhering to the Catholic credo on marriage will fail to register the worldviews of the majority of students who attend Catholic schools, regardless of their gender or sexual identification. Given such a situation, it is not surprising that the teens in our study expressed a belief in wide generational gaps on worldviews related to gender and sexuality.

In Ireland, the state is grappling with how to intervene in these debates. The results are somewhat contradictory. Like Australia, bullying related to homophobia and transphobia has been identified as unacceptable in nearly all schools in Ireland. But as Susan Bailey points out in her analysis of the Irish primary education system:

> It is entirely possible for a school to deal with transphobic and homophobic bullying behaviour as an instance of bullying while, at the same time, allowing for transphobic and homophobic beliefs to be perpetuated or go unchallenged.[12]

In Ireland and Australia, religious freedom and sexual freedom are clearly in tension. Students, teachers, administrators and parents perceive these tensions in curriculum provision, in policies related to bullying and in decisions made about staffing and school social events. Yet the vast majority of submissions to the recent review on religious freedom did not expressly address the views of young people regarding how they wanted to be educated about gender and sexual diversity. The teens in our survey have been clear about how they would like things to be done. This is evident no more so than when it comes to marriage equality.

Teens want marriage equality

In late 2017, Australian adults were invited to participate in a postal vote about marriage equality.[13] Adults, for and against marriage equality, worried about how young people might be impacted by the passage of marriage equality legislation, as well as by the ballot campaign itself. But young people's perspectives are often excluded from these debates and the focus turns to the rights of parents to determine how their children will be educated about diversity, including gender and sexual diversity. Therefore, we want to convey what young people had to say about marriage equality, especially because young people were largely excluded from official participation in the survey because they were not considered old enough.

Sixty-two per cent of adult Australians voted 'yes' to support this legislative change in November 2017, a majority of Australians in all states and territories (see Figure 9.1 below). Young people were keen to be part of this process. In the state of Victoria, for example, those aged 18–19 participated at high rates in the survey; 85 per cent of young women and 79 per cent of young men in this age group returned their postal surveys. Their rate of engagement was on par with people aged 50 and over. In the lead-up to the same-sex marriage survey, Victoria's electoral roll grew by over 16,000 young people aged 18–24, an increase in enrolments for this cohort of nearly 4 per cent.[14] This reflects this cohort of young people's strong interest in this issue and in having their voices heard. One researcher suggested that 'access to legal same-sex marriage was frequently seen [by young Australians they surveyed in 2013] as an indicator of equality in society in Australia'.[15]

Data collection for the AGZ survey coincidentally occurred at the same time as the non-compulsory survey on marriage equality was being administered in the second half of 2017. Despite employing different methods, and slightly different question phrasing, the postal vote and the AGZ survey are good

Figure 9.1 Gen Z teens' support for marriage equality versus Australian adults' support for marriage equality (% of the population).

barometers of sentiment.[16] As seen in Figure 9.1, young people in the AGZ study expressed incredibly strong support for marriage equality.

Teens' support for marriage equality was significantly higher than that of the adult population: **over 80 per cent of teens in our survey support marriage equality**, while only 62 per cent of the adult population expressed support for the laws to change. (Our chart leaves out those who were 18 at the time of the AGZ survey, as they had the opportunity to be part of the postal vote.) This strong support is echoed in other parts of the Anglosphere.[17] For young people in Australia, Ireland and Scotland, marriage equality was an issue around which there was much consensus.

There was also a clear relationship between how committed young people were in terms of religious affiliation and their support for marriage equality. Young people who we identified as Religiously Committed were least likely to support marriage equality (40 per cent of this type support it), while almost every person classified as This Worldly (95 per cent support), Indifferent (94 per cent support), SNBR (94 per cent support) or Seekers (95 per cent support) endorsed marriage equality.

Ashleigh (Religiously Committed) was the only interview participant to elaborate on having 'strict' and conservative religious parents, and she shared her view on marriage equality. Her worldview is quite distinct from her parents. Asked about her family's religious background and life, Ashleigh responded:

> My father is a very strong Catholic. He doesn't approve of gay marriage or gays at all. My mother, she is Catholic as well, but I don't think she is as religious, but she also to a certain point, doesn't believe in gay marriage. Like she – she said no to it, but she's not nasty if someone is gay, where my father is. He probably wouldn't shake a gay person's hand or something like that. So that's something that I disagree with, with my parents. Someone that is Catholic, I feel like – like God actually wouldn't like send them to hell because of it.

Though she strongly disagrees with her father on this issue of marriage equality, she described her understanding of why he is like this and doesn't 'hate him' for it:

> I feel that there's an actual issue that he was brought up with, and that's why he thinks like that. Like it – there's something that he can't change because that's the way he was taught.

Taylah (Seeker, and who identifies as LGBTQI+) actively campaigned for a 'yes' vote in the marriage equality survey and raised the issue of her reluctance to discuss controversial issues with friends who hold different views (on many topics), a pattern that emerged many times in the interviews:

> So I talked about it [same sex marriage] like with my close friends who are like all, you know, for it and all that. But with the friends who were a bit like 'I don't know what to do', I didn't really bring it up, because they didn't want to have that fight or that tension.

It appears that conversations about controversial issues with intimate friends are avoided because of tensions they might cause. Taylah supports same-sex marriage, enough to campaign for a 'yes' vote. But, like Ashleigh, she avoids confrontation with peers on the issue for fear of being seen to impose a particular way of thinking. As we have demonstrated abundantly in this book, for this generation of young Australians, having the freedom to hold different worldviews is something that is highly respected, even when those worldviews are not aligned with their own beliefs.

Teens on religious exemptions in Australian schools

In the week following the announcement of the 'Yes' result in the postal survey on same-sex marriage, the Liberal government (then led by Malcolm Turnbull) announced the review into religious freedom in Australia. The *Religious Freedom Review* was handed to the government in May 2018 but the findings were not released until the end of that year, no doubt being judged as too contentious by a conservative government battling internal conflicts.

However, parts of the expert panel's report were leaked in the lead up to the Wentworth by-election in October 2018,[18] a vote that saw the election of an openly lesbian candidate, Kerryn Phelps, in the seat of the former Prime Minister. According to an ABC news item:

> The report recommends that religious schools have the right to turn away LGBT+ students and teachers based on the school's religious beliefs. This is not new. Under section 38 of the Federal Sex Discrimination Act, religious schools are already permitted to discriminate against teachers and students on the grounds of sexual orientation and gender identity if this is 'in accordance with the doctrines ... of a particular religion'.[19]

The issue of religious exemptions is particularly salient in Australia where 20 per cent of students are enrolled in Catholic schools and a further 15 per cent are enrolled in independent schools, many of which have religious affiliations. For a brief moment after marriage equality was passed into law there was very strong public opposition to these exemptions. This is in contrast to a few years ago when most Australians were unaware that these exemptions even exist.[20] Recommendations 5 and 7 of the *Religious Freedom Review* expert panel support religious schools' right to discriminate against staff and students 'on the basis of sexual orientation, gender identity or relationship status' provided that:

(a) the discrimination is founded in the precepts of the religion;
(b) the school has a publicly available policy outlining its position in relation to the matter and explaining how the policy will be enforced; and
(c) the school provides a copy of the policy in writing to employees and contractors and prospective employees and contractors.[21]

Forecasting that religious exemptions in education would follow on from marriage equality, we were keen to discuss these issues directly with our participants. In post-survey interviews, we asked teens what they thought about religious exemptions for schools and the hiring/firing of staff in line with the school's position on religion. While they are keen to preserve religious freedoms, young people were adamant that minority beliefs should not be imposed on the broader community – something we demonstrated in Chapter 7.

Like many Australians, the teens we spoke to were generally not aware of the existence of religious exemptions. Surprise and shock was a common response to hearing about them. Most did not support religious exemptions. While a considerable amount was strongly opposed to them, some participants expressed an 'understanding' for the position faced by religious institutions while still being personally against them. The most prominent elements of religious exemptions criticized by young people were those relating to the right to discriminate against staff or students based on gender or sexual identity.

Taylah (Seeker) captured the sentiment of the majority of our participants in her response to our question about religious exemptions:

Taylah: Well, it makes me angry ... I don't think so ... I think they – it's equality and to say that this organization can discriminate you *for who you are* is wrong. You know, it happened like to a – something similar happened and it was like Aboriginal kids at schools and things like that, or just different races, and it's nowadays you would never say, you're Muslim so you can't be a teacher ... I think it should be, oh you're gay, you can't

	be a teacher should also be wrong to say. Regardless of what religious institution you're running, as long as that teacher isn't forcing what they believe, and they're still teaching to the Australian curriculum, and stuff like that, it shouldn't be an issue.
Q:	*Sort of the value, the value of equality should override sort of say for religious freedom?*
Taylah:	Like people can still have religious freedom, but they shouldn't be able to, like, you can still believe being gay is wrong, but you shouldn't be able to fire someone only on the basis that they are gay.

In response to a direct question about religious freedom, Taylah is supportive. Her opposition to religious freedom extends to protecting freedom of belief. But she draws a line when belief infringes on other people's right to employment. She also makes analogies to other groups in voicing her objection to exemptions. From her point of view, discrimination against people based on their sexuality is akin to discrimination based on race and religion. For her, discrimination based on 'who you are' is wrong. Lucinda (SBNR) also made parallels between discrimination based on age, race, and religion with discrimination associated with sexuality:

> Not hiring someone because of the way they are or their religious beliefs or stuff like that, I don't think that's something that should be allowed. You're not allowed to discriminate against people's age or race or anything so I don't think it should be any different with religion or sexuality.

Madison (This Worldly) argued that religious freedom is not logically related to a person's race or sexuality:

> I don't know if that makes sense, but just because you're religious doesn't mean that you have the right to express religious views over other spheres of people's lives. I understand if it's a highly religious school and someone maybe is highly opposed to that religion, sure, because it's a religious decision but it's a highly religious school and they have a problem based on some sort of other identification, whether it be race or sexuality, I don't think that's justified, because the two are not really logically related.

For Madison, logic trumps religious belief, even in religious contexts where beliefs are deeply held. We also asked participants in the post-survey interviews how they felt about students and teachers bringing same-sex partners to school events because we wanted to distinguish between how they felt about teachers and students on the subject of exemptions. Noah (This Worldly) responded to the question directly:

> Why the fuck not ... For what purpose would that serve? To not be allowed to do that is bizarre.

Julian (Seeker) expressed similar sentiments:

> Sure. I don't see what's wrong with that at all. If it's their partner then it's their partner, you know. People – you just deal with it, it's their decision.

Young people are not naïve about these topics. Like the rest of Australia, many of them received instruction about different ways of thinking about religious freedom and sexual freedom during the campaign for marriage equality. Paula Gerber, a specialist in human rights laws, observes:

> There was a stream of ads [during the campaign] asserting that boys would start wearing dresses to school, students would role-play being in same-sex relationships, and radical LGBT sex and gender education would become mandatory [if marriage equality was legalized].[22]

The young people we interviewed supported religious freedom and sexual freedom, but most objected when religious freedoms 'trumped' sexual freedoms. Yet, according to Gerber, sexual freedom within schools is becoming more restricted since the passage of the marriage equality legislation in November 2017. Federal and state governments in several Australian states have defunded programs specifically targeting school-based bullying related to gender and sexuality, and opposition parties have signalled an intention to do so on gaining office (Queensland, Tasmania, South Australia, New South Wales and Victoria).

This trend is particularly disturbing given young people's opposition to religious exemptions and a clearly articulated desire for more education about sexuality, including education about diverse sexual and gender identities. Vincent (Religiously Committed) believes education around sexual identities would help students to have empathy for others:

> I would definitely think that it is important to speak about ... for the same reason of just being able to put yourselves in other people's shoes and sort of, understanding the different hardships we all face ... you know, seek to understand as to be understood.

But not all our participants opposed religious exemptions. Annie (Nominally Religious) attended a Catholic school where a teacher was fired when they came out as gay. She reported that there was a lot of negativity about the decision, but she felt that the school was consistent in making this decision because it was consistent with Catholic teaching. At the same time, Annie affirmed her support of LGBTQI+ issues being taught at school:

> Q: *Yeah, so you don't have an issue with that, but by the same token feel that Christian schools have a right not to teach it if they wish to?*
>
> Annie: Yeah.

While Annie supports the inclusion of LGBTQI+ issues in education, she also supports the right of Christian schools not to teach these issues. In this respect, Annie seems to be an outlier among the young people we interviewed. As in the survey, the majority of young people thought that all schools should be inclusive of LGBTQI+ students.

In an Australian study of 342 primary school parents' views of sexuality education, Kerry Robinson and colleagues found that parents were supportive of sexuality education.[23] They saw it as providing media literacy to counter sexuality education young people might encounter online. They also appreciated that parents, including themselves, were sometimes reluctant to raise sensitive topics like LGBTQI+ issues with their children, and they were concerned that young people would educate themselves about such topics via alternative sources – in the absence of instruction in school or at home. Parents worried about sexuality education happening before young people were ready – they felt that kids need to be kids for as long as possible. Some parents also worried about how sexuality education delivered at school might teach their children things they 'felt were morally wrong'.[24]

None of the young people in our study had this concern for their wellbeing, though some of them did express concerns for the welfare of younger children if they thought this involved early exposure to sexuality education. To counter disconnects between parents, students and schools on sexuality education, Robinson and colleagues suggest a role for allied health groups in educating parents about sexuality using an evidence-based approach. They also suggest that schools need to engage more fulsomely with parents about how they plan sexuality education, both in terms of curriculum content and information offered to different year groups.

Young people in the AGZ study appear to express little ambiguity about what sort of education they want about gender and sexuality. Even those with strong religious affiliations generally support more inclusive education. Young people are increasingly nonreligious, and those who are religious often distance themselves from the teachings of their religious communities on topics such as gender and sexuality. At the same time, the expert panel associated with the Ruddock Review, prominent religious authorities and political figures, and what appears to be a very small minority of parents and young people, prioritize freedom of religion. *This undermines attempts to make education about gender and sexuality more inclusive in Australian schools.* As religious and independent schools defend the freedom to teach curriculum according to religious traditions, how much weight should be given to the majority perspective expressed by young people?

Conclusion

Teens care about what schools teach about gender and sexuality. Can schools do better? In presenting data on Australian young people's views about gender and sexuality in education, we hope our research might provide an evidence base to inform future debates about sexuality education curriculum and religious exemptions. For our participants, it still matters what schools are teaching with regards to gender and sexuality, even when they acknowledge their access to extensive alternative sources of knowledge. They recognize the symbolic importance of including this content in the curriculum and they strongly oppose religious exemptions.

Our study, like other research, underscores continuing concerns about childhood innocence and the fear that it could be compromised by school-based sexuality education. When the majority of young people already have access to resources that are far more explicit than anything they might hope to learn in the official curriculum, why do such concerns persist? Will it ever be possible to assuage concerns about childhood innocence and its relationship to school-based sexuality education?

Education about gender and sexuality needs to have a place in the curriculum that reflects young people's worldviews on religion, sex, sexuality and gender. Education about sexuality also needs to take account of young people's continuing retreat from religion and offer alternative ethical frameworks for the negotiation of abstinence, pleasure and consent.

Conclusion: The freedoms, faiths and futures of Australia's teens

The title of this work, *Freedoms, Faiths and Futures*, reflects three key takeaways from the book.

'Religious freedom' has been politicized in recent times, a cipher for those who support the 'right' of religious groups to exempt themselves from certain discrimination laws. The teens in our study don't think that this is an acceptable 'freedom' for any group to enjoy. For the majority, freedom is the right to be who you are and to not fear prejudice or discrimination at school or in the community, based on religion, sexuality, gender or any other part of one's identity. Teens also indicated to us that the freedom to hold different worldviews is something that is highly respected. Coincidentally, LGBTQI+ issues (such as marriage equality and religious schools' capacity to hire and fire LGBTQI+ teachers) were frequently in the news as we undertook this study, and our survey ran at the same time as the national adult postal survey on marriage equality. Teens were keen to have a say on these issues, perhaps especially because they were unable to have a voice in the postal survey. Young people as a whole are passionate about issues related to equality in the realm of sexual and gender identity.

'Faiths', because faith hasn't gone away, nor is faith singular. While young people increasingly say they have 'no religion', this doesn't mean they're rejecting religiosity or spirituality outright. Only about a quarter of Australia's teens have no belief at all in a transcendent being or God. The majority accept some kind of religious or spiritual belief or another, and almost all think that it's OK for others to have a religion if they want. And there's still a group of teens for whom religion plays an important and defining part in their lives. At the same time, many place their 'faith' in science.

The third word in our book's title alliteration is 'futures'. We finalized our manuscript against the backdrop of a global pandemic, that while proving more lethal to older people has hit young people hard. They have had their schooling, mental health and economic prospects impacted severely. This is true of young people across the globe and it will be a long, slow path back to a life that resembles something like it was before. One of the privileges of this research was talking to young people and hearing how sensible, progressive and optimistic they can be about all kinds of issues. If this generation of teens stays true to this course, then there is every reason to think widespread tolerance and acceptance of religious, sexual and gender diversity will be a hallmark of their futures. Maybe they can save the environment too.

We began this book setting out to answer some key questions about Australian teens and the complex, diverse world in which they come of age. How do they experience and understand diversity in its many forms? What proportion of teens has religious, spiritual or secular worldviews? How do teens learn about diversity in different school contexts and how does this impact on the ways that they relate to people who are different? And, we wondered, how do Gen Z teens differ in comparison to members of older generations concerning these issues? Below, we summarize our findings concerning these questions and discuss future research prospects.

Worldviews and six *types* of Australian teens

The key finding of our book is the discovery of the six worldview types of Australia's teens. Using a cutting-edge statistical approach, and underpinned by in-depth interviews and focus groups, we have moved beyond conventional understandings of young people and religion to offer an entirely new way of conceptualizing the worldviews of Australian teens. Reflecting their diverse commitments to religious, spiritual and nonreligious beliefs, we identified and named six different 'worldview types' of Australian Gen Z's (Religiously Committed, Nominally Religious, Spiritual but Not Religious, Seekers, Indifferent and This Worldly). We put types in italics in the subtitle of this section because we don't want to give the impression that these are somehow fixed categories into which all teens can straightforwardly be classified. As explained in Chapter 4, our worldview types are *implicit orientations* that teens have towards religious, spiritual and humanist beliefs, practices and ideas.

We used the types as a shorthand to convey persuasive patterns we found among the participants. Our six types are especially useful in thinking about young people beyond the categories of 'religious' or 'nonreligious' because such categories fail to apprehend the complex worldviews Australian teens express today. The types we have created and deployed illustrate some things that we already knew, for example, that some young people are Religiously Committed or Nominally Religious. Moving beyond this, we have demonstrated that a *majority* of young people in Australia do not fit into either of these two 'types'.

We have shown that Seekers are those most oriented towards the spiritual and metaphysical. Unlike their Spiritual but Not Religious peers, Seekers identify with a religious group. Together, these young people have a latent or active interest in an eclectic range of spiritual beliefs and associated practices and engage with these strictly on their terms.

Indifferent and This Worldly teens are two new categories specifically devised by our team to describe young people *outside* the language of 'nonreligious'. This is a descriptor that we wanted to avoid because it describes young people who express such views principally via a lack – their rejection of religion – rather than foregrounding how they encounter the world. At 23 per cent of all teens, the This Worldly type is the largest in our study. We found these young people stood apart from their peers because of the primacy of science in informing their worldview; for this group, science is the reliable source of knowledge and *meaning*. Not surprisingly, some teens didn't have a clear orientation; a significant finding in its own right. As with adults, some young people are fairly non-committal on the subject of belief; they are neither religious/spiritual, nor do they put their faith in science, and thus are genuinely Indifferent.

Stepping back, and placing these findings in the broader arc of recent social change, we suggest that Australian teens are emblematic of all the Anglosphere societies – places that are becoming less Christian, increasingly nonreligious *and* more religiously diverse. *Australia's Generation Z is the first-ever cohort who are more likely to have no religion than to affiliate with a religious group.* A small group of teens actively participate in the spiritual marketplace that expanded with the Boomers a few decades ago; a larger proportion agree they are 'spiritual but not religious'. Beyond that, a reasonable number nurture an interest in wellbeing practices, like yoga and meditation, which sit ambiguously in the terrain of the 'spiritual'. Some teens willingly call these activities 'spiritual', but many do not. Ideas and practices indebted to religion and spirituality circulate far more widely, but the bigger picture, and one captured by our types, is one of diversity and complexity.

There's religious diversity – *and religious discrimination hasn't gone away*

In early 2020, the Victorian state government decided to make education about the Holocaust, racism and prejudice compulsory in the curriculum of government-run secondary schools. This move happened in the same week as the Federal government reported a rising threat of neo-Nazi right-wing extremism. Our data are relatable to all of this. Teens are growing up differently to teens of previous generations: exposure to religious diversity is a part of teens' daily experience; teens are much more likely than previous generations to be mixing with peers who are from different religious backgrounds or with those who identify as having no religion. Put another way, Gen Z is less likely than previous generations to be Anglo-Australians or follow mainline Christian churches. We found that young people are immersed in diversity, but this isn't to say that discrimination based on religion is no longer an issue. We heard of instances of anti-Semitism, Islamophobia and other acts of religious discrimination. But Gen Z teens are significantly less likely than Australian adults to hold negative attitudes about different religions.

Teens don't like it when it seems religious people are impinging on the rights of others

Most Australian teens think that having people of many different religions makes Australia a better place to live, and they generally endorse the right of religious people to express their religion freely: about 90 per cent agreed that students should be allowed to wear religious clothes or jewellery to school. While they embrace diversity associated with religion, they are more cautious about religion when they perceive it as impinging on the rights of others. Half of Australia's teens think that people with very strong religious beliefs are often too intolerant of others; 34 per cent think that religion should have no place in our parliament or official ceremonies. This attitude was crystal clear on issues related to gender and sexual diversity. Most young people interviewed did not support religious exemptions or the right to discriminate against staff or students based on gender or sexual identity.

Getting educated about religion

Gen Z teens talked to us about their own and their peers' experiences of religious discrimination. Muslim and Jewish students in particular reported experiencing ongoing Islamophobia and anti-Semitism from their peers – on the street and at school. This is one of the most compelling arguments for raising the standard of education about religion in Australia's secondary schools. The existence of religious discrimination begs the question of where young people learn intolerance. If it is learned predominantly at home or online, can schools hope to counteract such forces? Alternatively, if young people are being exposed to discriminatory beliefs at home or in the media, the argument for such education at school is enhanced. Our research suggests that there is a positive correlation between education about diverse religions and more tolerance of religious and cultural difference. Hence, we argue for more thorough integration of GRE into the school curriculum.

However, making the case for education about religion is a 'hard sell'. First, religion is often associated in the public mind as a negative phenomenon. For example, online comments on media articles about our research frequently characterized any religious persons as superstitious, uneducated and uniformly intolerant of gender and sexual diversity. Second, schools are already dealing with a crowded curriculum, so religion is sidelined when placed alongside national priorities related to STEM and English. Third, even if GRE were to have greater prominence in schools, teacher education programs (except in Catholic universities) place little focus on religion, leaving prospective teachers ill-equipped to address education about religion. This gap has often been filled in primary schools by faith-based religious instruction, delivered in a voluntary capacity. We do not see this as the solution in primary or secondary schools. Our research makes a strong case for high school education about diverse worldviews, including the nonreligious, religious and spiritual, that is founded on *teens' ways of thinking and that matches their lived reality*. Importantly, this is an education that also doesn't see religious and sexual diversity as opposed.

Ideally, the question of how best to promote tolerance through education about religion and belief needs to be addressed at the level of government. Most importantly, teens need to be a part of the conversation regarding what provision looks like – how it is delivered, when, by whom and whether or not it should be compulsory. Many certainly want more diverse worldviews education, covering a wide range of perspectives and taught by qualified teachers.

But there is some disagreement among the authors of this book about how much education can play a part in fostering tolerance: there remains the question of whether education about diverse religions and beliefs can ameliorate religious discrimination *if other sources of disadvantage are not addressed concurrently*. We raise this question because our study found that teens who live in more socio-economically disadvantaged areas tend to have negative or neutral attitudes towards people who are followers of minority faiths. This is not surprising as higher individual income and educational attainment are positively correlated with tolerance, and disparity in income and experience of disadvantage are associated with a higher level of intolerance. From this perspective, if Australia remains an unequal society, we predict that intolerance will continue to thrive. Better education can counteract this, and not only in the domain of religion and spirituality. Therefore, as well as the integration of GRE into the curriculum, Australian education needs to be reformed so that it is equal for all and therefore less likely to leave young people feeling disenfranchised and susceptible to religious intolerance.[1]

Getting educated about gender and sexuality

As with education about religion, what young people learn about LGBTQI+ issues in the formal curriculum doesn't necessarily translate across school cultures. Young people also learn about discrimination and support for sexual and gender diversity through informal school cultures in the playground, classroom and at formal school events (dances, camps, sport). This is apparent in the recent, widely reported misogynistic chants of boys from an elite Victorian independent school.[2] Quite likely most of these young men would think of themselves as worldly and accepting of sexual and gender difference and supportive of gender equality. But informal school cultures frequently counteract the formal curriculum, and, just like in the broader community, young people's behaviour and education are not always consistent. So young people might receive education about sexual and gender equality, assimilate it and still engage in homophobic and misogynistic chants, or worry about openly expressing their sexual or gender identity at school.

All this being said, young people demand the right to learn about sexuality and gender in the curriculum; this reflects their everyday reality. Overall, the vast majority of teens – over 80 per cent – want schools to be places where it is not assumed that everybody is straight; they want to learn about gender and sexual diversity at school. (A minority of the teens who we classed as Religiously

Committed were the exception to this rule.) Young people told us that sexuality education doesn't sufficiently incorporate lessons about LGBTQI+ students. *Across all school types – state, religious and independent – they want this to change.* As per our advocacy of education about diverse religions, this underpins our strong support for school-based education that is inclusive of gender and sexual diversity – in the curriculum and within cultures of schooling. Most young people we interviewed strongly rejected attempts to legislate for the freedom of schools, on religious grounds, to discriminate against staff or students based on sexual and gender identity. They saw this as being at odds with the vast majority of teens' embrace of sexual and gender diversity.

Implications for and applications in future research

At the start of this book we noted that in the past three decades, there have been several major national-level or large-scale research projects on the religious and spiritual lives of teenagers throughout the Anglosphere. We drew gratefully on this research, particularly when it came to devising our worldview typology and how we might ask questions about attitudes to religious diversity. Like our counterparts in England and Wales, we found that teens who have close experience of religious diversity appreciate this aspect of their lives and tend to get along with each other. Our research confirms European findings of the benefits of inclusive, non-doctrinal education about religious and nonreligious worldviews.

We were fortunate to be able to build on a previous Australian survey of teens and our data show the benefits of repeated cross-sectional research in tracking shifting patterns of belief and practice, particularly the growth of Nones and the steady, but not increasing, belief in reincarnation, astrology and ghosts. Given how similar Australia is to places like Canada, New Zealand and Great Britain (even American youth), such findings should be instructive. We'd be curious to know how widespread the interest in yoga, meditation and wellbeing has become in these places and what meaning these activities have for young people. Our study, with a discrete focus on generational differences, suggests that this remains one of the best ways to explore patterns of religious change. British scholars have led the way in this kind of analysis and our Australian data confirm their findings, though we were able to show how rapid the pace of change has been, particularly the move away from Christian affiliation. The idea of Western societies representing 'religious complexity' was also born out in our analysis, and we have added to the evidence base explaining the causes of Christian decline and other shifts in religious affiliation, belief and practice.

A talking point at international conferences where we presented our worldview types was how this provides a nuanced way of making sense of the 'religious Nones'. Thinking of the Nones as spiritual but not religious, this-worldly or indifferent will hopefully prove a helpful advance in the burgeoning sociological study of non-religion. We are not the only ones attempting this task (as we noted in Chapter 6, we adopted the 'indifferent' label from a US study, one we heard about at a conference).[3] However, our approach shows the benefits of using a bespoke survey, latent-class analysis and in-depth interviews to explore types of no religion. Our research also highlights the value of exploring the connection between religion and sexuality and gender.

Taking the lead from Gen Z

Our work is predicated on the common-sense assumption that is valuable to know how young people are thinking about religious and other worldviews, and our findings reflect the complexities of the ways young Australians think about the world. It also explores, for the first time, a connection between religion, gender and sexuality, and how young people imagine the world around them. The AGZ project demonstrates that religion and belief, and gender and sexuality, are entangled in young people's lives.

Taking the pulse of teens' worldviews provides an opportunity for people working with this age group, within and outside schools, to tailor programs and curricula that better reflect the complexity and interests of this group. Already, young people are taking matters into their own hands. Gen Z is social media savvy and they are educating peers and the broader community about issues that matter to them. Education is now, more than ever, no longer a top-down affair.

As we completed this study, contentious questions of religious freedom continue to circulate as we await legislative reform from the incumbent government. Faith-based providers continue to argue the need to discriminate based on gender and sexual identity. The same providers assure the general public that they rarely, if ever, use such exemptions and that retaining them is ultimately about preserving the ethos of faith-based schools. The majority of young people we interviewed strongly opposed these religious exemptions. Young people want schools where they can feel safe regardless of how they identify and believe schools should not have the freedom to discriminate against teachers, parents or students based on gender, sex and sexuality. On this issue, we believe schools and the government need to listen to young people and follow their lead.

The AGZ study was the first of its kind in Australia and it should not be the last. Our study has been the subject of intense media interest – people are keen to know about how young people are developing attitudes and beliefs. This project demonstrates the importance of continuing to probe in this area. There needs to be funding for further robust research that can periodically take note of how young Australians' worldviews are developing and changing over time.

We hope readers will share and argue about these findings with young people they know, to provide a greater understanding of their complex worldviews and the issues confronting them and our broader society.

Appendix 1

2017 'Australia's Generation Z' national survey sample characteristics (unweighted)

Appendix Table 1: AGZ Survey 2017 characteristics: Age, gender, sexual orientation, Indigenous status, place of birth, parental place of birth, school type, study status, school year level, state of residence (n = 1200)

Category	Characteristic	Count	% of sample (n = 1200)
Age of respondent	13–15	518	43
	16–17	416	35
	18	266	22
Gender identification	Female	584	49
	Male	598	50
	Non-binary	15	1
Sexual orientation	Straight – Heterosexual	1031	86
	Gay/Lesbian/Bisexual/Questioning/Queer	160	13
	Don't know/can't say	12	1
Aboriginal or Torres Strait Islander background	Yes	57	5
	No	1123	94
	Don't know	20	2
Place of birth	Australia	1008	84
	Overseas	192	16
Mother's place of birth	Australia	785	65
	Overseas	410	34
Father's place of birth	Australia	782	65
	Overseas	398	33
	Not applicable/no male caregiver	13	1

Category	Characteristic	Count	% of sample (n = 1200)
School type (attends, or attended)	Catholic	250	21
	Independent	290	24
	Government	647	54
Current schooling/ education status (at time of survey)	Secondary school (up to and including Year 12)	963	80
	A tertiary institution (e.g. Uni, TAFE, etc.)	96	8
	Not attending an educational institution	141	12
Which year of schooling are you currently enrolled? (*Only those currently attending school*)	Year 7	89	9
	Year 8	165	17
	Year 9	183	19
	Year 10	176	18
	Year 11	153	16
	Year 12	194	20
State of residence	NSW	338	28
	VIC	344	29
	QLD	213	18
	SA	89	7
	WA	135	11
	TAS	32	3
	NT	12	1
	ACT	37	3

Source: AGZ Survey 2017.

Note: Proportions in the table may not add to 100 because of rounding, or because small proportions of 'Don't know' and 'No answer' responses have been omitted to simplify the table.

The survey questionnaire, a technical report and the data file are available at the Australian Data Archive: https://dataverse.ada.edu.au/.

(Search for it using the terms: Australia's Generation Z survey; or AGZ Survey)

Appendix 2

Correlates of membership in the worldview types

In Chapters 4–6, we discussed the sociocultural factors that are independently associated with membership of one worldview type or another. For example, in Chapter 6, we noted that males are twice as likely as females to be This Worldly, even after controlling for the effect of age, type of school attended, parental religion, parental place of birth and socio-economic status. This estimate was calculated using binary logistic regression, a statistical procedure which considers many variables at the same time and establishes which factors are distinct, significant 'predictors' of membership in any given worldview type. We chose these particular factors because previous research on teen religion and spirituality has shown them to be important sources of social influence in a teen's life (see Chapter 4). Our statistical procedure doesn't explain everything about why someone is This Worldly, or Religiously Committed (e.g. individual psychology; response to life events), but it does provide important clues about teen identity formation.

Space does not allow us to present all of the statistical output from our data analysis, so instead we have created a summary and presented this in Appendix Table 2. This table shows the relationship between the six spirituality types and the primary demographic variables that underpinned the multivariate analysis.

We have highlighted in bold font where one type varies notably from another type on any given sociocultural characteristic (there are others of note in any given row, but we have highlighted differences that are particularly meaningful). For example, in the **gender variable**, and the row for males, we can see that 66 per cent of This Worldly teens were male, compared to just 32 per cent of Seeker teens. Looking below, to the **age variable**, and the row for those aged 18, we can see that 30 per cent of the Seeker teens are aged 18, compared to 15 per cent of the Religiously Committed teens.

Appendix Table 2: Australians 13–18: Mean values or proportions for various demographic factors by worldview type (weighted)

		Worldview type (%)						Total for all teens (13–18)
		This Worldly	Indifferent	SBNR	Seekers	Nominally Religious	Religiously Committed	
SOCIO-DEMOGRAPHIC INDICATORS								
Gender	Male	66	44	44	32	55	50	51
	Female	34	56	56	66	45	50	48
Age	13–15	40	40	52	46	59	56	49
	16–17*	37	40	30	25	24	29	31
	18	23	20	18	30	17	15	20
School type	Catholic	13	22	11	42	33	23	22
	Independent	24	19	13	15	31	37	24
	Government	61	58	76	42	35	39	53
Parents' place of birth	Both born in Australia	63	60	62	44	56	43	56
	One born O/S*	23	19	23	19	16	16	19
	Both O/S	14	21	14	36	26	41	23
Religious ID	None	96	84	91	7	2	0	52
	Catholic	1	7	3	46	46	26	19
	Mainline Protestant	0	4	2	16	19	16	9

	Worldview type (%)						
Other Christian (i.e. Pentecostal)	0	1	0	11	17	42	11
Buddhist, Hindu, Jewish, Muslim, Sikh	2	2	1	19	13	13	7
Parental Religion							
Neither parent religious	58	43	53	11	11	5	33
One parent religious	25	25	30	34	23	9	24
Both parents religious	13	25	12	52	62	84	39
	Mean Value						
SEIFA average (1–5, with 5 the highest SEO status)	3.44	3.41	3.23	3.14	3.46	3.20	3.34

Source: AGZ Survey 2017.

Note: Proportions in the table may not add to 100 because of rounding, or because small proportions of 'Don't know' and 'No answer' responses have been omitted to simplify the table.

* None of the differences in this row are large enough to be statistically significant at the 0.05 level.

**SEIFA: Socio-Economic Index for Areas is an Australian Bureau of Statistic metric that scores postcodes in Australia according to relative socio-economic advantage.

Notes

1 The future makers: Teens in the age of diversity

1 There was a considerable media presence at Lakemba Mosque. This and similar photos of these scenes were circulated widely in the media. The image we are using was taken by Lisa Maree Williams.
2 Australian Curriculum, Assessment and Reporting Authority, 'Punchbowl High School, Punchbowl, NSW', My School. Available online: https://www.myschool.edu.au/school/41559/profile/2018 (accessed 6 May 2020).
3 Australian Bureau of Statistics, 'Punchbowl (Canterbury-Bankstown – NSW)', 2016 Census Quickstats. Available online: https://quickstats.censusdata.abs.gov.au/census_services/getproduct/census/2016/quickstat/SSC13273 (accessed 6 May 2020).
4 Gary D. Bouma, *Australian Soul: Religion and Spirituality in the 21st Century* (Melbourne: Cambridge University Press, 2006); Andrew Singleton, *Religion, Culture and Society: A Global Approach* (London: Sage, 2014).
5 Andriana Ramic et al., '900 Voices from Gen Z, America's Most Diverse Generation', *New York Times*. Available online: https://www.nytimes.com/interactive/2019/us/generation-z.html (accessed 16 May 2019).
6 Michael Mohammed Ahmad, 'Lebs Let Loose in Punchbowl "Prison"', *The Australian*. Available online: https://www.theaustralian.com.au/nation/inquirer/lebanese-on-the-loose-in-punchbowl-boys-high-school-prison/news-story/ac963cbf0f59c3c46ec6610effe484a0 (accessed 10 March 2017).
7 John Lyons et al., 'Inside Punchbowl Boys' High School: A battle for Hearts and Minds', *The Australian*. Available online: https://www.theaustralian.com.au/nation/education/inside-punchbowl-boys-high-school-a-battle-for-hearts-and-minds/news-story/f7145bf107c711647f2e1165fc84aa00 (accessed 10 March 2017).
8 Shandon Harris-Hogan and Kate Barrelle, 'Young Blood: Understanding the Emergence of a New Cohort of Australian Jihadists', *Terrorism and Political Violence* 32, no. 7 (2020): 1391–412, doi: 10.1080/09546553.2018.1473858.
9 These topics have not been explored much internationally either. In the UK, an important study of young adults is: Andrew Kam-Tuck Yip and Sarah-Jane Page, *Religious and Sexual Identities: A Multi-Faith Exploration of Young Adults* (Farnham: Ashgate, 2013). In the United States: Mark Regnerus, *Forbidden*

Fruit: Sex and Religion in the Lives of American Teenagers (New York: Oxford University Press, 2007).
10 This weighting simply reflects the balance of the team's research interests.
11 Meredith E. Coles et al., 'Adolescent Mental Health Literacy: Young People's Knowledge of Depression and Social Anxiety Disorder', *Journal of Adolescent Health* 58, no. 1 (2016): 57–62; Donna Cross et al., 'Longitudinal Impact of the Cyber Friendly Schools program on adolescents' cyberbullying behaviour', *Aggressive Behaviour* 42, no. 2 (2016): 166–81; Anita Harris, 'Belonging and the Uses of Difference: Young people in Australian Urban Multi-Culture', *Social Identities* 22, no. 4 (2016): 359–75; Tina Lam et al., 'Most Recent Risky Drinking Session with Australian Teenagers', *Aust NZ J Public* Health 41, no. 1 (2017): 105–10; Christopher M. Fisher and Sylvia Kauer, *National Survey of Australian Secondary Students and Sexual Health 1992-2018: Trends Over Time, (ARCSHS Monograph Series No. 118)* (Bundoora: Australian Research Centre in Sex, Health & Society, La Trobe University, 2019).
12 AIATSIS, 'Celebrating 2019 International Year of Indigenous Languages'. Available online: https://aiatsis.gov.au/whats-new/events/2019-international-year-indigenous-languages (accessed 18 November 2020).
13 Gary D. Bouma and Anna Halahoff, 'Australia's Changing Religious Profile – Rising Nones and Pentecostals, Declining British Protestants in Superdiversity: Views from the 2016 Census', *Journal for the Academic Study of Religion* 30, no. 2 (2017): 130.
14 Ibid., 130.
15 Russell King et al., *The Human Atlas of Migration* (Brighton: Earthscan, 2010).
16 Australian Bureau of Statistics, *Census of Population and Housing: Reflecting Australia – Stories from the Census, 2016*, Cat no. 2071.0 (Canberra: Australian Bureau of Statistics, 2016).
17 Ibid.
18 Singleton, *Religion, Culture and Society*, 92.
19 Australian Bureau of Statistics, *Census of Population and Housing*.
20 Bouma, *Australian Soul*.
21 Andrew Singleton, 'Strong Church or Niche Market? The Demography of the Pentecostal Church in Australia', in *Australian Pentecostal and Charismatic Movements: Arguments from the Margins*, ed. Christina Rocha et al. (Leiden: Brill, 2020), 99.
22 Singleton, *Religion, Culture and Society*.
23 Fisher and Kauer, *National Survey*.
24 Ibid., 2.
25 Michael Hogan, *The Sectarian Strand: Religion in Australian History* (Ringwood, Vic: Penguin, 1987).

26 Essential Media Communications, 'The Essential Report 25 March 2019'. Available online: https://www.essentialvision.com.au/wpcontent/uploads/2019/03/Essential-Report-250319-D2.pdf (accessed 7 May 2020).
27 Kevin Dunn et al., *The Resilience and Ordinariness of Australian Muslims: Attitudes and Experiences of Muslims Report* (Penrith: Western Sydney University and Islamic Sciences and Research Academy of Australia, 2015).
28 Nicola Madge et al., *Youth on Religion: Youth on Religion: The Development, Negotiation and Impact of Faith and Non-Faith* Identity (London: Routledge, 2014); Elizabeth Arweck (ed.), *Young People's Attitudes to Religious* Diversity (London: Routledge, 2016a).
29 Ibid., 213.
30 Robert Wuthnow, *After the Baby Boomers: How Twenty- and Thirty-Somethings Are Shaping the Future of American Religion* (New York: Oxford University Press, 2007); Tim Clydesdale and Kathleen Garces-Foley, *The Twentysomething Soul: Understanding the Religious and Secular Lives of American Young Adults* (New York: Oxford University Press, 2019).
31 Christian Smith and Melissa Lundquist Denton, *Soul Searching: The Religious and Spiritual Lives of Teenagers* (New York: Oxford University Press, 2005); Lisa Pearce and Melissa Lundquist Denton, *A Faith of Their Own: Stability and Change in the Religiosity of America's Adolescents* (New York: Oxford University Press, 2011).
32 Mandy Robbins and Lesley Francis, 'The Teenage Religion and Values Survey in England and Wales,' in *Religion and Youth*, ed. Sylvia Collins-Mayo and Pink Dandelion (Farnham: Ashgate, 2010), 47–54; Syvlia Collins-Mayo et al., *The Faith of Generation Y*, (London: Church House Publishing, 2010); Madge et al., *Youth on Religion*.
33 Michael Mason et al., *The Spirit of Generation Y: Young People's Spirituality in a Changing Australia* (Mulgrave: John Garratt Publishing, 2007); Reginald W. Bibby, *Emerging Millenials: How Canada's Newest Generation Is Responding to Change and Choice* (Lethbridge, Project Canada Books, 2009).
34 Collins-Mayo and Dandelion, *Religion and Youth*.
35 Linda Woodhead, 'The Rise of "No Religion": Towards an Explanation', *Sociology of Religion* 78, no. 3 (2017): 34.
36 Inger Furseth, 'Secularization, Deprivatization, or Religious Complexity?', in *Religious Complexity in the Public Sphere: Comparing Nordic Countries*, ed. Inger Furseth (Cham: Palgrave, 2018), 291–312.
37 See, e.g., David Hall (ed.), *Lived Religion in America: Toward a History of Practice* (Princeton, NJ: Princeton University Press, 1997); and Meredith B. McGuire, *Lived Religion: Faith and Practice in Everyday Life* (New York: Oxford University Press, 2008).

38 Line Nyhagen, 'The Lived Religion Approach in the Sociology of Religion and its Implications for Secular Feminist Analyses of Religion', *Social Compass* 64, no. 4 (2017): 495.

39 Australian Bureau of Statistics, *Schools, Australia, 2017*, Cat no. 2071.0 (Canberra: Australian Bureau of Statistics, 2017b).

40 Anna Halafoff, 'Special Religious Instruction and Worldviews Education in Victoria's Schools: Social Inclusion, Citizenship and Countering Extremism', *Journal of Intercultural Studies* 36, no. 3 (2015): 362–79; Robert Jackson, *'Signposts': Policy and Practice for Teaching about Religions and Non-Religious Worldviews in Intercultural Education* (Strasbourg: Council of Europe Publishing, 2014); Stephen Prothero, *Religious Literacy: What Every American Needs to Know – and Doesn't* (New York: HarperOne, 2007); Stephen Prothero and Lauren R. Kerby, 'The Irony of Religious Literacy in the USA', in *Religious Literacy in Policy and Practice*, ed. Adam Dinham and Matthew Francis (Bristol: Policy Press, 2015), 55–76; Adam Dinham and Matthew Francis (eds), *Religious Literacy in Policy and Practice* (Bristol: Policy Press, 2015).

41 Victorian Curriculum and Assessment Authority (VCAA), 'About the Humanities'. Available online: https://victoriancurriculum.vcaa.vic.edu.au/the-humanities/introduction/about-the-humanities (accessed 7 May 2020); VCAA, 'Learning about World Views and Religions'. Available online: https://victoriancurriculum.vcaa.vic.edu.au/static/docs/Learning%20about%20World%20Views%20and%20Religions.pdf (accessed 7 May 2020); VCAA, 'Learning in Ethical Capability'. Available online: https://victoriancurriculum.vcaa.vic.edu.au/ethical-capability/introduction/learning-in-ethical-capability (accessed 7 May 2020).

42 Barbara Baird, 'Child Politics, Feminist Analyses', *Australian Feminist Studies*, 23, no. 7 (2008): 291–305.

43 cf. Mason et al., *The Spirit of Generation Y*.

44 McCrindle Research, 'Gen Z/Alpha Infographic'. Available online: https://generationz.com.au/wp-content/uploads/2018/09/GenZGenAlpha.pdf (accessed 7 May 2020).

45 Michael Dimock, 'Defining Generations: Where Millennials End and Generation Z Begins', Pew Research Center, 17 January 2019. Available online: https://www.pewresearch.org/fact-tank/2019/01/17/where-millennials-end-and-generation-z-begins/ (accessed 7 May 2020).

46 Norman B. Ryder, 'The Cohort as a Concept in the Study of Social Change', *American Sociological Review* 30, no. 6 (1965): 843–61; Philip Schwadel, 'Period and Cohort Effects on Religious Nonaffiliation and Religious Disaffiliation: A Research Note', *Journal for the Scientific Study of Religion* 4, no. 2 (2010): 310–19.

47 Millennials are sometimes referred to as 'Generation Y', including in a major previous research project that informed this book (see Mason et al., *The Spirit of*

Generation Y). Because the name 'Millennials' is now used more widely, we will do so as well.

48 See Madge et al., *Youth on Religion*; Lesley J. Francis et al., 'Christian Affiliation, Christian Practice, and Attitudes to Religious Diversity: A Quantitative Analysis Among 13- to 15-year-old Female Students in the UK', *Journal of Contemporary Religion* 30, no. 2 (2015): 249–63; Arweck, *Young People's Attitudes*. We are particularly grateful to the *Young People's Attitudes to Religious Diversity* team (Warwick University) who graciously shared their survey instrument with us. Given the different survey modes (paper vs phone) we did not ask the same questions, but their approach was very helpful in guiding our survey design.
49 See Smith and Denton, *Soul Searching*; Mason et al., *The Spirit of Generation Y*.

2 Doing away with our Sunday best: Teenagers and the remaking of religion in Australia

1 David Aidone, 'Generation Z and Religion: Australia's Youths Turning their Back on God, Seeking Spirituality', *Daily Telegraph*, 24 December 2018. Available online: https://www.dailytelegraph.com.au/lifestyle/parenting/generation-z-and-religion-australias-youths-turning-their-back-on-god-seeking-spirituality/news-story/55dcd346f38bbc2f3feff737c64feb28?utm_campaign=EditorialSF&utm_content=SocialFlow&utm_medium=Twitter&utm_source=DailyTelegraph (accessed 8 May 2020); Lisa Murray, 'Fresh Answers to Old Questions', *Australian Financial Review*, 6 October 2018.
2 Ruth Powell et al., 'An Ageing Church, but Not Everywhere,' NCLS Research. Available online: https://www.ncls.org.au/ageing-church (accessed 13 March 2019).
3 Todd Johnson and Brian Grim, *The World's Religion in Figures: An Introduction to International Religious Demography* (Chichester: Wiley-Blackwell, 2013).
4 Randall J. Stephens, *The Devil's Music: How Christians Inspired, Condemned, and Embraced Rock 'n' Roll* (Cambridge, MA: Harvard University Press, 2018).
5 Singleton, 'Strong Church or Niche Market?'
6 Mason et al., *The Spirit of Generation Y*.
7 Bouma, *Australian Soul*; Hans Mol, *Religion in Australia: A Sociological Investigation* (Melbourne: Nelson, 1971); Andrew Singleton, 'Beyond Faith? Recent Trends in Religion and Spirituality among Teenagers', in *Re-Enchanting Education and Spiritual Wellbeing Fostering Belonging and Meaning-Making for Global Citizens*, ed. Marian de Souza and Anna Halafoff (New York: Routledge, 2017a), 23–35.
8 Billy Graham, 'Billy Graham Classic Crusades – Truth (1959)', YouTube, 30 December 2017. Available online: https://www.youtube.com/watch?v=ihIMWMZ-5AU (accessed May 16, 2019).

9. Judith Smart, 'The Evangelist as Star: The Billy Graham Crusade in Australia, 1959', *Journal of Popular Culture* 33, no. 1 (1999): 165–75.
10. Ibid.
11. David Hilliard, 'The Religious Crisis of the 1960s: The Experience of the Australian Church', *Journal of Religious History* 21, no. 2 (1997): 209–27.
12. See Jeffrey Jensen Arnett, 'Emerging Adulthood: A Theory of Development from the Late Teens through the Twenties', *American Psychologist* 55 (2000): 469–80; Smith and Denton, *Soul Searching*.
13. Michele Dillon and Paul Wink, *In the Course of a Lifetime: Tracing Religious Belief, Practice, and Change* (Berkeley: University of California Press, 2007).
14. See Peter Kaldor et al., *Build My Church: Trends and Possibilities for Australian Churches* (Adelaide: Openbook, 1999); Singleton, 'Strong Church or Niche Market?'
15. Bouma, *Australian Soul*; Singleton, *Religion, Culture and Society*.
16. Simon Brauer, 'The Surprising Predictable Decline of Religion in the United States', *Journal for the Scientific Study of Religion* 57, no. 4 (2018): 654–75; Alasdair Crockett and David Voas, 'Generations of Decline: Religious Change in 20th-century Britain,' *Journal for the Scientific Study of Religion* 45, no. 4 (2006): 567–84; Singleton, *Religion, Culture and Society*.
17. We calculated these percentages using 2016 ABS Census data. The age groups comprising each generation are shown in Table 1.1.
18. In a groundbreaking and highly influential paper, sociologist Norman Ryder ('The Cohort as a Concept') argued that birth cohorts are subject to socialization processes specific to their historic era. Looking at religion specifically, British sociologists Alasdair Crockett and David Voas, writing about Great Britain, argue: 'The fact that birth cohorts seem to be of far greater significance than either period or age … in accounting for levels of religiosity suggests that experience in childhood and adolescence is crucial' ('Generations of Decline', 577).
19. Hogan, *The Sectarian Strand*.
20. See Singleton, 'Beyond Faith?'.
21. Callum Brown, *Religion and the Demographic Revolution: Women and Secularisation in Canada, Ireland, UK and USA since the 1960s* (Woodbridge: Boydell Press, 2012), 30.
22. See Andrew Singleton, 'The Summer of the Spirits: Spiritual Tourism to America's Foremost Village of Spirit Mediums', *Annals of Tourism Research* 67 (2017): 48–57.
23. Christel Manning, *Losing Our Religion: How Unaffiliated Parents Are Raising Their Children* (New York: New York University Press, 2015).
24. Of the 46 per cent of Australian teens who identify with a religion, 8 per cent identify with a second religion (which is 3.8 per cent of the total teen population).

With so few teens in the sample claiming to identify with two religious traditions, it is not possible to identify any reliable patterns in these estimates.

25 The AGZ survey can meaningfully be compared to the Australian Census, which was conducted approximately a year before our data were collected. There are some differences if the same cohorts are compared – that is 12–17-year-olds from the 2016 census and 13–18-year-olds in our survey. We find a higher proportion are Nones (52 per cent cf. 31 per cent in the Census) and a lower proportion are Catholic (26 per cent cf. 19 per cent) or other Christian (27 per cent cf. 20 per cent). In the earlier study of Millennial spirituality – the SGY project – those researchers found *almost exactly* the same kind of discrepancies between their survey and the ABS Census. In that study, the researchers argued that it is usually the parent or guardian who completes the Census and the teen will usually have a religious identity conferred on them by that person. A confidential phone survey, by contrast, affords teens the opportunity to speak for themselves. Further, the fact that both the SGY and AGZ surveys have the same discrepancies from the Census validates the external reliability of the survey as way of accurately gauging the religious identification of teenagers.

26 Grace Davie, 'From Obligation to Consumption: A Framework for Reflection in Northern Europe', *Political Theology* 6, no. 3 (2005): 281–301.

27 A note about 'BHJMS'. In most national surveys of religion in Anglophone countries, there are not enough followers of the Buddhist, Sikh, Jewish, Muslim or Hindu traditions to make for reliable statistical comparison. In the AGZ survey, for example, we had thirty-four Muslims, eighteen Buddhists, fourteen Hindus, two Sikhs and nine Jewish teens, plus ten who followed another religion (e.g. Wicca; Chinese folk religion, or something that they wouldn't say). For the tables in this chapter, we've grouped them together. What to call this group? Sometimes they are called 'other religions' – that is, something 'other' than Christian. This seems rather imperialistic so we use 'BHJMS'.

28 The differences between Catholic and Mainline Protestant teens are not statistically significant at the 0.05 level. In other words, there is a greater than 5 per cent chance that the observed difference in belief in God (66 per cent for Catholics and 73 per cent for mainline Protestants) is due to sampling error. See notes in Chapter 4 for a discussion about statistical significance.

29 Evangelical Christians and some other Christian groups place a strong emphasis on the infallibility of Scripture and a personal relationship with Jesus, and frequently avoid traditional Catholic sacraments and rituals (apart from communion). Most Pentecostal Christians are evangelical in their religious expression, although not all evangelicals are Pentecostals.

30 See Singleton, 'Beyond Faith?'.

31 Michael Bird, 'Franklin Graham Is Coming to Australia: Here's Why I Won't be Attending', *ABC Religion and Ethics*, last revised 23 July 2018. Available online: https://www.abc.net.au/religion/franklin-graham-is-coming-to-australia-heres-why-i-wont-be-atten/10214340 (accessed 10 April 2019); Barney Zwartz, 'Franklin Graham Walks in His Father's Footsteps - and Trump's Shadow', *Sydney Morning Herald*, 9 February 2019. Available online: https://www.smh.com.au/national/franklin-graham-walks-in-his-father-s-footsteps-and-trump-s-shadow-20190204-p50vj0.html (accessed 10 April 2019).

32 British sociologists Crocket and Voas ('Generations of Decline') suggest that this intergenerational drift is likely to affect all the major religious groups, not just Christians.

3 Mind, body and spirit: Teenagers and spirituality

1 See Wade C. Roof, *Spiritual Marketplace: Baby Boomers and the Remaking of American Religion* (Princeton, NJ: Princeton University Press, 1999); Paul Heelas and Linda Woodhead, *The Spiritual Revolution: Why Religion Is Giving Way to Spirituality* (Oxford: Blackwell, 2005); Christopher Partridge, *The Re-enchantment of the West: Volume 1 Alternative Spiritualities, Sacralization, Popular Culture and Occulture* (London: T&T Clark, 2004).

2 See Nancy Ammerman, *Sacred Stories, Spiritual Tribes: Finding Religion in Everyday Life* (New York: Oxford University Press, 2013).

3 Mason et al., *The Spirit of Generation Y*, 34.

4 Ibid., 35.

5 Singleton, 'The Summer of the Spirits', 51.

6 Ibid., 51.

7 See Roof, *Spiritual Marketplace*; Robert Wuthnow, *After the Baby Boomers*.

8 Mason et al., *The Spirit of Generation Y*, 180.

9 See Roof, *Spiritual Marketplace*.

10 See Heelas and Woodhead, *The Spiritual Revolution*; Paul Heelas, *Spiritualities of Life: New Age Romanticism and Consumptive Capitalism* (Oxford: Blackwell, 2008).

11 For a discussion of the American context, see Christopher D. Bader et al., *Paranormal America: Ghost Encounters, UFO Sightings, Bigfoot Hunts, and other Curiosities in Religion and Culture* (New York: New York University Press, 2017). These supernatural and mystical beliefs are often derided by the sceptical as 'woo' beliefs—see Sadri Hassani, '"Post-Materialist" Science? A Smokescreen for Woo', *Skeptical Inquirer* 39, no. 5 (2015): 123–7.

12 Rachel Carson's 1962 book, *Silent Spring*, was instrumental in raising Western consciousness about environmental issues. The 1979 book by James Lovelock, *Gaia: A New Look at Life on Earth* (Oxford: Oxford University Press, 1979), the 1986 Chernobyl nuclear disaster, the 1992 United Nations Conference on Environment and Development (also known as the Rio de Janeiro Earth Summit), and Al Gore's film *An Inconvenient Truth* have all furthered environmental activism. See Paul F. Knitter, *One Earth Many Religions: Multifaith Dialogue and Global Responsibility* (Maryknoll: Orbis Books, 1995); Laurel Kearns and Catherine Keller (eds.), *Ecospirit: Religions and Philosophies for the Earth* (New York: Fordham University Press, 2007); Anna Halafoff, *The Multifaith Movement: Global Risks and Cosmopolitan Solutions* (Dordrecht: Springer, 2013a).
13 See Halafoff, *The Multifaith Movement*.
14 See Rosemary Hancock, *Islamic Environmentalism: Activism in the United States and Great Britain* (London: Routledge, 2018).
15 See Anna Kirkland, 'What is Wellness Now?' *Journal of Health Politics, Policy and Law* 39, no. 5 (2014): 957–70.
16 E.g. see BerkeleyWellness.com; also, the podcast *The Dream*, season 2, www.stitcher.com/podcast/stitcher/the-dream (accessed 15 May 2020).
17 See Mark Singleton, 'Salvation through Relaxation: Proprioceptive Therapy and Its Relationship to Yoga', *Journal of Contemporary Religion* 20, no. 3 (2005): 289–304; Mark Singleton, *Yoga Body: The Origins of Modern Posture Practice* (London: Oxford University Press, 2010); Andrea R. Jain, *Selling Yoga: From Counterculture to Pop Culture* (Oxford: Oxford University Press, 2015).
18 Jon Kabat-Zinn, who pioneered secular mindfulness in the West, expresses caution about framing mindfulness as a spiritual practice, given its often vague and imprecise meaning. He notes: 'Perhaps, ultimately, spiritual simply means experiencing wholeness and interconnectedness directly, a seeing that individuality and the totality are interwoven, that nothing is separate or extraneous' (*Wherever You Go, There You Are* [London: Piatkus, 2004], 266).
19 Even the authors of this book disagree about the spiritual nature of these practices.
20 See Annette Hill, *Paranormal Media: Audiences, Spirits and Magic in Popular Culture* (London: Routledge, 2010).
21 cf. Karen Ager et al., 'Mindfulness in Schools Research Project: Exploring Students' Perspectives of Mindfulness: What Are Students' Perspectives of Learning Mindfulness Practices at School?' *Psychology* 6, no. 7 (2015): 896–914.
22 See Itai Ivtzan and Sivaja Jegatheeswaran, 'The Yoga Boom in Western Society: Practitioners' Spiritual vs. Physical Intentions and Their Impact on Psychological Wellbeing', *Yoga and Physical Therapy* 5, no. 3 (2014): 1–7; Jain, *Selling Yoga*, 2015; Cheah Whye Lian et al., 'Commitment and Motivation in Practicing Yoga among Adults in Kuching, Sarawak', *Indian Journal of Traditional Knowledge* 16 (Suppl) (June 2017): 81–7.

23 That project, 'Social Engagement in Spiritualism', is a collaboration with Matt Tomlinson (University of Oslo). Coincidently, Andrew wrote large parts of Chapter 7 of *this book* while conducting fieldwork at the historic American Spiritualist camps, Lily Dale, New York, and Camp Chesterfield, Indiana, in July 2019. Matt and Andrew sat in two dark séances at Lily Dale. Those in attendance were over the age of 40.

24 See Andrew Singleton, 'Beyond Heaven? Young People and the Afterlife', *Journal of Contemporary Religion* 27, no. 3 (2012): 453–68; Andrew Singleton, 'Seven Heavens? The Character and Importance of Afterlife Belief among Contemporary Australians', *Mortality* 21, no. 2 (2016): 167–84.

25 See Paul K. McClure, 'Faith and Facebook in a Pluralistic Age: The Effects of Social Networking Sites on the Religious Beliefs of Emerging Adults', *Sociological Perspectives* 59, no. 4 (2016): 818–34.

26 See Mason et al., *The Spirit of Generation Y*.

27 It is named the 'Hardy question', after biologist Sir Alistair Hardy who developed it. See Alistair Hardy, *The Spiritual Nature of Man: A Study of Contemporary Religious Experience* (Oxford: Clarendon Press, 1979), 20; David Hay, *Exploring Inner Space: Scientists and Religious Experience* (London: Continuum, 1982), 114.

28 See David Hay and Ann Morisy, 'Secular Society, Religious Meanings: A Contemporary Paradox', *Review of Religious Research* 26, no. 3 (March 1985): 213–27.

29 See Ammerman, *Sacred Stories, Spiritual Tribes*. In her study of American adults, Ammerman describes the importance of nature in many people's lived experience of spirituality, whether they identify as religious or not.

30 As the AGZ survey and interviews were conducted in 2017–18, this was before the School Climate Strike movement gained momentum.

31 The evidence base for this assertion is unclear – astrology has long been popular, as have all kinds of other 'alternatives'. Social researchers Mass Observation surveyed a London borough throughout the early 1940s and found that as many as 40–50 per cent of people believed in astrology at any given time, while Spiritualism has had many boom periods since the late 1800s. The 'Occult Craze' of the late 1970s is further evidence of the enduring appeal of the occult and paranormal. For the assertion about astrology, see Rebecca Nicholson, 'Star Gazing: Why Millennials Are Turning to Astrology', *The Guardian*, 11 March 2018. Available online: https://www.theguardian.com/global/2018/mar/11/star-gazing-why-millennials-are-turning-to-astrology?CMP=share_btn_link (accessed 12 March 2018).

32 See Roof, *Spiritual Marketplace*; Heelas and Woodhead, *The Spiritual Revolution*; Partridge, *The Re-enchantment of the West*.

33 Mason et al., *The Spirit of Generation Y*, 35.

34 Michael Lipka and Claire Gecewicz, 'More Americans Now Say They're Spiritual but Not Religious', Pew Research Center, 6 September 2017. Available online: https://www.pewresearch.org/fact-tank/2017/09/06/more-americans-now-say-theyre-spiritual-but-not-religious/ (accessed 7 September 2017).
35 Robert Wuthnow, *Inventing American Religion: Polls, Surveys and the Tenuous Quest for a Nation's Faith* (New York: Oxford University Press, 2015).

4 A personal point of view: Discovering teenage worldviews

1 See Mason et al., *The Spirit of Generation Y*.
2 Examples include Smith and Denton, *Soul Searching*; Pearce and Denton, *A Faith of Their Own*.
3 Mason et al., *The Spirit of Generation Y*, 171.
4 We prefer to refer to our model as a 'typology' rather than a 'taxonomy'. It is based on a conceptual model, and justified empirically, rather than being based solely on post-hoc empirical classification. For a technical discussion of the difference, see Kenneth D. Bailey, *Typologies and Taxonomies: An Introduction to Classification Techniques* (Thousand Oaks, CA: Sage, 1994).
5 A person-centred approach is different to 'variable-centred' statistical approaches, which map the scores, rank or grades that people have (e.g. IQ; weight; a wellbeing scale). With the variable-centred approach, people are treated as an item on a continuum that is measuring something else about them. For teens in Australia, the pre-eminent measurement of this kind is the Australian Tertiary Admission Rank (ATAR). Certainly, this is helpful in deciding who gets an offer to study medicine or sociology, but it tells us nothing of the clusters of disciplinary interest teens have, i.e. whether that is towards the humanities, sciences or social sciences. For a helpful discussion of latent-class statistical analysis (LCA) as a person-centred approach, see Linda M. Collins and Stephanie T. Lanza, *Latent Class and latent Transition Analysis: With Applications in the Social Behavioral, and Health Sciences* (New Jersey: Wiley, 2010); Pearce and Denton, *A Faith of Their Own*; Linda E. Pearce, E. Michael Foster and Jessica Halliday Hardie, 'A Person-Centred Examination of Adolescent Religiosity using Latent Class Analysis', *Journal for the Scientific Study of Religion* 52, no. 1 (2013): 57–79.
6 Technically speaking, Table 4.1 shows item response probabilities, i.e. the probabilities of each response for every variable, conditional on six latent classes.
7 See Hardy, *The Spiritual Nature of Man*; David Hay, *Exploring Inner Space: Scientists and Religious Experience* (London: Continuum, 1982).
8 See Hay and Morisy, 'Secular Society, Religious Meanings'.
9 See Singleton, 'Beyond Heaven?'.

10 See Mason et al., *The Spirit of Generation Y*.
11 A Bayesian estimate of model specificity had a p-value of 0.000.
12 Cf. Madge et al., *Youth on Religion*, which is a major study of teen religion in England.
13 'Significant': by this, we mean statistically significant, but we also mean 'socially significant'. Inferential statistical procedures of the kind used in this section calculate a p-value, and most social scientists zoom in on findings that are 'statistically significant' i.e. a p-value of less than 0.05 or 0.01. Such calculations determine the probability that an estimate is likely true of the population or likely due to sampling error. To declare that a finding is 'significant' at the 0.05 level means that there is a less than 5 per cent chance that the finding is due to sampling error and more than a 95 per cent chance it is likely true of the population being sampled, assuming a 100 per cent response rate of those asked to participate in the survey. *It does not actually mean the finding is true of the real world, interesting or even worth reporting.* But many scholars have missed that vital point. They hunt for the significant relationships in their data and assume that this finding is the final word. They ignore things like the strength, character and magnitude of relationships between variables, or biases in their survey (like non-response rates). Some researchers even calculate p-values on non-probability samples, which, technically and mathematically speaking, makes no sense. There are other substantive issues with p-values: they can be easily manipulated (called 'p-hacking') and are also subject to the vagaries of sample size. Our approach is to calculate statistical significance, think of what it means and then comment on the robust, important – significant – findings.
14 We have mainly used binary logistic regression, or in some instances, multinominal logistic regression.
15 A table that summarizes all of these relationships is presented in Appendix 2 of this book.
16 See Smith and Denton, *Soul Searching*; Mason et al., *The Spirit of Generation Y*; Ralph W. Hood Jr., Peter C. Hill and Bernard Spilka, *The Psychology of Religion: An Empirical Approach*, 4th edn (New York: The Guilford Press, 2009).
17 This phrase comes from Pearce and Denton's 2011 study of teen religion in America, *A Faith of Their Own*.
18 See Richard J. Petts, 'Trajectories of Religious Participation from Adolescence to Young Adulthood', *Journal for the Scientific Study of Religion* 48, no. 4 (2009): 552–71; Christian Smith and Patricia Snell, *Souls in Transition: The Religious and Spiritual Lives of Emerging Adults* (New York: Oxford University Press, 2009).
19 See Smith and Snell, *Souls in Transition*.
20 Mason et al., *The Spirit of Generation Y*, 165.
21 See Singleton, 'Strong Church or Niche Market?'.
22 For a helpful summary, see Hood et al., *The Psychology of Religion*.

5 'A higher order out there': Seekers and the spiritual but not religious

1 See, e.g., Ammerman's work on spiritual communities in *Sacred Stories, Spiritual Tribes*.
2 All the major studies of New Age and alternative spiritualities throughout the Anglosphere suggest that it is Boomers and Gen Xers who have driven this movement. See Robert Wuthnow, *After Heaven: Spirituality in America since the 1950s* (Berkeley: University of California Press, 1998); Heelas and Woodhead, *The Spiritual Revolution*; Mason et al., *The Spirit of Generation Y*; Ammerman, *Sacred Stories, Spiritual Tribes*.
3 See Wuthnow, *After Heaven*.
4 Mason et al., *The Spirit of Generation Y*, 197.
5 This point is discussed in Christian Smith et al., *Young Catholic America: Emerging Adults in, out of, and Gone from the Church* (New York: Oxford University Press, 2014).
6 Stuart Rose, 'Is the Term "Spirituality" a Word that Everyone Uses, but Nobody Knows What Anyone Means by it?' *Journal of Contemporary Religion* 16, no. 2 (2001): 193–207.
7 On this point, see Singleton, 'Salvation through Relaxation', and *Yoga Body*.
8 This was the finding from previous studies on these topics. See Mason et al., *The Spirit of Generation Y*; Singleton, 'Beyond Heaven?'; Singleton, 'Seven Heavens?'; Bader et al., *Paranormal America*.
9 See Guy Redden, 'Revisiting the Spiritual Supermarket: Does the Commodification of Spirituality Necessarily Devalue It?' *Culture and Religion* 17, no. 2 (2016): 231–49, for an excellent discussion of this point.
10 Yoga and meditation were not practices we included in the worldview types model.
11 Seekers and the 'spiritual marketplace' subset of SBNR teens are the ones most likely to have done yoga or meditation. There is certainly an association between these practices and these groups, but we can't state unambiguously how 'spirituality' figures in all of this. The Seeker and marketplace teens offered various answers when asked why they did these activities, and if they were thought of as 'spiritual'. The different points of view reflect the fact that spirituality is a highly personal construct. Complicating the picture is the gendered nature of these activities. Females are more likely than males to have practised yoga or meditation and to be members of the categories we have identified as more likely to do these practices. Age is also an important predictor of interest in these activities. These associations hold true when many potential influences are considered. We can say with confidence that age, gender *and* worldview type predict interest in these activities.

12 Cf. the earlier SGY study (Mason et al.). The qualitative evidence from that research suggests that spiritually eclectic teens, particularly those engaged in a range of spiritual practices, typically have one or both parents who are also interested in these kinds of things.

13 Studies in various Anglophone countries show that UFO belief is persistently more common among males than females. UFO belief is associated with anti-authoritarian conspiracy theories, and men tend to be drawn more to these than women. See Bader et al., *Paranormal America*; Clay Routledge et al., 'We Are Not Alone: The Meaning Motive, Religiosity, and Belief in Extra-Terrestrial Intelligence', *Motivation and Emotion* 41, no. 2 (2017): 135–46.

6 Immanent gods: This Worldly and Indifferent teens

1 Alain de Botton, *Religion for Atheists: A Non-Believer's Guide to the Uses of Religion* (New York: Pantheon Books, 2012).

2 Ibid., 2.

3 'Welcome' Sunday Assembly London Available online: https://sundayassembly.online/ (accessed 13 May 2020).

4 Faith Hill, 'They Tried to Start a Church without God. For a While, It Worked', *The Atlantic*, 21 July 2019. Available online: https://www.theatlantic.com/ideas/archive/2019/07/secular-churches-rethink-their-sales-pitch/594109/ (accessed 21 July 2019).

5 See Joseph O. Baker and Buster G. Smith, *American Secularism: Cultural Contours of Nonreligious Belief Systems* (New York: New York University Press, 2015).

6 See Jesse M. Smith and Ryan T. Cragun, 'Mapping Religion's Other: A Review of the Study of Nonreligion and Secularity', *Journal for the Scientific Study of Religion* 58, no. 2 (2019): 319–35.

7 E.g. Mason et al., *The Spirit of Generation Y*; Pearce and Denton, *A Faith of Their Own*; Madge et al., *Youth on Religion*.

8 Smith and Cragun, 'Mapping Religion's Other', 327.

9 American Atheists, 'What is Atheism?'. Available online: https://www.atheists.org/activism/resources/about-atheism/ (accessed 13 May 2020).

10 Armin W. Geertz and Guðmundur Ingi Markússon, 'Religion is Natural, Atheism is Not: On Why Everybody is Both Right and Wrong', *Religion* 40, no. 3 (2010): 153.

11 Singleton, *Religion, Culture and Society*, 201.

12 In 2006, 31,305 people wrote in the Australian Census that they were atheists (0.15 per cent of the population), rising to 58,899 in the 2011 (0.27 per cent of the population). By 2016, this had fallen to 32,298 people (0.13 per cent of the population).

13 See Elizabeth Arweck, '"I've Been Christened, but I Don't Really Believe in It": How Young People Articulate Their (Non-)Religious Identities and Perceptions of (Non-)Belief', in *Social Identities Between the Sacred and the Secular*, ed. Abby Day, Giselle Vincett and Christopher R. Cotter (London: Routledge, 2016b), 103–26; Rebecca Catto and Janet Eccles, 'Dis(Believing) and Belonging: Investigating the Narrative of Young British Atheists', *Temenos* 49, no. 2 (2013): 37–63.
14 See Appendix 2.
15 Manning, *Losing Our Religion*, 105.
16 While a lot has been written about this, the best recent summary is Brett Mercier et al., 'Belief in God: Why People Believe, and Why They Don't', *Current Directions in Psychological Science* 27, no. 4 (2018): 263–8.
17 See ibid.
18 See Hood et al., *The Psychology of Religion*.
19 See Penny Edgell et al., 'From Existential to Social Understandings of Risk: Examining Gender Differences in Nonreligion', *Social Currents* 4, no. 6 (2017): 556–74.
20 Musk's official name for the rocket is 'Big Falcon Rocket', pet name 'Big Fucking Rocket', which is how Noah describes it.
21 See Mason et al., *The Spirit of Generation Y*; Smith and Denton, *Soul Searching*, have found that peer influence is an important influence on teen religion.
22 Manning, *Losing Our Religion*, 34.
23 Ibid., 24.
24 Mercier et al., 'Belief in God', 265.

7 Awash but not adrift: Teen attitudes to religious diversity

1 Erin Pearson, 'Jewish Teens Racially Abused on Bus', *The Age*, 3 February 2019.
2 Adam Carey, 'Teen Charged with Threatening to Kill Bullied Jewish Student, Boy's Mum', *The Age*, 24 October 2019. Available online: https://www.theage.com.au/national/victoria/teen-charged-with-threatening-to-kill-bullied-jewish-student-boy-s-mum-20191024-p533wg.html (accessed 16 March 2020).
3 Given the time constraints with our survey, we could only ask respondents about their attitudes to the four largest religions in Australia, and no religion. As the example at the start of the chapter shows, we used the focus groups to explore the issue of anti-Semitism.
4 Andrew Markus, *Mapping Social Cohesion: The Scanlon Foundation Surveys 2018*. Available online: https://scanlonfoundation.org.au/wp-content/uploads/2018/12/Social-Cohesion-2018-report-26-Nov.pdf (accessed 20 May 2019), 62.

5   See Jan G. Janmaat and Avril Keating, 'Are Today's Youth More Tolerant? Trends in Tolerance among Young People in Britain', *Ethnicities* 19, no. 1 (2019): 44–65. We are not sure if this will change as they age for those we surveyed. There's some evidence to suggest that people do become more socially conservative with age: see James Tilley and Geoffrey Evans, 'Ageing and Generational Effects on Vote Choice: Combining Cross-sectional and Panel Data to Estimate APC Effects', *Electoral Studies* 33, no. 1 (2018): 19–27.

6   Markus, *Mapping Social Cohesion*, 7.

7   Cf. Courtney Kennedy et al., 'Are Telephone Polls Understating Support for Trump?', Pew Research Center, 31 March 2017. Available online: https://www.pewresearch.org/methods/2017/03/31/are-telephone-polls-understating-support-for-trump/ (accessed 12 December 2019).

8   Americans, for example, notoriously overestimate attendances at religious services. On this point, see C. Kirk Hadaway et al., 'What the Polls Don't Show: A Closer Look at U.S. Church Attendance', *American Sociological Review* 58, no. 6 (1993): 741–52.

9   See Scott Keeter et al., 'What Low Response Rates Mean for Telephone Surveys', Pew Research Center, 15 May 2017. Available online: https://www.pewresearch.org/methods/2017/05/15/what-low-response-rates-mean-for-telephone-surveys/ (accessed 12 December 2019).

10 Twenty per cent of teens have a 'neutral to negative' attitude towards minority religions: we did some data reduction (combining several individual measures into a single measure) to arrive at this estimate.

11 Joanne Simone-Davies, 'Population and Migration Statistics in Australia', Parliament of Australia, 7 December 2018. Available online: https://www.aph.gov.au/About_Parliament/Parliamentary_Departments/Parliamentary_Library/pubs/rp/rp1819/Quick_Guides/PopulationStatistics/ (accessed 15 January 2019).

12 According to our calculation of the 2016 ABS Census data, 3.8 per cent of Gen Zs identify as Muslim compared to 1.1 per cent of Baby Boomers.

13 See Janmaat and Keating, 'Are Today's Youth More Tolerant?'.

14 Department of the Prime Minister and Cabinet, Australian Government, *Religious Freedom Review: Report of the Expert Panel*, 18 May 2018. Available online: https://www.ag.gov.au/RightsAndProtections/HumanRights/Documents/religious-freedom-review-expert-panel-report-2018.pdf (accessed 15 January 2019).

15 Stephanie Corsetti, 'Bendigo Mosque Appeal Request Thrown Out by High Court', *ABC News*, 15 June 2016. Available online: https://www.abc.net.au/news/2016-06-15/bendigo-mosque-high-court-challenge/7511690 (accessed 16 May 2019).

16 Pauline Hanson's One Nation Party, 'Pauline Hanson Moves to Ban Burqa – Voted Down by Out of Touch Politicians', 13 September 2018. Available online: https://

www.onenation.org.au/pauline-hanson-moves-to-ban-burqa-voted-down-by-out-of-touch-politicians/ (accessed 16 May 2019).
17 Katherine Stewart and Caroline Fredrickson, 'Bill Barr Thinks America Is Going to Hell', *New York Times*, 29 December 2019. Available online: https://www.nytimes.com/2019/12/29/opinion/william-barr-trump.html (accessed 29 December 2019).
18 Using the statistical procedure known as factor analysis, we concluded that the five items included in Table 7.2 are measuring an underlying construct whereby people are variously supportive or not supportive of the right of religious groups to freely practise their religion. The Cronbach's alpha score for this scale was 0.70 (unweighted and rounded), which is adequate – scores above 0.70 are preferred.

8 Taking it to school: Worldviews and religious education

1 Marion Maddox, *God under Howard: The Rise of the Religious Right in Australian Politics* (Sydney: Allen and Unwin, 2005); Marion Maddox, *Taking God to School* (Sydney: Allen and Unwin, 2014); Anna Halafoff, 'UnAustralian Values' (paper presented at UNAustralia conference: Cultural Studies Association of Australasia annual conference, University of Canberra, Canberra, 4–6 December 2006); Anna Halafoff, 'Education about Religions and Beliefs in Victoria', *Journal for the Academic Study of Religion* 26, no. 2 (2013b): 172–97; Gary D. Bouma et al., *Managing the Impact of Global Crisis Events on Community Relations in Multicultural Australia: Part I (Background Report) and Part II (Community Relations Toolkit) for Victoria* (Melbourne: Monash University, 2007); Jackson, 'Signposts'; Prothero and Kerby, 'The Irony of Religious Literacy in the USA'; Francis and Dinham, *Religious Literacy in Policy and Practice*.
2 Victorian Department of Education and Training, 'School Policy on Special Religious Instruction'. https://www2.education.vic.gov.au/pal/special-religious-instruction/policy (accessed 22 April 2020).
3 For policies pertaining to specific jurisdictions, see: Government of Western Australia Department of Education, 'Special Religious Education (SRE)', last modified 22 September 2015. Available online: http://det.wa.edu.au/curriculumsupport/religiouseducation/detcms/navigation/special-religious-education/; New South Wales Government, 'Religion and Ethics', last modified 13 February 2020. Available online: https://education.nsw.gov.au/teaching-and-learning/curriculum/learning-across-the-curriculum/religion-and-ethics; Northern Territory Government Department of Education, 'Religious Instruction', last modified 10 July 2017. Available online: https://education.nt.gov.au/policies/religious-instruction; Tasmanian Government Department of Education, 'Religious

Instruction'. Available online: https://www.education.tas.gov.au/parents-carers/parent-fact-sheets/religious-instruction/ (all accessed 16 May 2019).
4. See Maddox, *Taking God to School*.
5. Victorian Department of Education and Training, 'School Policy'.
6. Ministerial Council on Education, Employment, Training and Youth Affairs, *Melbourne Declaration on Educational Goals for Young Australians*, December 2008. Available online: http://www.curriculum.edu.au/verve/_resources/National_Declaration_on_the_Educational_Goals_for_Young_Australians.pdf.
7. VCAA, 'About the Humanities'; VCAA, 'Learning about World Views and Religions'; VCAA, 'Learning in Ethical Capability'; Victorian Curriculum and Assessment Authority, *Victorian Certificate of Education Religion and Society Study Design*, 2006. Available online: https://www.vcaa.vic.edu.au/Documents/vce/religion/2017ReligionSocietySD.pdf; Queensland Curriculum and Assessment Authority, 'Religion and Ethics Applied Senior Syllabus 2019: Syllabus', last modified 16 January 2019. Available online: https://www.qcaa.qld.edu.au/senior/senior-subjects/humanities-social-sciences/religion-ethics/syllabus; School Curriculum and Standards Authority, 'Religion and Life'. Available online: https://senior-secondary.scsa.wa.edu.au/syllabus-and-support-materials/humanities-and-social-sciences/religion-and-life (accessed 16 May 2019).
8. Jackson, *'Signposts'*; Halafoff, 'Special Religious Instruction'.
9. Prothero, *Religious Literacy*.
10. A survey of Australian adults' knowledge of Islam asked participants (n = 613) five questions that tested their knowledge of Islam. Only a minority answered these three questions correctly: 'Is Jesus a revered Prophet in Islam?'; 'Is Islam an Abrahamic religion as are Judaism and Christianity?'; and 'Are the majority of Muslims Shia, Sufi or Sunni?'. Most respondents said they didn't know, or got the wrong answer. See Fethi Mansouri and Matteo Vergani, 'Intercultural Contact, Knowledge of Islam, and Prejudice against Muslims in Australia', *International Journal of Intercultural Relations* 66 (2018): 85–94.
11. Anna Halafoff and Enqi Weng, 'Religion on an Ordinary Day: Australia', in *An Ordinary Day: An International Study of Religion in the Media*, eds. David Michels and Mathilde Vanasse-Pelletier (forthcoming).
12. In the survey, we defined GRE as 'general education about religions, that is, lessons or information about the major religions of the world, like Islam, Christianity, Buddhism or Aboriginal religions'. This is distinct from Specific Religious Instruction (SRI), which we defined as 'specific religious education, that is, lessons on the beliefs and practices of [a particular faith]'. Depending on the kind of school the respondent attended, these questions were modified to be appropriate for that schooling context.

13 See, e.g., Jackson, *'Signposts'*.
14 Mansouri and Vergani found that among Australian adults, better factual knowledge of Islam is associated with more positive views of Muslims. See Mansouri and Vergani, 'Intercultural Contact'.

9 Harry Potter, homophobia and human rights: Teens talk about sexuality education, religious exemptions and gay rights

1 For a discussion of Prime Minister Morrison's tweet related to trans students, see Tyrone Butson, ' "Gender Whisperers": Scott Morrison Criticised for "Hateful" Tweet about Trans Students', *SBS News*, last modified 5 September 2018. Available online: https://www.sbs.com.au/news/gender-whisperers-scott-morrison-criticised-for-hateful-tweet-about-trans-students (accessed 5 September 2018).
2 See Department of the Prime Minister and Cabinet, Australian Government, 'Religious Freedom Review – Submissions'. Available online: https://www.pmc.gov.au/domestic-policy/religious-freedom-review/review-submissions (accessed 18 May 2020).
3 See Paul Karp, 'Scott Morrison Will Change the Law to Ban Religious Schools Expelling Gay Students', *The Guardian*, 13 October 2018. https://www.theguardian.com/australia-news/2018/oct/13/morrison-caves-to-labor-on-gay-students-in-discrimination-law-reform-push (accessed 13 October 2018).
4 For a detailed discussion of the survey methodology we used in relation to recruitment of participants please, see Mary Lou Rasmussen et al., 'Methodological Challenges of Designing a Survey to Capture Young People's (Non-binary) Affiliations in Relationship to Religion, Sexuality and Gender', *International Journal of Social Research Methodology* 23, no. 6 (May 2020): 695–709.
5 For example, the question in the survey on sexual identity was asked by the telephone interviewer in this way: 'The next question is about your sexual identity. If you would prefer, please just say the number before each option I read out. [Please remember your answers are strictly confidential] Do you think of yourself as? One, Straight, that is heterosexual; Two, Lesbian/Homosexual/Gay; Three, Bisexual; Four, Questioning; Five, Queer; Something else – SPECIFY?'.
6 Tom Wilson and Fiona Shalley, 'Estimates of Australia's Non-heterosexual Population', *Australian Population Studies* 2, no. 1 (2018): 26–38. Their estimates are based on the Census and two large-scale national surveys. It should be noted that the two surveys asked the question about sexual identity differently to us.
7 Ibid.

8   This term relates to those aspects of the curriculum which schools do not teach, as well as affective, economic and political elements of schooling. The term is generally attributed to Phillip W. Jackson, *Life in Classrooms* (New York: Holt, Rinehart and Winston, 1968).
9   For a discussion of this issue, see Anna Hickey-Moody, 'Youth Agency and Adult Influence: A Critical Revision of Little publics', *Review of Education, Pedagogy and Cultural Studies* 38, no. 1 (2016): 58–72.
10 Butson, '"Gender Whisperers".'
11 See Association of Heads of Independent schools of Australia, *AHISA Submission: Religious Freedom Review*, 9 February 2018. Available online: https://www.pmc.gov.au/sites/default/files/religious-freedom-submissions/4950.pdf (accessed 15 March 2019).
12 Susan Bailey, 'From Invisibility to Visibility: A Policy Archaeology of the Introduction of Anti-transphobic and Anti-homophobic Bullying Guidelines into the Irish Primary Education System', *Irish Educational Studies* 36, no. 1 (2017): 34.
13 This was not a strictly 'plebiscite' or a referendum, rather, a survey to gauge public opinion that then might guide the parliament.
14 Jessie Mitchell, 'National Marriage Equality Survey – What Do the Results Tell Us about Young People?' *Youth Affairs Council of Victoria*, 20 November 2017. Available online: https://www.yacvic.org.au/blog/national-marriage-equality-survey-what-do-the-results-tell-us-about-young-people/ (accessed 15 March 2019).
15 Ariadne Vromen et al., 'Beyond Lifestyle Politics in a Time of Crisis? Comparing Young Peoples' Issue Agendas and Views on Inequality', *Policy Studies* 36, no. 6 (2015): 541.
16 The adult postal vote asked: 'Should the law be changed to allow same-sex couples to marry?' The AGZ survey asked: 'Do you support marriage equality? (CLARIFY IF NEEDED: By that we mean same-sex marriage).' The sampling was different too: the postal survey was sent to every person on the electoral role and got a response rate of 80 per cent; ours was a telephone survey sample of 1200, and a margin of error of about 2.5 per cent. Thus, while the methods of data collection and question are not directly comparable, we do get a good indication of how different groups think about this issue.
17 Similar levels of support were evident in Scotland where the Scottish Social Attitudes 2014 survey revealed that support for marriage equality was highest among young people (83 per cent of 18–24-year-olds) (see Equality Network, 'Record Support for Same-Sex Marriage in Scotland', 15 December 2014. Available online: https://www.equality-network.org/record-support-for-same-sex-marriage-in-scotland/) (accessed 15 March 2019). In Ireland, voter turnout in the marriage equality referendum was higher among 18- to 24-year-olds than was true of the same age group in the 2011 general election (see Johan A. Elkink

et al., 'Understanding the 2015 Marriage Referendum in Ireland: Constitutional Convention, Campaign, and Conservative Ireland', *UCD Geary Institute for Public Policy Discussion Paper Series*, 9 November 2015. Available online: http://www.ucd.ie/geary/static/publications/workingpapers/gearywp201521.pdf) (accessed 15 March 2019).

18 To view all the recommendations from the review, see *The Sydney Morning Herald*, 'Read the Full 20 Recommendations from the Religious Freedom Review', 12 October 2018. Available online: https://www.smh.com.au/politics/federal/read-the-full-20-recommendations-from-the-religious-freedom-review-20181011-p50918.html (accessed 20 March 2019).

19 Liam Elphick et al., 'Ruddock Report Constrains, Doesn't Expand, Federal Religious Exemptions', *ABC News*, last modified 11 October 2018. Available online: https://www.abc.net.au/news/2018-10-11/ruddock-report-constrains-federal-religious-exemptions/10363248 (accessed 20 March 2019).

20 Markus Mannheim, 'Few Know of Religious Exemption', *The Sydney Morning Herald*, 19 November 2012. Available online: https://www.smh.com.au/national/few-know-of-religious-exemption-20121118-29kns.html (accessed 20 March 2019).

21 See Department of the Prime Minister and Cabinet, Australian Government, *Religious Freedom Review: Report of the Expert Panel*.

22 Paula Gerber, 'Six Months after Marriage Equality There's Much to Celebrate – and Still Much to Do', *The Conversation*, 3 July 2018. Available online: https://theconversation.com/six-months-after-marriage-equality-theres-much-to-celebrate-and-still-much-to-do-97783 (accessed 20 March 2019).

23 Kerry H. Robinson et al., 'Responsibilities, Tensions and Ways Forward: Parents' Perspectives on Children's Sexuality Education', *Sex Education* 17, no. 3 (2017): 333–47.

24 Ibid., 341.

Conclusion: The freedoms, faiths and futures of Australia's teens

1 See David Zyngier, 'Stop All Government Funding for Private Schools. (Why and How We Could Do It)', *EduResearch Matters*, 27 January 2020. Available online: https://www.aare.edu.au/blog/?p=5056 (accessed 25 May 2020).

2 See Australian Broadcasting Corporation, 'Boys Club', Four Corners, last modified 25 February 2020. Available online: https://www.abc.net.au/4corners/boy-club/11994640 (accessed 25 May 2020).

3 80th Annual Meeting of the Association for the Sociology of Religion, 11–13 August 2018, Hotel Sofitel Philadelphia, Philadelphia, PA.

Bibliography

Ager, Karen, Nicole Albrecht and Marc Cohen. 'Mindfulness in Schools Research Project: Exploring Students' Perspectives of Mindfulness: What Are Students' Perspectives of Learning Mindfulness Practices at School?' *Psychology* 6, no. 7 (2015): 896–914.

AGZ (Australia's Generation Z) Survey. *Young Australians' Perspectives on Religious and Non-religious Worldviews Survey Version 1*. Unpublished Research Questionnaire, Australian National University, Deakin University, Monash University, 2017.

Ahmad, Michael M. 'Lebs Let Loose in Punchbowl "Prison"'. *The Australian*. https://www.theaustralian.com.au/nation/inquirer/lebanese-on-the-loose-in-punchbowl-boys-high-school-prison/news-story/ac963cbf0f59c3c46ec6610effe484a0 (accessed 10 March 2017).

Aidone, David. 'Generation Z and Religion: Australia's Youths Turning their Back on God, Seeking Spirituality'. *Daily Telegraph*, 24 December 2018. https://www.dailytelegraph.com.au/lifestyle/parenting/generation-z-and-religion-australias-youths-turning-their-back-on-god-seeking-spirituality/news-story/55dcd346f38bbc2f3feff737c64feb28?utm_campaign=EditorialSF&utm_content=SocialFlow&utm_medium=Twitter&utm_source=DailyTelegraph (accessed 8 May 2020).

American Atheists. 'What is Atheism?'. https://www.atheists.org/activism/resources/about-atheism/ (accessed 13 May 2020).

Ammerman, Nancy. *Sacred Stories, Spiritual Tribes: Finding Religion in Everyday Life*. New York: Oxford University Press, 2013.

Arnett, Jeffrey J. 'Emerging Adulthood: A Theory of Development from the Late Teens through the Twenties'. *American Psychologist* 55 (2000): 469–80.

Arweck, Elizabeth (ed.). *Young People's Attitudes to Religious Diversity*. London: Routledge, 2016a.

Arweck, Elizabeth. '"I've Been Christened, but I Don't Really Believe in It": How Young People Articulate Their (Non-)Religious Identities and Perceptions of (Non-)Belief'. In *Social Identities Between the Sacred and the Secular*, edited by Abby Day, Giselle Vincett and Christopher R. Cotter, 103–26. London: Routledge, 2016b.

Association of Heads of Independent Schools of Australia. *AHISA Submission: Religious Freedom Review*, 9 February 2018. https://www.pmc.gov.au/sites/default/files/religious-freedom-submissions/4950.pdf.

Australian Broadcasting Corporation. 'Boys Club'. Four Corners. Last modified 25 February 2020. https://www.abc.net.au/4corners/boy-club/11994640.

Australian Bureau of Statistics. 'Punchbowl (Canterbury-Bankstown – NSW)'. 2016 Census Quickstats. https://quickstats.censusdata.abs.gov.au/census_services/getproduct/census/2016/quickstat/SSC13273 (accessed 6 May 2020).

Australian Bureau of Statistics. *Census of Population and Housing: Reflecting Australia – Stories from the Census, 2016*. Cat no. 2071.0. Canberra: Australian Bureau of Statistics, 2016.

Australian Bureau of Statistics. *Census Reveals a Fast Changing, Culturally Diverse Nation* (Media Release, 27 June 2017). http://www.abs.gov.au/ausstats/abs@.nsf/lookup/Media%20Release3. Canberra: Australian Bureau of Statistics, 2017a.

Australian Bureau of Statistics. *Schools, Australia, 2017*. Cat no. 4221.0. Canberra: Australian Bureau of Statistics, 2017b.

Australian Curriculum, Assessment and Reporting Authority. 'Punchbowl High School, Punchbowl, NSW'. My School. https://www.myschool.edu.au/school/41559/profile/2018 (accessed 6 May 2020).

Bader, Christopher D., Joseph O. Baker and Carson F. Mencken. *Paranormal America: Ghost Encounters, UFO Sightings, Bigfoot Hunts, and other Curiosities in Religion and Culture*. New York: New York University Press, 2017.

Bailey, Kenneth D. *Typologies and Taxonomies: An Introduction to Classification Techniques*. Thousand Oaks, CA: Sage, 1994.

Bailey, Susan. 'From Invisibility to Visibility: A Policy Archaeology of the Introduction of Anti-transphobic and Anti-homophobic Bullying Guidelines into the Irish Primary Education System'. *Irish Educational Studies* 36, no. 1 (2017): 25–42. DOI: 10.1080/03323315.2016.1243066.

Baird, Barbara. 'Child Politics, Feminist Analyses'. *Australian Feminist Studies* 23, no. 7 (2008): 291–305.

Baker, Joseph O., and Buster G. Smith. *American Secularism: Cultural Contours of Nonreligious Belief Systems*. New York: New York University Press, 2015.

Bibby, Reginald W. *The Emerging Millennials: How Canada's Newest Generation Is Responding to Change and Choice*. Lethbridge: Project Canada Books, 2009.

Bird, Michael. 'Franklin Graham Is Coming to Australia: Here's Why I Won't be Attending'. *ABC Religion and Ethics*, last revised 23 July 2018. https://www.abc.net.au/religion/franklin-graham-is-coming-to-australia-heres-why-i-wont-be-atten/10214340.

Bouma, Gary D. *Australian Soul: Religion and Spirituality in the 21st Century*. Melbourne: Cambridge University Press, 2006.

Bouma, Gary D., and Anna Halafoff. 'Australia's Changing Religious Profile – Rising Nones and Pentecostals, Declining British Protestants in Superdiversity: Views from the 2016 Census'. *Journal for the Academic Study of Religion* 30, no. 2 (2017): 129–43. https://doi.org/10.1558/jasr.34826.

Bouma, Gary D., Sharon J. Pickering, Anna Halafoff and Hass Dellal. *Managing the Impact of Global Crisis Events on Community Relations in Multicultural Australia: Part I (Background Report) and Part II (Community Relations Toolkit) for Victoria*. Melbourne: Monash University, 2007.

Brauer, Simon. 'The Surprising Predictable Decline of Religion in the United States'. *Journal for the Scientific Study of Religion* 57, no. 4 (2018): 654–75. https://doi.org/10.1111/jssr.12551.

Brown, Callum. *Religion and the Demographic Revolution: Women and Secularisation in Canada, Ireland, UK and USA since the 1960s*. Woodbridge: Boydell Press, 2012.

Butson, Tyrone. '"Gender Whisperers": Scott Morrison Criticised for "Hateful" Tweet about Trans Students'. *SBS News*, last modified 5 September 2018. https://www.sbs.com.au/news/gender-whisperers-scott-morrison-criticised-for-hateful-tweet-about-trans-students.

Carey, Adam. 'Teen Charged with Threatening to Kill Bullied Jewish Student, Boy's Mum'. *The Age*, 24 October 2019. https://www.theage.com.au/national/victoria/teen-charged-with-threatening-to-kill-bullied-jewish-student-boy-s-mum-20191024-p533wg.html (accessed 16 March 2020).

Carson, Rachel. *Silent Spring*. Boston, MA: Harcourt, 1962.

Catto, Rebecca, and Janet Eccles. 'Dis(Believing) and Belonging: Investigating the Narrative of Young British Atheists'. *Temenos* 49, no. 2 (2013): 37–63.

Clydesdale, Tim, and Kathleen Garces-Foley. *The Twentysomething Soul: Understanding the Religious and Secular Lives of American Young Adults*. New York: Oxford University Press, 2019.

Coles, Meredith E., Ariel Ravid, Brandon Gibb, Daniel George-Denn, Laura R. Bronstein and Sue McLeod. 'Adolescent Mental Health Literacy: Young People's Knowledge of Depression and Social Anxiety Disorder'. *Journal of Adolescent Health* 58, no. 1 (2016): 57–62.

Collins-Mayo, Sylvia, and Pink Dandelion (eds). *Religion and Youth*. Farnham: Ashgate, 2010.

Collins-Mayo, Sylvia, Bob Mayo, Sally Nash and Christopher Cocksworth. *The Faith of Generation Y*. London: Church House Publishing, 2010.

Collins, Linda M., and Stephanie T. Lanza. *Latent Class and Latent Transition Analysis: With Applications in the Social Behavioral, and Health Sciences*. New Jersey: Wiley, 2010.

Corsetti, Stephanie. 'Bendigo Mosque Appeal Request Thrown Out by High Court'. *ABC News*, 15 June 2016. https://www.abc.net.au/news/2016-06-15/bendigo-mosque-high-court-challenge/7511690 (accessed 16 May 2019).

Crockett, Alasdair, and David Voas. 'Generations of Decline: Religious Change in 20th-Century Britain'. *Journal for the Scientific Study of Religion* 45, no. 4 (2006): 567–84.

Cross, Donna, Theresa Shaw, Kate Hadwen, Patricia Cardoso, Phillip Slee, Clare Roberts, Laura Thomas and Amy Barnes. 'Longitudinal impact of the Cyber Friendly Schools Program on Adolescents' Cyberbullying Behaviour'. *Aggressive Behavior* 42, no. 2 (2016): 166–81. DOI:10.1002/ab.21609.

Davie, Grace. 'From Obligation to Consumption: A Framework for Reflection in Northern Europe'. *Political Theology* 6, no. 3 (2005): 281–301.

De Botton, Alain. *Religion for Atheists: A Non-Believer's Guide to the Uses of Religion*. New York: Pantheon Books, 2012.

Department of the Prime Minister and Cabinet, Australian Government. *Religious Freedom Review: Report of the Expert Panel*, 18 May 2018. https://www.ag.gov.au/RightsAndProtections/HumanRights/Documents/religious-freedom-review-expert-panel-report-2018.pdf.

Department of the Prime Minister and Cabinet, Australian Government. 'Religious Freedom Review – Submissions'. https://www.pmc.gov.au/domestic-policy/religious-freedom-review/review-submissions (accessed 18 May 2020).

Dillon, Michele, and Paul Wink. *In the Course of a Lifetime: Tracing Religious Belief, Practice, and Change*. Berkeley: University of California Press, 2007.

Dimock, Michael. 'Defining Generations: Where Millennials End and Generation Z Begins'. Pew Research Center, 17 January 2019. https://www.pewresearch.org/fact-tank/2019/01/17/where-millennials-end-and-generation-z-begins/ (accessed 7 May 2020).

Dinham, Adam, and Matthew Francis, eds. *Religious Literacy in Policy and Practice*. Bristol: Policy Press, 2015.

Dunn, Kevin, Rosalie Atie, Virginia Mapedzahama, Mehmet Ozalp and Adem F. Aydogan. *The Resilience and Ordinariness of Australian Muslims: Attitudes and Experiences of Muslims Report*. Penrith: Western Sydney University and Islamic Sciences and Research Academy of Australia (ISRA), 2015.

Edgell, Penny, Jacqui Frost and Evan Stewart. 'From Existential to Social Understandings of Risk: Examining Gender Differences in Nonreligion'. *Social Currents* 4, no. 6 (2017): 556–74.

Elkink, Johan A., David M. Farrell, Theresa Reidy and Jane Suiter. 'Understanding the 2015 Marriage Referendum in Ireland: Constitutional Convention, Campaign, and Conservative Ireland'. *UCD Geary Institute for Public Policy Paper Discussion Series*, 9 November 2015. http://www.ucd.ie/geary/static/publications/workingpapers/gearywp201521.pdf.

Elphick, Liam, Amy Maguire and Anja Hilkemeijer. 'Ruddock Report Constrains, Doesn't Expand, Federal Religious Exemptions'. *ABC News*, last modified 11 October 2018. https://www.abc.net.au/news/2018-10-11/ruddock-report-constrains-federal-religious-exemptions/10363248.

Equality Network. 'Record Support for Same-Sex Marriage in Scotland', 15 December 2014. https://www.equality-network.org/record-support-for-same-sex-marriage-in-scotland/.

Essential Media Communications. 'The Essential Report 25 March 2019'. https://www.essentialvision.com.au/wpcontent/uploads/2019/03/Essential-Report-250319-D2.pdf (accessed 7 May 2020).

Fisher, Christopher M., and Sylvia Kauer. *National Survey of Australian Secondary Students and Sexual Health 1992–2018: Trends Over Time (ARCSHS Monograph*

Series No. 118). Bundoora: Australian Research Centre in Sex, Health & Society, La Trobe University, 2019.

Francis, Lesley J., Alice Pyke and Gemma Penny. 'Christian Affiliation, Christian Practice, and Attitudes to Religious Diversity: A Quantitative Analysis Among 13- to 15-Year-Old Female Students in the UK'. *Journal of Contemporary Religion* 30, no. 2 (2015): 249–63. DOI: 10.1080/13537903.2015.1026116.

Francis, Matthew and Adam Dinham, eds. *Religious Literacy in Policy and Practice*. Bristol: Policy Press, 2015.

Furseth, Inger. 'Secularization, Deprivatization, or Religious Complexity?' In *Religious Complexity in the Public Sphere: Comparing Nordic Countries*, edited by Inger Furseth, 291–312. Cham: Palgrave, 2018.

Geertz, Armin W., and Guðmundur Ingi Markússon. 'Religion Is Natural, Atheism is Not: On Why Everybody Is Both Right and Wrong'. *Religion* 40, no. 3 (2020): 152–65.

Gerber, Paula. 'Six Months after Marriage Equality There's Much to Celebrate – and Still Much to Do'. *The Conversation*, 3 July 2018. https://theconversation.com/six-months-after-marriage-equality-theres-much-to-celebrate-and-still-much-to-do-97783.

Government of Western Australia Department of Education. 'Special Religious Education (SRE)', last modified 22 September 2015. http://det.wa.edu.au/curriculumsupport/religiouseducation/detcms/navigation/special-religious-education/.

Graham, Billy. 'Billy Graham Classic Crusades - Truth (1959)'. YouTube, 30 December 2017. https://www.youtube.com/watch?v=ihIMWMZ-5AU (accessed 16 May 2019).

Hadaway, C. Kirk, Penny Long Marler and Mark Chaves. 'What the Polls Don't Show: A Closer Look at U.S. Church Attendance'. *American Sociological Review* 58, no. 6 (1993): 741–52.

Halafoff, Anna, and Enqi Weng. 'Religion on an Ordinary Day: Australia'. In *An Ordinary Day: An International Study of Religion in the Media*, edited by David Michels and Mathilde Vanasse-Pelletier (forthcoming).

Halafoff, Anna. 'UnAustralian Values'. Paper presented at UNAustralia conference: Cultural Studies Association of Australasia annual conference, University of Canberra, Canberra, 4–6 December 2006.

Halafoff, Anna. *The Multifaith Movement: Global Risks and Cosmopolitan Solutions*. Dordrecht: Springer, 2013a.

Halafoff, Anna. 'Education about Religions and Beliefs in Victoria'. *Journal for the Academic Study of Religion* 26, no. 2 (2013b): 172–97.

Halafoff, Anna. 'Special Religious Instruction and Worldviews Education in Victoria's Schools: Social Inclusion, Citizenship and Countering Extremism'. *Journal of Intercultural Studies* 36, no. 3 (2015): 362–79.

Hall, David, ed. *Lived Religion in America: Toward a History of Practice*. Princeton, NJ: Princeton University Press, 1997.

Hancock, Rosemary. *Islamic Environmentalism: Activism in the United States and Great Britain*. London: Routledge, 2018.

Hardy, Alistair. *The Spiritual Nature of Man: A Study of Contemporary Religious Experience*. Oxford: Clarendon Press, 1979.

Harris, Anita. 'Belonging and the Uses of Difference: Young people in Australian Urban Multi-Culture'. *Social Identities* 22, no. 4 (2016): 359–75.

Harris-Hogan, Shandon, and Kate Barrelle. 'Young Blood: Understanding the Emergence of a New Cohort of Australian Jihadists'. *Terrorism and Political Violence* 32, no. 7 (2020): 1391–412. DOI: 10.1080/09546553.2018.1473858.

Hassani, Sadri. '"Post-Materialist" Science? A Smokescreen for Woo'. *Skeptical Inquirer* 39, no. 5 (2015): 123–7.

Hay, David. *Exploring Inner Space: Scientists and Religious Experience*. London: Continuum, 1982.

Hay, David, and Ann Morisy. 'Secular Society, Religious Meanings: A Contemporary Paradox'. *Review of Religious Research* 26, no. 3 (March 1985): 213–27.

Heelas, Paul, and Linda Woodhead. *The Spiritual Revolution: Why Religion Is Giving Way to Spirituality*. Oxford: Blackwell, 2005.

Heelas, Paul. *Spiritualities of Life: New Age Romanticism and Consumptive Capitalism*. Oxford: Blackwell, 2008.

Hill, Annette. *Paranormal Media: Audiences, Spirits and Magic in Popular Culture*. London: Routledge, 2010.

Hill, Faith. 'They Tried to Start a Church without God. For a While, It Worked'. *The Atlantic*, 21 July 2019. https://www.theatlantic.com/ideas/archive/2019/07/secular-churches-rethink-their-sales-pitch/594109/.

Hickey-Moody, Anna. 'Youth Agency and Adult Influence: A Critical Revision of Little Publics'. *Review of Education, Pedagogy and Cultural Studies* 38, no. 1 (2016): 58–72.

Hilliard, David. 'The Religious Crisis of the 1960s: The Experience of the Australian Church'. *Journal of Religious History* 21, no. 2 (1997): 209–27.

Hogan, Michael. *The Sectarian Strand: Religion in Australian Life*. Ringwood: Penguin, 1987.

Hood, Ralph W., Jr., Peter C. Hill and Bernard Spilka. *The Psychology of Religion: An Empirical Approach* (4th edn). New York: The Guilford Press, 2009.

Ivtzan, Itai, and Sivaja Jegatheeswaran. 'The Yoga Boom in Western Society: Practitioners' Spiritual vs. Physical Intentions and Their Impact on Psychological Wellbeing'. *Yoga and Physical Therapy* 5, no. 3 (2014): 1–7.

Jackson, Phillip W. *Life in Classrooms*. New York: Holt, Rinehart and Winston, 1968.

Jackson, Robert. *'Signposts': Policy and Practice for Teaching about Religions and Non-Religious Worldviews in Intercultural Education*. Strasbourg: Council of Europe Publishing, 2014.

Jain, Andrea R. *Selling Yoga: From Counterculture to Pop Culture*. Oxford: Oxford University Press, 2015.

Janmaat, Jan G., and Avril Keating. 'Are Today's Youth More Tolerant? Trends in Tolerance among Young People in Britain'. *Ethnicities* 19, no. 1 (2019): 44–65.

Johnson, Todd, and Brian Grim. *The World's Religion in Figures: An Introduction to International Religious Demography*. Chichester: Wiley-Blackwell, 2013.

Kabat-Zinn, Jon. *Wherever You Go, There You Are*. London: Piatkus, 2004.

Kaldor, Peter, John Bellamy, Ruth Powell, Keith Castle and Bronwyn Hughes. *Build My Church: Trends and Possibilities for Australian Churches*. Adelaide: Openbook, 1999.

Karp, Paul. 'Scott Morrison Will Change the Law to Ban Religious Schools Expelling Gay Students'. *The Guardian*, 13 October 2018. https://www.theguardian.com/australia-news/2018/oct/13/morrison-caves-to-labor-on-gay-students-in-discrimination-law-reform-push.

Kearns, Laurel, and Catherine Keller, eds. *Ecospirit: Religions and Philosophies for the Earth*. New York: Fordham University Press, 2007.

Keeter, Scott, Nick Hatley, Courtney Kennedy and Arnold Lau. 'What Low Response Rates Mean for Telephone Surveys'. Pew Research Center, 15 May 2017. https://www.pewresearch.org/methods/2017/05/15/what-low-response-rates-mean-for-telephone-surveys/.

Kennedy, Courtney, Scott Keeter, Andrew Mercer, Nick Hatley, Nick Bertoni and Arnold Lau. 'Are Telephone Polls Understating Support for Trump?' Pew Research Center, 31 March 2017. https://www.pewresearch.org/methods/2017/03/31/are-telephone-polls-understating-support-for-trump/.

King, Russell, Richard Black, Michael Collyer, Anthony J. Fielding and Ronald Skeldon. *The Human Atlas of Migration*. Brighton: Earthscan, 2010.

Kirkland, Anna. 'What is Wellness Now?' *Journal of Health Politics, Policy and Law* 39, no. 5 (2014): 957–70.

Knitter, Paul F. *One Earth Many Religions: Multifaith Dialogue and Global Responsibility*. Maryknoll: Orbis Books, 1995.

Lam, Tina, Simon Lenton, Rowan Ogeil, Lucinda Burns, Alexandra Aiken, Tanya Chikritzhs, William Gilmore, Belinda Lloyd, James Wilson, Dan Lubman, Richard Mattick and Steve Allsop. 'Most Recent Risky Drinking Session with Australian Teenagers'. *Aust NZ J Public Health* 41, no. 1 (2017): 105–10.

Lian, Cheah Whye, Chang Kam Hock, Muhammed Affan Azmi, Najihah Ayuni Md Hamsani, Yek En Ci, Yeap Yi Ni. 'Commitment and Motivation in practicing Yoga among Adults in Kuching, Sarawak'. *Indian Journal of Traditional Knowledge* 16 (Suppl) (June 2017): 81–7. http://nopr.niscair.res.in/handle/123456789/42276.

Lipka, Michael, and Claire Gecewicz. 'More Americans Now Say They're Spiritual but Not Religious'. Pew Research Center, 6 September 2017. https://www.pewresearch.org/fact-tank/2017/09/06/more-americans-now-say-theyre-spiritual-but-not-religious/.

Lovelock, James. *Gaia: A New Look at Life on Earth*. Oxford: Oxford University Press, 1979.

Lyons, John, Paul Maley and Jennine Khalik. 'Inside Punchbowl Boys' High School: A Battle for Hearts and Minds'. *The Australian*, 10 March 2017. https://www.theaustralian.com.au/nation/education/inside-punchbowl-boys-high-school-a-battle-for-hearts-and-minds/news-story/f7145bf107c711647f2e1165fc84aa00.

Maddox, Marion. *God under Howard: The Rise of the Religious Right in Australian Politics*. Sydney: Allen & Unwin, 2005.

Maddox, Marion. *Taking God to School*. Sydney: Allen & Unwin, 2014.

Madge, Nicola, Peter Hemming and Kevin Stenson. *Youth on Religion: The Development, Negotiation and Impact of Faith and Non-Faith Identity*. London: Routledge, 2014.

Mannheim, Markus. 'Few Know of Religious Exemption'. *The Sydney Morning Herald*, 19 November 2012. https://www.smh.com.au/national/few-know-of-religious-exemption-20121118-29kns.html.

Manning, Christel. *Losing Our Religion: How Unaffiliated Parents Are Raising Their Children*. New York: New York University Press, 2015.

Mansouri, Fethi, and Matteo Vergani. 'Intercultural Contact, Knowledge of Islam, and Prejudice against Muslims in Australia'. *International Journal of Intercultural Relations* 66 (2018): 85–94. https://doi.org/10.1016/j.ijintrel.2018.07.001.

Markus, Andrew. *Mapping Social Cohesion: The Scanlon Foundation Surveys 2018*. https://scanlonfoundation.org.au/wp-content/uploads/2018/12/Social-Cohesion-2018-report-26-Nov.pdf (accessed 20 May 2019).

Mason, Michael, Andrew Singleton and Ruth Webber. *The Spirit of Generation Y: Young People's Spirituality in a Changing Australia*. Mulgrave: John Garratt Publishing, 2007.

McClure, Paul K. 'Faith and Facebook in a Pluralistic Age: The Effects of Social Networking Sites on the Religious Beliefs of Emerging Adults'. *Sociological Perspectives* 59, no. 4 (2016): 818–34.

McCrindle Research. 'Gen Z/Alpha Infographic'. https://generationz.com.au/wp-content/uploads/2018/09/GenZGenAlpha.pdf (accessed 7 May 2020).

McGuire, Meredith B. *Lived Religion: Faith and Practice in Everyday Life*. New York: Oxford University Press, 2008.

Mercier, Brett, Stephanie R. Kramer and Azim F. Sharif. 'Belief in God: Why People Believe, and Why They Don't'. *Current Directions in Psychological Science* 27, no. 4 (2018): 263–8.

Ministerial Council on Education, Employment, Training and Youth Affairs. *Melbourne Declaration on Educational Goals for Young Australians*, December 2008. http://www.curriculum.edu.au/verve/_resources/National_Declaration_on_the_Educational_Goals_for_Young_Australians.pdf.

Mitchell, Jessie. 'National Marriage Equality Survey — What Do the Results Tell Us about Young People?' *Youth Affairs Council of Victoria*, 20 November 2017.

https://www.yacvic.org.au/blog/national-marriage-equality-survey-what-do-the-results-tell-us-about-young-people/.

Mol, Hans. *Religion in Australia: A Sociological Investigation*. Melbourne: Nelson, 1971.

Murray, Lisa. 'Fresh Answers to Old Questions'. *Australian Financial Review*, 6 October 2018.

New South Wales Government. 'Religion and Ethics', last modified 13 February 2020. https://education.nsw.gov.au/teaching-and-learning/curriculum/learning-across-the-curriculum/religion-and-ethics.

Nicholson, Rebecca. 'Star Gazing: Why Millennials Are Turning to Astrology'. *The Guardian*, 11 March 2018. https://www.theguardian.com/global/2018/mar/11/star-gazing-why-millennials-are-turning-to-astrology?CMP=share_btn_link.

Northern Territory Government Department of Education. 'Religious Instruction'., last modified 10 July 2017. https://education.nt.gov.au/education/policies/religious-instruction.

Nyhagen, Line. 'The Lived Religion Approach in the Sociology of Religion and its Implications for Secular Feminist Analyses of Religion'. *Social Compass* 64, no. 4 (2017): 495–511.

Partridge, Christopher. *The Re-enchantment of the West: Volume 1 Alternative Spiritualities, Sacralization, Popular Culture and Occulture*. London: T&T Clark, 2004.

Pauline Hanson's One Nation Party. 'Pauline Hanson Moves to Ban Burqa – Voted Down By Out Of Touch Politicians'. https://www.onenation.org.au/pauline-hanson-moves-to-ban-burqa-voted-down-by-out-of-touch-politicians/ (accessed 16 May 2019).

Pearce, Lisa D., and Melissa Lundquist Denton. *A Faith of Their Own: Stability and Change in the Religiosity of America's Adolescents*. New York: Oxford University Press, 2011.

Pearce, Lisa D., E. Michael Foster and Jessica Halliday Hardie. 'A Person-Centred Examination of Adolescent Religiosity Using Latent Class Analysis'. *Journal for the Scientific Study of Religion* 52, no. 1 (2013): 57–79.

Pearson, Erin. 'Jewish Teens Racially Abused on Bus'. *The Age*, 3 February 2019.

Petts, Richard J. 'Trajectories of Religious Participation from Adolescence to Young. Adulthood'. *Journal for the Scientific Study of Religion* 48, no. 4 (2009): 552–71.

Powell, Ruth, Miriam Pepper and Kathy Jacka Kerr. 'An Ageing Church, but Not Everywhere'. NCLS Research. https://www.ncls.org.au/ageing-church (accessed 13 March 2019).

Prothero, Stephen. *Religious Literacy: What Every American Needs to Know - and Doesn't*. New York: HarperOne, 2007.

Prothero, Stephen, and Lauren R. Kerby. 'The Irony of Religious Literacy in the USA'. In *Religious Literacy in Policy and Practice*, edited by Adam Dinham and Matthew Francis, 55–76. Bristol: Policy Press, 2015.

Queensland Curriculum and Assessment Authority (QCAA). 'Religion and Ethics Applied Senior Syllabus 2019: Syllabus', last modified 16 January 2019. https://www.qcaa.qld.edu.au/senior/senior-subjects/humanities-social-sciences/religion-ethics/syllabus.

Ramic, Andriana, Antonio de Luca, Lauretta Charlton and Lindsey Underwood. '900 Voices from Gen Z, America's Most Diverse Generation'. *New York Times*. https://www.nytimes.com/interactive/2019/us/generation-z.html (accessed 16 May 2019).

Rasmussen, Mary Lou, Sulamith Graefenstein, Andrew Singleton, Anna Halafoff and Gary Bouma. 'Methodological Challenges of Designing a Survey to Capture Young People's (Non-binary) Affiliations in Relationship to Religion, Sexuality and Gender'. *International Journal of Social Research Methodology* 23, no. 6 (May 2020): 695–709. https://doi.org/10.1080/13645579.2020.1763692.

Redden, Guy. 'Revisiting the Spiritual Supermarket: Does the Commodification of Spirituality Necessarily Devalue It?' *Culture and Religion* 17, no. 2 (2016): 231–49. DOI: 10.1080/14755610.2016.1183690.

Regnerus, Mark. *Forbidden Fruit: Sex and Religion in the Lives of American Teenagers*. New York, Oxford University Press, 2007.

Robbins, Mandy, and Lesley Francis. 'The Teenage Religion and Values Survey in England and Wales'. In *Religion and Youth*, edited by Sylvia Collins-Mayo and Pink Dandelion, 47–54. Farnham: Ashgate, 2010.

Robinson, Kerry H., Elizabeth Smith and Cristyn Davies. 'Responsibilities, Tensions and Ways Forward: Parents' Perspectives on Children's Sexuality Education'. *Sex Education* 17, no. 3 (2017): 333–47. DOI: 10.1080/14681811.2017.1301904.

Roof, Wade C. *Spiritual Marketplace: Baby Boomers and the Remaking of American Religion*. Princeton, NJ: Princeton University Press, 1999.

Rose, Stuart. 'Is the Term "Spirituality" a Word that Everyone Uses, but Nobody Knows What Anyone Means by it?' *Journal of Contemporary Religion* 16, no. 2 (2001): 193–207. DOI: 10.1080/13537900120040663.

Routledge, Clay, Andrew A. Abeyta and Christina Roylance. 'We Are Not Alone: The Meaning Motive, Religiosity, and Belief in Extra-Terrestrial Intelligence'. *Motivation and Emotion* 41, no. 2 (2017): 135–46.

Ryder, Norman B. 'The Cohort as a Concept in the Study of Social Change'. *American Sociological Review* 30, no. 6 (1965): 843–61.

School Curriculum and Standards Authority (SCSA). 'Religion and Life'. https://seniorsecondary.scsa.wa.edu.au/syllabus-and-support-materials/humanities-and-social-sciences/religion-and-life (accessed 16 May 2019).

Schwadel, Philip. 'Period and Cohort Effects on Religious Nonaffiliation and Religious Disaffiliation: A Research Note'. *Journal for the Scientific Study of Religion* 4, no. 2 (2010): 310–19. SGY (Spirt of Generation Y) Survey. *PR0178 Youth Spirituality Main Study Version (D12) Final*. Unpublished Research Questionnaire, Australian Catholic University, Christian Research Association, Monash University, 2005.

Simone-Davies, Joanne. 'Population and Migration Statistics in Australia'. Parliament of Australia, 7 December 2018. https://www.aph.gov.au/About_Parliament/ Parliamentary_Departments/Parliamentary_Library/pubs/rp/rp1819/ Quick_Guides/PopulationStatistics/.

Singleton, Andrew. 'Beyond Heaven? Young People and the Afterlife'. *Journal of Contemporary Religion* 27, no. 3 (2012): 453–68.

Singleton, Andrew. *Religion, Culture and Society: A Global Approach*. London: Sage, 2014.

Singleton, Andrew. 'Seven Heavens? The Character and Importance of Afterlife Belief among Contemporary Australians'. *Mortality* 21, no. 2 (2016): 167–84.

Singleton, Andrew. 'Beyond Faith? Recent Trends in Religion and Spirituality among Teenagers'. In *Re-Enchanting Education and Spiritual Wellbeing Fostering Belonging and Meaning-Making for Global Citizens*, edited by Marian de Souza and Anna Halafoff, 23–35. New York: Routledge, 2017a.

Singleton, Andrew. 'The Summer of the Spirits: Spiritual Tourism to America's Foremost Village of Spirit Mediums'. *Annals of Tourism Research* 67 (2017b): 48–57. https://doi.org/10.1016/j.annals.2017.08.002.

Singleton, Andrew. 'Strong Church or Niche Market? The Demography of the Pentecostal Church in Australia'. In *Australian Pentecostal and Charismatic Movements Arguments from the Margins*, edited by Christina Rocha, Mark P. Hutchinson and Kathleen Openshaw, 88–105. Leiden: Brill, 2020.

Singleton, Mark. 'Salvation through Relaxation: Proprioceptive Therapy and Its Relationship to Yoga'. *Journal of Contemporary Religion* 20, no. 3 (2005): 289–304. DOI: 10.1080/13537900500249780.

Singleton, Mark. *Yoga Body: The Origins of Modern Posture Practice*. London: Oxford University Press, 2010.

Smart, Judith. 'The Evangelist as Star: The Billy Graham Crusade in Australia, 1959'. *Journal of Popular Culture* 33, no. 1 (1999): 165–75.

Smith, Christian, and Melissa Lundquist Denton. *Soul Searching: The Religious and Spiritual Lives of Teenagers*. New York: Oxford University Press, 2005.

Smith, Christian, and Patricia Snell. *Souls in Transition: The Religious and Spiritual Lives of Emerging Adults*. New York: Oxford University Press, 2009.

Smith, Christian, Kyle Longest, Jonathan Hill and Kari Christoffersen. *Young Catholic America: Emerging Adults in, out of, and Gone from the Church*. New York: Oxford University Press, 2014.

Smith, Jesse M., and Ryan T. Cragun. 'Mapping Religion's Other: A Review of the Study of Nonreligion and Secularity'. *Journal for the Scientific Study of Religion* 58, no. 2 (2019): 319–35.

Stephens, Randall J. *The Devil's Music: How Christians Inspired, Condemned, and Embraced Rock 'n' Roll*. Cambridge, MA: Harvard University Press, 2018.

Stewart, Katherine, and Caroline Fredrickson. 'Bill Barr Thinks America Is Going to Hell'. *New York Times*, 29 December 2019. https://www.nytimes.com/2019/12/29/opinion/william-barr-trump.html.

The Sydney Morning Herald. 'Read the Full 20 Recommendations from the Religious Freedom Review'. 12 October 2018. https://www.smh.com.au/politics/federal/read-the-full-20-recommendations-from-the-religious-freedom-review-20181011-p50918.html.

Tasmanian Government Department of Education. 'Religious Instruction'. https://www.education.tas.gov.au/parents-carers/parent-fact-sheets/religious-instruction/ (accessed 16 May 2019).

Tilley, James, and Geoffrey Evans. 'Ageing and Generational Effects on Vote Choice: Combining Cross-sectional and Panel Data to Estimate APC Effects'. *Electoral Studies* 33, no. 1 (2018): 19–27. DOI: 10.1016/j.electstud.2013.06.007.

Victorian Curriculum and Assessment Authority (VCAA). 'About the Humanities'. https://victoriancurriculum.vcaa.vic.edu.au/the-humanities/introduction/about-the-humanities (accessed 7 May 2020).

Victorian Curriculum and Assessment Authority (VCAA). 'Learning about World Views and Religions'. https://victoriancurriculum.vcaa.vic.edu.au/static/docs/Learning%20about%20World%20Views%20and%20Religions.pdf (accessed 7 May 2020).

Victorian Curriculum and Assessment Authority (VCAA). 'Learning in Ethical Capability'. https://victoriancurriculum.vcaa.vic.edu.au/ethical-capability/introduction/learning-in-ethical-capability (accessed 7 May 2020).

Victorian Curriculum and Assessment Authority (VCAA). *Victorian Certificate of Education Religion and Society Study Design*, 2006. https://www.vcaa.vic.edu.au/Documents/vce/religion/2017ReligionSocietySD.pdf.

Victorian Department of Education and Training. 'School Policy on Special Religious Instruction'. https://www.education.vic.gov.au/school/principals/spag/curriculum/Pages/sri.aspx (accessed 22 April 2020).

Vromen, Ariadne, Brian D. Loader and Michael A. Xenos. 'Beyond Lifestyle Politics in a Time of Crisis? Comparing Young Peoples' Issue Agendas and Views on Inequality'. *Policy Studies* 36, no. 6 (2015): 532–49. DOI/10.1080/01442872.2015.1095283.

Wilson, Tom, and Fiona Shalley. 'Estimates of Australia's Non-heterosexual Population'. *Australian Population Studies* 2, no. 1 (2018): 26–38.

Woodhead, Linda. 'The Rise of "No Religion": Towards an Explanation'. *Sociology of Religion* 78, no. 3 (2017): 247–62. https://doi.org/10.1093/socrel/srx031.

Wuthnow, Robert. *After Heaven: Spirituality in America since the 1950s*. Berkeley: University of California Press, 1998.

Wuthnow, Robert. *After the Baby Boomers: How Twenty- and Thirty-Somethings are Shaping the Future of American Religion*. Princeton, NJ: Princeton University Press, 2007.

Wuthnow, Robert. *Inventing American Religion: Polls, Surveys and the Tenuous Quest for a Nation's Faith*. New York: Oxford University Press, 2015.

Yip, Andrew Kam-Tuck, and Sarah-Jane Page. *Religious and Sexual Identities: A Multi-Faith Exploration of Young Adults*. Farnham: Ashgate, 2013.

Zwartz, Barney. 'Franklin Graham walks in his Father's Footsteps – and Trump's Shadow'. *The Sydney Morning Herald*. February 9, 2019. https://www.smh.com.au/national/franklin-graham-walks-in-his-father-s-footsteps-and-trump-s-shadow-20190204-p50vj0.html.

Zyngier, David. 'Stop All Government Funding for Private Schools. (Why and How We Could Do It)'. *EduResearch Matters*, 27 January 2020. https://www.aare.edu.au/blog/?p=5056.

Index

Abbott, Tony 157
Abdel-Magied, Yassmin 141, 143
Aboriginal peoples
   see Indigenous Australians
agnostic 96, 110
Aly, Anne 141
Association of Heads of Independent Schools of Australasia (AHISA) 169–70
astrology
   see spirituality and spiritual movements
atheists and atheism 3, 18, 30, 93–4, 95, 110
   attitudes toward 123–4
   New Atheist movement 96
   see also Dawkins, Richard; Harris, Sam; Hitchens, Christopher
Australian Bureau of Statistics (ABS) 21
   census 75, 96
   1961 census 20
   2016 census 11, 12, 14, 22
Australian curriculum 10, 139, 161, 175
Australia's Generation Z (AGZ) study 19, 24, 115, 140, 178, 186–7
   comparisons with other studies 3–4, 26–7, 171–2
   see also research methods

Baha'i faith 9
Bailey, Susan 170
Baird, Barbara 11
belief in a higher being 28, 30, 34, 40, 63–4, 66, 94, 96, 107
   social risk and 105
   see also teens
birth cohorts 11, 54
   Baby Boomers 22, 23, 39, 40, 83, 90, 122, 165, 166, 181
   Generation X 22, 24, 40, 83, 90, 122
   Generation Z 2, 3, 4, 11–12, 15, 19, 24, 26–7, 28, 34–5, 38, 54, 94, 122

Millennials 22, 24, 26–7, 33, 34, 54
'Silent' generation 20, 22–3, 25
   see also teens
Brennan, Frank 169
Brown, Callum 23
Buddhists and Buddhism 5, 13, 39, 43, 56
   attitudes toward 115, 117, 129
   see also Dalai Lama; karma; teens

Catholics and Catholicism 13, 20, 21–2, 28, 32–3, 47–8, 169–70
   see also denominational fidelity; education; Francis, Pope; karma; schools and school systems; teen worldviews; teens
Chinese religions 5
Christians and Christianity 5–6, 8, 13, 17, 19–24, 28–32, 35, 47, 55
   attitudes toward 115, 146
   see also individual entries
Church of Scientology 38, 144
Crockett, Alasdair 200 n.18
communicating with the dead
   see spirit communication
COVID-19 pandemic 4, 180

Dalai Lama 140, 141
Darwin, Charles 143
Dawkins, Richard 96, 101, 141, 143–4
de Botton, Alain 93
denominational fidelity 22
   Dimock, Michael 11
discrimination and intolerance 7, 126, 128, 179
   anti-Semitism 7, 113, 127, 182, 183
   experiences of 16, 146–7
   homophobia, transphobia and LGBTQI+ 135, 163–4, 166, 167–8, 170, 172, 173–8, 186–7
   Islamophobia 1, 3, 7, 117–19, 127–8, 182, 183

places of worship and 130, 131, 136
vilification and 113, 114, 126–30, 133, 137
see also Sex Discrimination Act
diversity in Australia 4–11, 16, 130, 185–6
cultural and linguistic 59, 120, 121, 137, 139
see also LGBTQI+ issues

Edgell, Penny 105
education
about religion and diversity 4, 9–11, 16, 126, 144–55, 163, 183–5
LGBTQI+ issues and 160–5, 166–9, 176–8, 184–5
nonreligious perspectives 9, 139, 148, 149, 154
wellness/wellbeing programs 42
see also ethics and ethical lives; gender; General Religious Education (GRE); Special Religious Education/Instruction (SRI); Worldviews Education (WE)
Edward, John 40
environmental concerns 3, 39, 53, 91, 94
equality and inequality 91, 100, 102, 171, 175, 176, 179, 184
ethics and ethical lives 16, 98, 100, 103, 108
education 139, 148, 149, 158, 161

feminism 148
Fitzpatrick, Ruth 106
Francis, Pope 140, 141
Furseth, Inger 8

gender 9, 14, 85, 105, 159–60, 178–80
education about 154, 157, 161–5, 166–7, 169–71, 176, 178
freedom of expression 157, 159, 163
politics 157–8, 167, 176
religious views and 3–4, 10–11, 12, 91, 92, 158, 166–7, 169–70
see also feminism; Sex Discrimination Act
General Religious Education (GRE) 9–10, 126, 139, 144–5, 147–55, 184
generational difference in beliefs and practices 19, 21–7, 33–5, 76, 110

Gerber, Paula 176
ghosts 47, 49, 50–1, 66, 103
Gillard, Julia 157
Global Atheist Conventions 96
Graham, Billy 19, 22, 34
Greek Orthodox faith 84, 120

Hall, David 8
Hanson, Pauline 7, 127, 130
Harris, Sam 96
Hilliard, David 20
Hillsong Church 17–18, 141, 143
Hindus and Hinduism 5, 13, 82, 115, 117, 147
see also education; karma; teens
Hitchens, Christopher 96
holistic practices 37, 40, 81, 90, 92
horoscopes
see spirituality and spiritual movements
Houston, Brian 17
human rights 130, 133, 135, 136, 176
humanists and humanism 10, 19, 30, 67, 94, 96, 98, 148, 149

Immigration Restriction Act (1901)
see White Australia Policy
Indigenous Australians 1–2, 4–5, 14, 141, 147
see also Uluru
Intelligent Design 97
Islam
see Muslims and Islam

Jews and Judaism 13, 47, 56, 59, 128
see also education; teens; Wailing Wall

karma 81
Buddhism and 47, 48, 49, 50, 79
Catholics and 47, 49
Hinduism and 47, 48
see also spirituality and spiritual movements

Lakemba Mosque 1, 2
Lesbian, Gay, Bisexual, Transgender, Queer, Intersex, and other non-heterosexual people
see LGBTQI+
Leyonhjelm, David 130

Index

LGBTQI+ issues 4, 6, 16, 87, 101, 108–9, 111, 131, 138, 157, 179
   generational differences 160, 165–70
   marriage equality 2, 6, 16, 101, 108, 133, 158, 167, 169, 170–3, 179
   religion 161, 163, 164, 165, 166–7, 168, 169, 172, 173–8, 186
   rights 4, 101, 111, 163, 167
   sexual freedom 169, 170, 176
   see also discrimination and intolerance; education; gender
life after death 33–4, 61, 63, 66–7, 86, 95, 100, 107
   see also mediums; Spiritualism; spirituality and spiritual movements

McGuire, Meredith 8
MacKillop, Mary 140
magic and mysticism 39, 40, 54
   see also spiritual experiences; spirituality and spiritual movements
Manning, Christel 103, 106
marriage equality
   see LGBTQI+ issues
Marxism 94, 148
meditation 38, 54, 80, 89, 106
   beliefs and 39, 40, 43
   wellbeing and 16, 41–3, 44, 181
mediums 33, 37–8, 40, 46, 87
   see also Edward, John
Mercier, Brett 110
migrants and migration 5, 21–2, 23, 74–5, 82, 85
'MindBodySpirit Festival' 37
Mormons and the Church of Jesus Christ of Latter-day Saints 25, 68–9
   see also teen worldviews
Morrison, Scott 157–8, 167
multiculturalism 1, 6, 23
   see also White Australia Policy
Musk, Elon 105
Muslims and Islam 1, 7, 13, 35, 47
   attitudes toward 115–16, 117–19, 120, 127, 128, 130–1, 137–8, 150–2
   see also Abdel-Magied, Yassmin; Aly, Anne; discrimination and intolerance; education; teen worldviews; teens

new religious movements (NRMs) 23
Nones 20–1, 22, 24, 25, 28, 30, 31–2, 34, 46–8, 53, 105, 106, 109, 186
   attitudes toward 115
   see also atheists and atheism; spiritual identity; Sunday Assembly
Nyhagen, Line 8–9

Orthodox Church, 25

Pastafarianism 96, 97–8, 135
Pentecostal-Charismatic Christian (PCC) movement 17–18, 23
Pentecostals 13, 17–18, 21, 25, 30–1, 35, 133–5, 146
   see also education; Hillsong Church
Phelps, Kerryn 173
prayer 30, 68
Protestants and Protestantism 13, 20, 21, 23, 28, 31, 47, 143–4
   see also education
psychics 37, 54, 87
Punchbowl Boys' High School 1–2, 3

Radcliffe, Daniel 167–8
radicalization 3
rationalism 149
reiki
   see spirituality and spiritual movements
reincarnation 46–8, 49–50, 51, 54, 80, 81, 95
   see also Buddhists and Buddhism; spirituality and spiritual movements
religious attendance 19, 20, 22, 30–2, 34, 61, 64–6, 76–7
religious diversity 1, 2–6, 15, 22, 24, 25, 71, 97, 111, 114, 179
   attitudes toward 10, 12, 15, 109, 113–19, 130–6, 137–40, 149–53, 182
   generational differences 6, 8, 9, 11, 15, 19, 22, 23, 26–7, 116, 122, 185
   living with 120–6
   religious freedom and 130–1, 158, 166, 169–70, 175, 176, 178, 179, 183, 186
   religious literacy and 138–44, 148, 155
   understanding and 138, 149, 150–2, 155
   see also Australian Bureau of Statistics (ABS); diversity in Australia;

education; teen worldviews; teens; tolerance; and individual entries
religious education
see education
religious expression, freedom of 130–6
Religious Freedom Review 130, 169–70, 173–4, 178
research methods 8, 12–15, 30, 63, 67, 106, 116–17, 140, 157, 159
Ruddock, Philip 169, 178
Ryder, Norman 200 n.18

schools 120–1, 138–9, 145–7 159, 161–4
　bullying and 4, 91, 129, 163, 170, 176
　experiences in 9, 13, 25–6, 129, 137–8
　religious exemptions 10, 16, 173–8, 182, 186
　systems/types 13, 14, 73–5, 76, 85, 92, 100, 102, 105, 125
　see also education
scientism 100
Sex Discrimination Act 169, 173
sexuality 2, 9, 14, 175–80
　education about 154, 157, 161–5, 166–7, 169–70, 176, 177–8
　freedom of expression 157, 159, 163
　politics 157–8, 167, 176
　religious views and 3–4, 10–11, 12, 158, 166–7, 169–70
Sikhs and Sikhism 5, 6, 26, 30, 47, 128
Special Religious Education/Instruction (SRI) 9, 10, 139, 144–7, 154, 155
spirit communication 37, 40, 46, 47, 49, 54, 81
　see also ghosts; mediums; spiritual experiences
Spirit of Generation Y (SGY) project 8, 26–7, 67
spiritual eclecticism 49, 67, 68, 79, 81, 84, 90, 92
spiritual experiences 51–3, 80, 141
spiritual identity 54–8, 64–5, 67, 80, 81
spiritual marketplace 38–40, 67, 83, 87, 90–1, 92, 181
　see also spirituality and spiritual movements
Spiritualism 6, 37, 38, 39, 54
　see also spirit communication
spirituality and spiritual movements 15, 19, 23, 24, 35, 37–41, 65–6, 179

beliefs 44–6, 53–4, 55, 63, 67, 81, 86–8, 181
practices 37–8, 39–40, 44–6, 53–4, 55, 67, 83, 87, 90, 92
see also individual entries
Sunday Assembly 93–4

tarot cards 44–6, 83–4
teen worldviews 3–4, 7–11, 13, 14, 15–16, 58–67, 180–2, 187
　belief in higher being 61, 63–4, 66, 73, 82, 94–6, 107, 110
　Catholicism and 69–70, 72–3
　Indifferent 93–4, 105–11
　influences on 72, 73–4, 78, 84, 91–2, 102, 103–5, 158
　Islam and 70–1
　Mormonism and 69, 72
　Nominally Religious 67, 68, 73, 75–8, 83, 105, 117, 133
　religion and diversity 136–40
　Religiously Committed 67–71, 72–5, 83, 105, 131, 133, 163, 166–7
　Seekers 79–86, 90, 91
　science and scientific thinking 95, 98, 107, 111, 179, 181
　six types of 60–5, 99, 106, 111, 161, 162, 180–2
　Spiritual but Not Religious (SBNR) 77, 79, 80, 85–92
　This Worldly 94–105, 106–7, 110–11, 131, 133
　see also individual entries
teens 20, 55, 76
　engagement with religion 15, 17–19, 24, 30–4
　in age of diversity 1–4
　importance of religion in daily life 61–2, 64, 66, 68, 74, 75, 81
　religious beliefs 27–35, 64–6, 69–71, 180–1
　religious diversity and religious identity 7–9, 53, 59–60, 64–6, 80–1, 109
　spiritual, paranormal and supernatural beliefs 46–51, 86–7
　see also education; schools and school systems; spiritual identity; spirituality and spiritual movements
terrorism 117–19, 138–9, 150–2
Theosophy 6, 38

Thunberg, Greta 91
tolerance 103, 109, 122–3, 125–6, 130, 165, 180, 183–4
   Harmony Day/Week 147, 148, 149, 155
transcendent experiences
   see spiritual experiences
Turnbull, Malcolm 157, 173

Uluru 140, 141

Voas, David 200 n.18

Wailing Wall 141, 143
wellbeing 4, 16, 37, 40, 41–3, 55
   see also meditation; yoga
White Australia Policy 5
Woodhead, Linda 8
Worldviews Education (WE) 139, 148, 153–5
Wuthnow, Robert 56

yoga 38, 39, 40, 41–3, 48, 54, 80, 86, 87, 181

www.ingramcontent.com/pod-product-compliance
Lightning Source LLC
Chambersburg PA
CBHW072147290426
44111CB00012B/2003